SACRED MUSIC IN SECULAI

As both a sacred musician and a scholar of historical theology, Jonathan Arnold is uniquely qualified to write this lucid and informed book. He tackles one of the most mysterious and fascinating questions in the area of theology and the arts: what is it about music that still appeals so vividly to modern people's sense of the spiritual? He explores this question in an engaging, open, accessible and enthusiastic way, bringing his own insights into conversation with some of the best-known composers, performers and theorists of sacred music at work today.

Ben Quash, King's College London, UK

Jonathan Arnold explores the phenomenon of sacred music as a potent force, whether heard in its liturgical setting or the concert hall, to lead us beyond ourselves to the transcendent and the numinous. His thought-provoking survey draws upon the experience of those who create sacred music as composers or performers, whether as people of profound, uncertain or no faith, providing rich insights into the compelling mysteries and beauties of this treasure trove of music.

John Scott, Organist and Director of Music,
St Thomas Church, New York City, USA

An intriguing, fresh look at the existence and role of music and its sublime effect. What is it that is so special about sacred music?

Ralph Allwood, Director, Eton Choral Courses

A valuable contribution to the study of sacred music in our world today.

Stephen Leyton, Trinity College, Cambridge, UK

If music has ever given you 'a glimpse of something beyond the horizons of our materialism or our contemporary values' (James MacMillan), then you will find this book essential reading. Asking why Christian sacred music is now appealing afresh to a wide and varied audience, both religious and secular. Jonathan Arnold offers unique insights as a professional singer of sacred music in liturgical and concert settings worldwide, as an ordained Anglican priest and senior research fellow.

Blending scholarship, theological reflection and interviews with some of the greatest musicians and spiritual leaders of our day, including James MacMillan and Rowan Williams, Arnold suggests that the intrinsically theological and spiritual nature of sacred music remains an immense attraction particularly in secular society. Intended by the composer and inspired by religious intentions this theological and spiritual heart reflects our inherent need to express our humanity and search for the mystical or the transcendent. Offering a unique examination of the relationship between sacred music and secular society, this book will appeal to readers interested in contemporary spirituality, Christianity, music, worship, faith and society, whether believers or not, including theologians, musicians and sociologists.

For Thomas and Katie

Sacred Music in Secular Society

JONATHAN ARNOLD
Worcester College, University of Oxford, UK

Routledge
Taylor & Francis Group

LONDON AND NEW YORK

First published 2014 by Ashgate Publishing

Published 2016 by Routledge
2 Park Square, Milton Park, Abingdon, Oxon OX14 4RN
711 Third Avenue, New York, NY 10017, USA

Routledge is an imprint of the Taylor & Francis Group, an informa business

British Library Cataloguing in Publication Data
A catalogue record for this book is available from the British Library

The Library of Congress has cataloged the printed edition as follows:
Arnold, Jonathan.
  Sacred music in secular society / by Jonathan Arnold.
     pages cm
  Includes index.
  ISBN 978-1-4094-5170-9 (hardcover : alk. paper) — ISBN 978-1-4094-5171-6 (pbk. : alk. paper)
  1. Music—Religious aspects. 2. Music—Social aspects. I. Title.
  ML3921.A76 2014
  781.71—dc23

                                                                                    2013026725

ISBN 9781409451709 (hbk)
ISBN 9781409451716 (pbk)

Bach musicological font developed by © Yo Tomita

Contents

Acknowledgements

I would like to thank all those who have helped and encouraged the completion of this book, especially those who kindly gave their time by agreeing to be interviewed: Harry Christophers, Stephen Farr, James MacMillan, James O'Donnell, Peter Phillips, Robert Saxton, Roger Scruton, Francis Steele and Rowan Williams. I am immensely grateful to them for their insights and wisdom, without which this book would have been impossible.

My sincere appreciation is offered to those who have assisted my research by reading extracts from my thesis and offering helpful criticism and advice. In particular, I would like to thank Rebecca Adams, of Worcester College, Oxford for transcribing the interview material, which saved me an enormous amount of time. I am deeply grateful, once again, for the meticulous work of historian Tim Stuart-Buttle of Worcester College for his painstaking proofreading, editing and sound advice, and to Sarah Lloyd and Barbara Pretty, my editors at Ashgate for all their support and help, as well as the anonymous peer-reviewers who offered such helpful guidance on both the proposal and the manuscript. Their work has assisted me immeasurably and any mistakes that remain are entirely my own.

As with any project I undertake, it would get nowhere without the love, support and faith of Emma, and the constantly stimulating company of our children, Thomas and Katie. I am delighted that Amy the cat managed to stay with us for this book as she entered genuine old age. I wish to thank my parents, Brenda and Christopher, who encouraged my love of music and supported my career choice of music. And so, lastly, I wish to thank all those musicians with whom I was, and am, fortunate to work, for many happy times making music throughout the world.

Interviewees

Harry Christophers is known internationally as founder and conductor of *The Sixteen* as well as a regular guest conductor for many of the major symphony orchestras and opera companies worldwide. He has directed *The Sixteen* choir and orchestra throughout Europe, America and the Asia-Pacific region, gaining a distinguished reputation for his work in Renaissance, Baroque and twentieth-century music. He has made a significant contribution to the recording catalogue (already comprising over 100 titles) for which he has won numerous awards including the coveted Gramophone Award for Early Music and the prestigious Classical Brit Award in 2005 for his disc *Renaissance*.

Harry Christophers has been Artistic Director of Boston's Handel and Haydn Society since 2008, is Principal Guest Conductor of the Granada Symphony Orchestra and regularly appears with the Academy of St Martin-in-the-Fields. As well as performing on the concert stage, Harry Christophers continues to lend his artistic direction to opera.

Harry Christophers received a CBE in the Queen's 2012 Birthday Honours List. He is an Honorary Fellow of Magdalen College, Oxford, as well as the Royal Welsh College of Music and Drama, and has an Honorary Doctorate in Music from the University of Leicester.

Stephen Farr is Director of Music at St Paul's Church, Knightsbridge, a post that he combines with a varied career as soloist, continuo player and conductor. He was Organ Scholar of Clare College Cambridge, graduating with a double first in Music and an MPhil in Musicology. He then held appointments at Christ Church, Oxford and at Winchester and Guildford Cathedrals. From 2007 until 2012 he was Director of Chapel Music at Worcester College, Oxford.

A prizewinning performer at international level, he has an established reputation as one of the leading recitalists of his generation with numerous recordings to his credit; he has appeared in the UK in venues including the Royal Albert Hall (where he gave the première of Judith Bingham's 'The Everlasting Crown' at the 2011 BBC Proms), Bridgewater Hall and Symphony Hall, Birmingham; he also appears frequently on BBC Radio 3. He has performed widely in North and South America, Australia, and throughout Europe. He has also worked with many other leading ensembles including the Berliner Philharmoniker, Florilegium, the Bach Choir, Holst Singers, BBC Singers, Polyphony, English Concert, London Baroque Soloists, City of London Sinfonia, City of Birmingham Symphony Orchestra, Royal Philharmonic Orchestra, Philharmonia, Academy of Ancient Music, Britten Sinfonia and Orchestra of the Age of Enlightenment.

James MacMillan is one of today's most successful living composers and is also internationally active as a conductor. His musical language is flooded with influences from his Scottish heritage, Catholic faith, social conscience and close connection with Celtic folk music, blended with influences from Far Eastern, Scandinavian and Eastern European music.

He first became internationally recognized after the extraordinary success of *The Confession of Isobel Gowdie* at the BBC Proms in 1990. His prolific output has since been performed and broadcast around the world, placing him in the front rank of today's composers. His major works include percussion concerto *Veni, Veni, Emmanuel*, which has received more than 400 performances, a cello concerto for Mstislav Rostropovich, large-scale choral-orchestral work *Quickening*, and three symphonies. Recent major works include his *St John Passion*, Violin Concerto and his Piano Concerto No.3, *Mysteries of Light,* which received its world premiere in 2011.

James MacMillan's music has been the focus of many major festivals and residencies over the years, such as the London Symphony Orchestra's 2009–10 season 'Artist Portrait'. He has directed many of his own works on disc. The year 2013 included the premiere of *The Death of Oscar* in Stuttgart conducted by Stéphane Denève; the UK premiere of Piano Concerto No.3 with Jean-Yves Thibaudet and Royal Scottish National Orchestra in Edinburgh and new recordings to be released on Hyperion, Challenge Classics and Linn. James MacMillan was awarded a CBE in January 2004.

James O'Donnell is Organist and Master of the Choristers of Westminster Abbey and (until July 2013) President of the Royal College of Organists. Internationally recognized as a conductor and organ recitalist, he has given concerts all over the world, including the United States, Japan, Australia, New Zealand, and throughout Europe, and appeared as organ soloist in the BBC Proms and at many other festivals.

Alongside his responsibilities at Westminster Abbey, James O'Donnell has worked widely as soloist and director with many of the country's leading orchestras and ensembles. In 2011 he became Music Director of St James's Baroque. He is Visiting Professor of Organ and of Choral Conducting at the Royal Academy of Music. In November 2010 he was Artist in Residence at Yale University. He was awarded the papal honour of Knight Commander of the Order of St Gregory in 1999. He received Honorary Membership of the Royal Academy of Music in 2002, and a Fellowship of the Royal College of Music in 2009. He was elected an Honorary Fellow of Jesus College, Cambridge in 2011.

Peter Phillips is the founder and director of *The Tallis Scholars*, with whom he has now appeared in nearly 2000 concerts and made sixty discs, encouraging interest in polyphony all over the world. As a result of his work, through concerts, recordings, magazine awards and publishing editions of the music and writing articles, Renaissance music has come to be accepted for the first time as part of the mainstream classical repertoire. Peter has recently been appointed a Reed Rubin Director of Music and Bodley Fellow at Merton College, Oxford, where the new choral foundation he helped to establish began singing services in October 2008. They gave their first live broadcast on BBC Radio 3's Choral Evensong in October 2011.

In 2005 Peter Phillips was made a *Chevalier de l'Ordre des Arts et des Lettres* by the French Minister of Culture, a decoration intended to honour individuals who have contributed to the understanding of French culture in the world. He is active as a writer, having contributed a music column to the *Spectator* for over 30 years.

Robert Saxton is a leading composer and figure in British Contemporary music. Guidance in early years from Benjamin Britten and four years of intensive study with Elisabeth Lutyens (1970–74) was followed by periods of study at both Cambridge and Oxford Universities with Robin Holloway and Robert Sherlaw Johnson, and later Luciano Berio. He won the Gaudeamus International Composers prize in Holland at the age of twenty-one. In 1986 he was awarded the Fulbright Arts Fellowship to the United States, where he was in residence at Princeton.

Robert Saxton was Head of Composition at the Guildhall School of Music and Drama from 1991 to 1997, and Head of Composition and Contemporary Music at the Royal Academy of Music from 1998 to 1999. He is currently Professor of Composition and Tutorial Fellow in Music at Worcester College at the University of Oxford and is a Trustee of the Mendelssohn/Boise Foundation. He became a DMus at Oxford in 1992.

Commissions for 2013 included a song cycle for the Oxford Lieder Festival and a trumpet concerto, *Shakespeare Scenes* for Simon Desbruslais and the Orchestra of the Swan, and *Hortus Musicae*, a piano cycle for Clare Hammond, commissioned by the City of London Festival. His radio opera, *The Wandering Jew*, was released on NMC in June 2011. Since September 2013, he has also been Composer-in-Assocation to the Purcell School for Young Musicians. He is married to the soprano Teresa Cahill.

Roger Scruton is a senior research fellow of Blackfriars Hall, Oxford and a visiting research professor at St Andrews University, Scotland. He is well known on both sides of the Atlantic as a prolific writer and public intellectual, author of over 30 books, including works of criticism, political theory and aesthetics, as well as novels and short stories. In addition to his authoritative compendia, *Modern Philosophy: An Introduction and Survey* (1994), and *A Dictionary of Political Thought* (3rd edition, 2007), Roger Scruton has written three important studies in applied philosophy: *The Aesthetics of Architecture* (1979), *Sexual Desire* (1986) and *The Aesthetics of Music* (1997). Roger Scruton is a Fellow of the Royal Society of Literature, a Fellow of the European Academy of Arts and Sciences, and a Fellow of the British Academy.

Francis Steele is Musical Director of La Maison Verte in the South of France, a centre for residential courses and was, for thirty years, a professional vocalist, singing bass for such groups as *The Tallis Scholars* and *The Sixteen*, of whom he was a founder member, as well as the choir of St Paul's Cathedral in London. He edits and reconstructs Renaissance music for the Oxford University Press series, *Musica Dei Donum*, and has produced many editions for performance, as well as appearing on many award-winning recordings. Since 2003 he has developed a worldwide reputation as a vocal group coach/tutor and has also produced many CDs. He enjoys working with less experienced singers as much as with professionals.

Rowan Williams is Master of Magdalene College, Cambridge and former Archbishop of Canterbury, who was educated at Wadham College, Oxford. He is an outstanding theological writer, scholar and teacher and has been involved in many theological, ecumenical and educational commissions. He has written extensively across a very wide range of related fields of professional study – philosophy, theology (especially early and patristic Christianity), spirituality and religious aesthetics – as evidenced by his bibliography. He has also written throughout his career on moral, ethical and social topics and, while Archbishop of Canterbury, turned his attention increasingly to contemporary cultural and interfaith issues. His most recent book, *Faith in the Public Square* (2012), is a collection of public talks and lectures on the implications of religion for politics and social policy. He is also an accomplished poet and translator.

In 1983 he was appointed as a Lecturer in Divinity in the University of Cambridge, and the following year became Dean and Chaplain of Clare College. 1986 saw a return to Oxford as Lady Margaret Professor of Divinity and Canon of Christ Church; he was awarded the degree of Doctor of Divinity in 1989, and became a Fellow of the British Academy in 1990.

In 1991 Rowan Williams accepted election and consecration as Bishop of Monmouth and, in 1999, was elected Archbishop of Wales. Archbishop Williams was confirmed on 2 December 2002 as the 104th bishop of the See of Canterbury: the first Welsh successor to St Augustine of Canterbury. In 2012 he was made a life peer, becoming Baron Williams of Oystermouth in the City and County of Swansea. His interests include music, fiction and languages.

Preface

We apprehend Him in the alternate voids and fullness of a cathedral; in the space that separates the salient features of a picture; in the living geometry of a flower, a seashell, an animal; in the pauses and intervals between the notes of music, in their difference of tones and sonority; and finally, on the plane of conduct, in the love and gentleness, the confidence and humility, which give beauty to the relationships between human beings.

Aldous Huxley[1]

A Day in the Life ...

On a summer's day a few years ago, I left my home in Oxfordshire to embark upon a long drive. Far from being an unusual way to spend my Saturday this was, and for my professional singer colleagues still is, the norm. Travel is part of the musician's life, whether within one's own country or around the world; and one of the great advantages of that life is the enjoyment of new experiences at one's destination. On this particular warm day, it was a delight to get out of the car at York Minster (having parked in the Archbishop of York's space which, I was assured, he would not need that day) and enter the vast and beautiful building: a sermon in stone, whose very arches, buttresses and vaulted roof echo the melodious phrasing of the Renaissance music composed at the time of, and after, its construction.

I was in York with a choir, *The Sixteen*, for one of over twenty performances of sacred Renaissance music we performed in British cathedrals that year, a tradition started at the millennium. As I had done many times before, I found myself on a stage at the east end of the nave, ready to rehearse, albeit briefly, the familiar programme. In this vast and cavernous space, we were eighteen[2] distant voices in harmony above the tourist hum.

It was my custom in those days, if there was an opportunity, to find a cathedral service to attend and hear some choral music as well as sing it. This day my luck was in for, between the rehearsal and the concert, there was a service of Choral Evensong sung by the Minster Choir. I followed the Verger's directions and found myself in the more intimate (but still very grand) setting of the Choir, beyond the

---

[1] A. Huxley, 'Seven Meditations' in C. Isherwood (ed.), *Vedanta for the Western World* (Hollywood, CA: The Vedanta Society of Southern California, 1945), pp. 163–70. Here at p. 164.

[2] *The Sixteen* has contained a regular choir of eighteen for many years now.

screen and closer to the east-end altar. Far from being tiny figures, as the men and boys of the choir and clergy processed in with their flowing robes, I could scrutinize each of their faces, see their folders of music and hear their voices distinctly as they began the *Preces and Responses*. This was not a concert. Instead, those present were worshipping together, with all that the concept implied: standing, sitting, turning east for the Creed, kneeling to pray – a sort of contract between priest, reader, musician, listener, worshipper and God. The music enhanced the worship, giving beauty and character to the heartfelt words of the Psalms, to the joyful thanksgiving in Mary's song of praise and liberation, the *Magnificat*, and to the prayers of the Collects. The music of worship was interspersed with words and silence, in which our own thoughts and petitions crept in and became part of the tapestry of the liturgy. This experience was an oasis in my day; not because it was an escapist hour away from the noise of the street and motorway, but as a participation in something new and other. It was a pointer towards the divine, and a collective expression from all who were there that day of thanks for the gift of life. As the choir and clergy left, I felt glad that I had joined with those fellow worshippers in York. People I did not know and would probably never see again, but with whom I now had a bond forged by the shared experience of that liturgical rite and in what had brought us there.

Shortly afterwards I returned to the real purpose of my visit: I was there to perform. Less than two hours after Evensong, the nave and side-aisles were completely full of people who had paid to hear sacred music at the opening concert of the York Early Music Festival. As we stepped onto the stage, not in cassock and surplice but in our concert white-tie-and-tails and ladies' dresses, with music in our folders, around 1700 faces greeted us in expectation of the music to come. This situation was not new to me: from concert halls in Asia to North and South America to Europe, the creative art of Renaissance polyphony and its successors to the present day has an enduring appeal in today's culture.

It had cost me nothing to attend Evensong but, in this concert setting with a paying audience rather than a praying congregation, what was the contract now? The money paid had released those in front of us from any obligation to stand, sit, and turn east (or any other direction). No prayer was required or encouraged. We were not singing in order to enhance prayer or spiritual well-being. Each one of us, as performers, may have had a different attitude to the music we were singing. For some it was simply good music, the fine pieces by Thomas Tallis or William Byrd considered on a par with a Beethoven piano sonata or a Haydn quartet. For others, the interest might have lay in the historical context from which the pieces emerged: the religious and political upheavals of the Reformation, when Catholicism and Protestantism were battling for divine truth and for people's hearts and minds. For others, the spirituality of the words may have been paramount. Whatever the case, that day in York, and many others like it in Britain and throughout the world, highlighted the seeming paradox that, in today's so-called secular society, sacred choral music is as powerful, compelling and popular as it has ever been. For instance, whilst I was writing this work, *The Tallis Scholars'* recording of

Thomas Tallis's magnificent *Spem in alium,* for 40 unaccompanied voices, reached Number 1 on the UK's Official Classical Singles Chart. In doing so it ended a three-week run at the top of the chart for Luciano Pavarotti, and overcame a strong challenge from Andrea Bocelli and Sarah Brightman. Composed in the reign of the Queen Elizabeth I (*c.* 1570), *Spem in alium* is written for eight unaccompanied choirs of five voices each, and is one of the most wonderful and ambitious choral works ever produced. Peter Phillips, director of *The Tallis Scholars,* said:

> I am thrilled that *Spem in alium* has attracted such a large new audience. It is one of the most remarkable achievements of the human mind, an extra-ordinary and moving piece written for 40 individual singers. After performing *Spem in alium* for nearly 40 years I still cannot conceive how Thomas Tallis set about writing it. Even with 21st century computers it would be a daunting task. For me it ranks alongside the best works of Michelangelo and Leonardo da Vinci and confirms Tallis as England's greatest composer. It's on my iPod![3]

There has been a surge in classical track download sales in the UK in the last two years.[4] The Internet, digital technology, and the airtime and broad audience it accesses through popular radio stations such as Classic FM has ensured that sacred music has remained a strong force in the public consciousness. But it is not just in the digital world where sacred music is thriving. Attendance at religious services sung by professional choirs in British cathedrals has increased by a huge 30 per cent in the last decade.[5]

Indeed, outside my own area of choral music, many different types of sacred Christian music are performed at extremely high levels of competence on the concert platforms of the world. In short, sacred music is thriving. This book simply asks: 'Why?'

Jonathan Arnold

---

[3] Quoted in *Gimell* Records press release, August 2012.

[4] Ibid.

[5] http://www.churchofengland.org/media-centre/news/2012/03/cathedral-attendance-statistics-enjoy-over-a-decade-of-growth.aspx.

Introduction

Du holde Kunst, in wieviel grauen Stunden,	O gracious Art, in how many grey hours
Wo mich des Lebens wilder Kreis umstrickt,	When life's fierce orbit encompassed me,
Hast du mein Herz zu warmer Lieb' entzunden,	Hast thou kindled my heart to warm love,
Hast mich in eine beßre Welt entrückt!	Hast charmed me into a better world!
Oft hat ein Seufzer, deiner Harf' entflossen,	Oft has a sigh, issuing from thy harp,
Ein süßer, heiliger Akkord von dir	A sweet, blest chord of thine,
Den Himmel beßrer Zeiten mir erschlossen,	Thrown open the heaven of better times;
Du holde Kunst, ich danke dir dafür!	O gracious Art, for that I thank thee!

Franz von Schober[1]

For years I made my living from singing sacred Christian choral music in both liturgical and non-liturgical settings, and for years I had been baffled by certain questions. Why is sacred music so popular in the twenty-first century in a secular society whilst religion is being attacked by atheists and church attendance is on the wane? In other words, what is the status of sacred music in contemporary life? And what is sacred music anyway? Where does it come from, what does it mean and what is it for? Who writes it, sings it or plays it and who listens and with what motives? What is its role and what is its future?

As a singer and now an Anglican priest, I ask why Western Christian sacred music of the classical tradition, perhaps now more than ever, appeals to such a wide and varied audience of both religious and secular listeners and how theology can (or must) deal with this phenomenon. In seeking to address these issues I have undertaken interviews with several leading exponents of sacred music today who have endeavoured to convey the essence of sacred music in religious and secular settings. I have interviewed a number of composers: James MacMillan, a Roman Catholic who has spoken publicly about the Christian heritage of his music and the counter-culturalism of being a believer today; Robert Saxton, Professor of Music Composition at the University of Oxford, who, as a Jewish composer, provides a fascinating insight into religious music; and I also use material from interviews with the late composers Sir John Tavener and Jonathan Harvey.[2] From a performer's point of view, conductors Harry Christophers (*The Sixteen*), Peter Phillips (*The Tallis Scholars*), James O'Donnell (Organist and Master of the

---

[1]   Set to music by Franz Schubert. Translation by Gerarad Mackworth-Young: http://www1.cpdl.org/wiki/index.php/An_die_Musik_(Franz_Schubert).

[2]   Who both died in 2013.

Choristers at Westminster Abbey) and Stephen Farr (Director of Music at St Paul's Knightsbridge), as well as singer Francis Steele (formerly of *The Tallis Scholars* and *The Sixteen*, who now runs courses for choirs in the South of France), all speak openly and richly about their passion for sacred music and its place in the world today. My conclusions are also drawn from personal interviews with the theologian and former Archbishop of Canterbury, Dr Rowan Williams and the philosopher Professor Roger Scruton.

These conversations acknowledge the fact that, far from moving away from the sacred in music and culture, society is embracing it through more media, and on a bigger scale, than ever before.[3] Live concerts, CD recordings, digital downloadable tracks from the Internet, live pod-casts, and broadcasts of religious choral services and concerts have meant that many millions of people across the world are encountering not just music, composed and performed by the best musicians, but also the sacred every day. Our so-called 'secular' society is apparently saturated with the sacred and thus I am intrigued by the issue of what sacred music means for people today. I will give a brief consideration of the relationship between sacred music and Western society and the sacramental role music has played in religion, as well as the changing function of music in recent centuries, which will hopefully serve as a background to the subsequent interviews. I begin by identifying music's fundamental place in our consciousness and culture.

Music and Civilization

In his recent ground-breaking work on the divided brain, Iain McGilchrist has persuasively argued that the activity of the left and right hemispheres of the brain is very distinctive. The left hemisphere has largely been depicted as the most important, dealing as it does with practical, organizational, analytical and theoretical 'serious business', with the right hemisphere adding 'a little colour' in the areas of emotion, religion the arts.[4] But McGilchrist argues that the right hemisphere is much more important for our culture than has been previously acknowledged:

> My thesis is that for us as human beings there are two fundamentally opposed realities, two different modes of experience; that each is of ultimate importance in bringing about the recognisably human world; and that their difference is

---

[3]   For a discussion of the 'sacralization' of music in society, see T. Blanning, *The Triumph of Music: Composers, Musicians and their Audiences, 1700 to the Present* (Harmondsworth: Penguin, 2008), pp. 89–91, 122–46; C. Dahlhuas, *The Idea of Absolute Music*, trans. R. Lustig (Chicago: University of Chicago Press, 1990); M.E. Bonds, *Music as Thought: Listening to the Symphony in the Age of Beethoven* (Princeton: Princeton University Press, 2006).

[4]   I. McGilchrist, *The Master and His Emissary* (New Haven and London: Yale University Press, 2012), p. 92.

rooted in the bihemispheric structure of the brain. It follows that the hemispheres need to co-operate, but I believe they are in fact involved in a sort of power struggle, and that this explains many aspects of contemporary Western culture.[5]

McGilchrist argues that, in today's society, the left hemisphere has dominated almost all aspects of our culture creating 'a sort of self-reflexive virtual world', which has excluded us from 'a reality which the right hemisphere could enable us to understand'.[6] But he explains why this has become difficult for us compared to our ancestors:

> In the past, this tendency was counterbalanced by forces from outside the enclosed system of the self-conscious mind; apart from the history incarnated in our culture, and the natural world itself, from both of which we are increasingly alienated, these were principally the embodied nature of our existence, the arts and religion. In our time each of these has been subverted and the routes of escape from the virtual world have been closed off. An increasingly mechanistic, fragmented, decontextualized world, marked by unwarranted optimism mixed with paranoia and a feeling of emptiness, has come about, reflecting, I believe, the unopposed action of a dysfunctional hemisphere.[7]

It is this emptiness in our consciousness, perhaps aggravated by our over-dependence upon our left-hemisphere brain, that music can fill: 'Music, being grounded in the body, communicative of emotion, implicit, is a natural expression of the nature of the right hemisphere', suggests McGilchrist, and he explains why:

> It is the relations *between* things, more than entities in isolation, that are of primary importance to the right hemisphere. Music consists entirely of relations, 'betweenness'. The notes mean nothing in themselves: the tensions between the notes, and between notes and the silence with which they live in reciprocal indebtedness, are everything.[8]

It is this 'betweenness' that relates to realities other than ourselves and, in music of every culture, it is used to encounter the 'supernatural' or 'Other than' ourselves, or what Roger Scruton describes as music's power to evoke the 'real presence' of something spiritual.[9]

---

[5] Ibid., p. 3.

[6] Ibid., p. 6.

[7] Ibid.

[8] Ibid., p. 72

[9] Ibid., p. 77; R. Scruton, *The Face of God: The Gifford Lectures 2010* (London: Continuum, 2012), p. 53; idem, *Beauty: A Very Short Introduction* (Oxford: OUP, 2009), p. 45.

But music also lies at the heart of our civilization in another sense, in that there is good evidence to suggest that music existed long before language and that, in fact, music is the basis for language. Fossil records show that 'the control of voice and respiration needed for singing came into being long before they would ever have been required by language'.[10] Moreover the simpler syntax of music suggests an earlier origin, as does the observation that in children musicality develops before the spoken word: 'intonation, phrasing and rhythm develop first; syntax and vocabulary come only later'.[11] Communication via music is expressive of the emotions, therefore 'our love of music reflects the ancestral ability of our mammalian brain to transmit and receive basic emotional sounds'.[12]

For McGilchrist music was the ancestor of language that arose largely in the right hemisphere of the brain, which was concerned with communication, social cohesion and harmony and helped bond people together in community. Today we have lost the primal sense of music, because language and the printed word have dominated society for generations. Music is increasingly the exclusive domain of the specialist composer and performer, to be heard in a concert or a church or on a recording. Nevertheless, when we hear such music, we instinctively recapture that basic bonding experience with the community around us.[13] Thus, McGilchrist's thesis is that, before historical records began, music was essential for communication and cohesion in society. If this is true, then it certainly adds weight to the notion that music is somehow at the centre of our consciousness and culture. However, in recent centuries, the relationship between religion and music's function has altered, which I shall turn to now by first considering music's sacramental function.

Sacred by Context: Music as Sacrament

'Sacramental' is perhaps an unpopular term to apply to music these days, and one that is not easily understood. When people speak of music as echoing transcendent beauty or communicating divine blessing, as Albert Blackwell argues, then it is sacramental. There are two types of sacramentality relevant here. First, the Pythagorean, which defines music as a gift from God transcending history; and, second, an incarnational depiction of sacrament, which defines music as the manifestation of the divine to human hearts. Just as fallen humanity is encapsulated by the image of cacophony and dissonance, so music is seen as a companion in our (self-inflicted) suffering and our salvation, and brings healing and harmony to the individual, community and cosmos. In this sense, Blackwell's interpretation complements Begbie's emphasis on the incarnational aspect of

---

[10]   McGilchirst, *The Master and his Emissary*, p. 102.

[11]   Ibid, p. 103.

[12]   Ibid.

[13]   Ibid., p. 105.

music, embodying as it does art and beauty through time, by means of a series of tensions and resolutions. Blackwell depicts music as with us (like Christ) in our world of suffering now, but also to be defined in eschatological terms as the final bliss and spiritual fulfilment of humanity.[14]

'Sacramental' is also defined by Paul Tillich as 'Objects which are vehicles of the Divine Spirit', which 'become sacramental materials and elements in a sacramental act ... The largest sense of the term denotes everything in which the Spiritual Presence has been experienced'.[15] George Steiner describes sacramental music as that which 'puts our being as men and women in touch with that which transcends the sayable, which outstrips the analysable',[16] whereas Simone Weil defines sacrament simply as 'contact with God' or the 'real presence of God in matter'. All three of these definitions can be applied to a theistic and sacramental role of music. For instance, Weil's definition music enables us to make contact with divinity, where beauty becomes a 'sacrament in the full sense of the word.'[17] For her, music, in its incarnational role, brings about harmony in humanity, just as the pre-Christian Pythagoras considered music to be a reflection of the cosmic harmony in the spheres: 'The incarnation of Christianity implies a harmonious solution of the problem of the relations between the individual and the collective. Harmony in the Pythagorean sense: the just balance of contraries.'[18] But the notion of sacrament, for Weil, also implies an element of contemplation of beauty that comes naturally when we are confronted by great sacred music:

> When we listen to Bach or to a Gregorian melody, all the faculties of the soul become still and tense in order to apprehend this thing of perfect beauty ... The mysteries of faith are degraded if they are made a subject of affirmation and negation, when in reality they should be a subject of contemplation.[19]

William James recognized that music was the best of the arts for accessing spirituality: 'Not conceptual speech but music rather, is the element through which

---

[14] A. Blackwell, *The Sacred in Music* (Cambridge: Lutterworth Press, 1999), pp. 13–14; J. Begbie, *Theology, Music and Time* (Cambridge: CUP, 2000), p. 100.

[15] P. Tillich, *Systematic Theology*, 3 vols. (Chicago: Chicago University Press, 1951–63), Vol. 3, pp. 120–21, quoted in Blackwell, *Sacred in Music*, p. 26.

[16] G. Steiner, *Real Presences* (Chicago: Chicago University Press, 1989), p. 218, quoted in Blackwell, *Sacred in Music*, p. 29.

[17] S. Weil, *Waiting for God*, trans. E, Cranford (New York: Putnam, 1951), p. 214 and S. Weil, *Gravity and Grace*, trans. E. Cranford (London: ARK, 1987), pp. 138 and 169, quoted in Blackwell, *Sacred in Music*, p. 30.

[18] Weil, *Waiting for God*, p. 77.

[19] S. Weil, *Notebooks of Simone Weil*, ed. A Wills, 2 vols (London: Routledge, 1956), Vol. I, p. 245, quoted in Blackwell, *Sacred in Music*, p. 45.

we are best spoken to by mystical truth'.[20] Blackwell posits a workable definition of both 'mystical' and 'sacramental' that can be applied to sacred music. A mystical experience is one in which we have a 'sense of intimate communion with reality infinitely greater than ourselves'. A sacrament is a 'finite reality through which the divine is perceived and disclosed and communicated and through which our human response takes shape, form and structure'. In this context worship is our response to the divine.[21] Thus, in Blackwell's study, sacred music is defined by its liturgical purpose:

> The musical tradition of the Universal Church is a treasure of inestimable value, greater even than that of any other art. The main reason for this pre-eminence is that, as sacred melody united in words, it forms a necessary or integral part of the solemn liturgy ... Therefore sacred music increases in holiness to the degree that it is intimately linked with liturgical action, winningly expresses prayerfulness, promotes solidarity, and enriches sacred rites with heightened solemnity.[22]

But this earthly response to God is no more than a reflection of the celestial praise of God in heaven, as described in Hildegard of Bingen's vision:

> Then I saw the lucent sky, in which I heard different kinds of music marvellously embodying all the meanings I had heard before. I heard the praises of the joyous citizens of Heaven, steadfastly persevering in the ways of Truth; and laments calling people back to those praises and joys; and the exhortations of the virtues.[23]

Thus, music's sacramental and liturgical function is one facet of its sacredness. But sacred music is not just heard and used in religious settings and for religious purposes: music is a thread that binds the spheres of sacred and secular together, a characteristic that is more true now than it has ever been before, as I shall consider now.

Changing Ideas of the Sacred

For the Florentine Christian Platonist Marsilio Ficino (1433–99) the word *spiritus* meant neither body nor soul but something that unites them.[24] Therefore, music

---

[20]   W. James, *The Varieties of Religious Experience: A Study in Human Nature*, ed. M.E. Marty (New York: Longmans, Green and Co., 1902; New York: New American Library, 1958), p. 322, quoted in Blackwell, *Sacred in Music*, p. 215.

[21]   Blackwell, *Sacred in Music*, pp. 215 and 223.

[22]   Ibid., p. 15.

[23]   Hildegard von Bingen, Sixth Vision of the *Scivias*, quoted in Blackwell, *Sacred in Music*, p. 228.

[24]   J. Godwin, *Harmonies of Heaven and Earth: The Spiritual Dimension of Music from Antiquity to the Avant-Garde* (London: Thames and Hudson, 1987), p. 81; M. Cobussen,

could perform an intermediary role between the two, and exercise a beneficial effect on both the emotions and the senses.[25] Thus, musical sound becomes a bridge between heaven and earth. Blanning remarks that this is still, in many ways, the objective of music today:

> The purpose of music has remained the same throughout its history. One constant has been redemption, transporting human beings closer to God by encouraging their spirits to soar to a sonic heaven. Music still performs that function for organised religions, although its transcendental embrace has now expanded to include almost everyone.[26]

One example of how this expansion has occurred is to look at how the music of J.S. Bach is received today. Bach travelled very little during his lifetime; and in contrast to his contemporary Handel (1685–1759), whose music was performed in the largest cities in Europe, Bach's main periods of creativity were focussed upon the relatively small towns of Weimar in Saxony (1713–16) and Leipzig (1723–29), where, in the latter, he wrote for the liturgy of St Thomas' Church, the Thomas Kirke. Therefore, there is some irony in the popularity of Bach today:

> It is one of the great ironies of history that Bach's religious music should be so much more available and so much more esteemed in a secular age than at any other time. In 1727, when he wrote the *St Matthew Passion* ... the community's values and world view were steeped in religion. Yet the *St Matthew Passion* was performed only four times during Bach's lifetime, and then sank without a trace [until 1829] ... Today, when in Europe at least only a small and dwindling proportion of the population goes anywhere near a church, the *St Matthew Passion* is universally regarded as one of the greatest achievements of European culture, is performed regularly across the globe and is available in scores of different countries.[27]

This explanation for the relative obscurity of Bach in the years after his death, compared with Handel, is to be found in the metropolitan contexts in which the men worked. Whereas Bach wrote his *St Matthew Passion* for a 'captive audience' of religious worshippers in Leipzig on Good Friday 1727, Handel wrote the *Messiah* for a 'voluntary' paying audience at Neale's New Musick Hall in Dublin in 1742.[28] Bach wrote music for worshippers, who may also have appreciated the music;

Thresholds: Rethinking Spirituality Through Music (Aldershot: Ashgate, 2008), p. 44.

[25] M. Ficino, *De Vita Coelitus Comparanda: Marsilio Ficino, Three Books on Life*: A Critical Edition and Translation with Introduction and Notes, by Carol V. Kaske and John R. Clark (Binghamton, NY: Medieval and Renaissance Texts and Studies, 1989), Book 3, Chapter XXI.

[26] Blanning, *Triumph of Music*, pp. 73–4.

[27] Ibid., pp. 82–3.

[28] Ibid., p. 84.

Handel wrote for a paying audience who may, or may not, also have been seeking spiritual transcendence. The practice of sacred music being performed in concert had a huge and lasting impact:

> An important step in the elevation of music and its creators was to divorce them from service to a third party. In the case of *opera seria*, that party was the prince [the wealthy patron]; in the case of religious music, it was God. Although Handel appears to have been every bit as devout as Bach, his staging of oratorios in theatres for the paying public pointed the way to music's eventual emancipation from function.[29]

Society has devoted an increasing amount of space, money, buildings, technology, radio airwaves and visual broadcasting to music. Since the rise of the concert hall in the eighteenth century it is unsurprising that much of the musical emphasis in composition since then has been focussed upon non-religious forms: symphony, sonata, concerto, and so on. But with the advent of long-playing records, the 1950s saw a resurgence of interest in 'early music', meaning that dating from the Renaissance period and earlier, which was largely, by its very nature, sacred. Since then, CDs, digital technology and the Internet have helped generate an unprecedented and truly global interest in European Renaissance and Baroque sacred music, and furnished it with an audience both larger and broader than at any time in history.[30]

Sir John Eliot Gardiner's record label *Soli Deo Gloria*, founded to produce CDs of his Bach Pilgrimage in the year 2000 and Harry Christophers' Choral Pilgrimage[31] concert series allude to religious devotion in their titles, and yet what is being performed is in no way a religious service. It is a concert: respectable, solemn, serious and, to the attentive listener, extremely moving. As such, its transcendental nature has been widened to embrace a secular world. So, how does that fact alter our perception of the music's sacredness?

The Nature of Sacred Music

In his poem, 'Church Going', Philip Larkin wrote about a time when he stopped at a village church, concluding with the thought that 'A serious house on serious earth it is'.[32]

---

[29]   Ibid., p. 85.

[30]   T. Croucher, *Early Music Discography: From Plainsong to the Sons of Bach*, 2 vols (London: The Library Association, 1981), p. vi; John Milsom, 'Soundclips and *Early Music*', *Early Music*, 31, no.1 (2003), p. 3; Blanning, *Triumph of Music*, p. 327.

[31]   Ibid., p. 328.

[32]   P. Larkin, 'Church Going' (1955), in *Philip Larkin: Collected Poems*, ed. Anthony Thwaite (London: Faber & Faber, 1988), p. 97.

Since the nineteenth century at least, sacredness has often been related to the seriousness and likewise sacred music has been viewed, for the most part, as a serious business: it is played or sung at solemn occasions, in religious buildings and often with a spiritual purpose. The serious nature of the music may be reflected in its content, words or harmony. Thus, in Larkin's poem, one senses that the only music appropriate to the scene would be that which is fitting to the seriousness of the church building and what it stands for. Larkin was no Christian believer; nevertheless, his language of gravity, wisdom and death acknowledges the solemnity of the place. From another agnostic point of view Peter Phillips similarly emphasizes the seriousness of the religious music his choir performs:

> I want to deal with serious stuff. I'm engaged in very serious-minded activity. It's not a jokey business putting on a concert. We don't dress up in Medieval costumes, we've never done that. Even in our approach to the serious stuff, we've never tried to dress it up so that it's more easily listened to, we've delivered it straight. And it's serious music, very. Standing there on stage and doing a whole concert is a very taxing and business … we never make the [audience] laugh. I don't think we've ever made them laugh.[33]

But seriousness only describes one current approach to the music rather than defines sacred music for us, leaving us with the questions: is it the religious words that are set to the music that suggest something spiritual, transcendent, or speak of God, or is there a divine element within music itself? What do we mean when we say that some music sounds 'sublime', or 'divine', or 'out-of-this-world'? How is it that instrumental music, without any religious text or context, can provide a 'spiritual' experience? Can we really separate sacred from secular anyway?

Three Possibilities

Sacred music might be defined by the *intentions* of the composer: music that is explicitly intended for the purpose of expressing (and stimulating in the listener) one's devotion to a specifically Christian God in all his ineffability. This might be music with a sacred or religious subject, but without, necessarily, a liturgical context. For instance, Brahms' *Requiem* is a piece of sacred music without a liturgical function (i.e. it was not written to be performed in a religious service), but a Mass setting by Giovanni Perluigi da Palestrina has both a sacred text and a liturgical context in mind. By contrast, a pop song by *U2* may be influenced by the faith of the band members who wrote and perform it, and therefore might be labelled as religious, but is neither sacred, as in the Brahms and Palestrina examples, nor is it liturgical (although it might be used in certain kinds of religious services).

Thus, sacred music might be defined by the *context* in which it is performed: in a church or cathedral service, such as the Evensong at York Minster that I

---

[33] Interview with Peter Phillips, Merton College, 21 February 2012.

mentioned in the preface, or indeed as part of a domestic devotion or for religious purposes beyond the church. For instance, practices of domestic piety in the Early Modern period made use of music, such as hymn singing, or performance of songs with instrumental accompaniment by lute or virginal. There was also use of artistic music in the 'domestic' religious practices of the nobility. In fact, many Renaissance motets were not composed for church liturgy but for other occasions. For example, Orlando di Lasso's *Penitential Psalms*, from the later sixteenth century were not composed as liturgical pieces, even though we might use them in the liturgy today. Claudio Monteverdi states that his *Vespers* of 1610 could be performed in church or in the chambers of the nobility. Whether in church or home, in liturgy or private devotion, such music is inherently sacred by virtue of its text, intention of the composer and the devotional response it was intended to invoke in the listener.

However, since the liberation of music from its religious function over the centuries, we must now entertain another approach, namely that sacred music may be most properly defined by its nature: by the *genius* of an art form that, when perfected, appeals to those needs, desires and doubts that are experienced by all thinking and truly human individuals. Perhaps great music always touches upon concerns common to all self-conscious humans, by pointing towards themes, ideas and ideals of mystery, transcendence, sin and forgiveness, love and hope that are eternal. The current popularity, in a secular age, of specifically 'sacred' music composed by avowed Christians such as Tallis and Byrd attests to Christianity's specific capacity in Western society to respond to and express these needs and desires. Thus, a twenty-first century listener may hear a piece of classical Western sacred music with, as it were, 'secular ears', while at the same time discovering a spiritual message in a work of secular instrumental music.

Thus, in Western society today, *all* music that evokes a genuine affective response also appeals to the themes mentioned above to a lesser or greater degree. As Roger Scruton relates in Chapter 5 of this volume,[34] this is not least because Western culture owes an enormous amount to, and cannot be understood in isolation from, the Judeo-Christian tradition, and this is especially true for our appreciation of music. When touched upon, these desires and doubts stimulate a creative and, in an important respect, a *participatory* response from all who allow themselves to engage with them. It is for this reason that music reveals its true beauty and resonance only to those who will listen attentively or 'seriously', as Rowan Williams emphasizes in Chapter 4 of this volume.[35] In this regard, music cannot, clearly enough, be defined as an object of reverence in itself, or at least not in the West; rather, it only affects the composer, performer or individual to the degree that it points towards something far greater than itself, but that it alone can begin to express.

---

[34]   See below, pp. 121–9.

[35]   See below, pp. 91–101.

Understood in this manner, the current popularity of 'sacred music' – that is, music that touches upon themes eternal and essential to human existence as we perceive them from a Western aesthetic – represents a great opportunity for Christian apologists. To set limitations on definitions of 'sacred music' as only that which is intended of the composer, or the text, or the religious context in which it is performed is, in effect, to miss this opportunity; to recognize it, by contrast, will lead the Christian to give the admirer of sacred music (whether they consider themselves atheist, Christian, agnostic or other) what they in effect would welcome even in this secular age.

It is in this context that greater accessibility to sacred music through various media is so beneficial to society: by providing access not just to the music, but also to information about the composer's intentions in his age, as well as an idea of why the religious context (worship, the architecture of churches and cathedrals) in an important respect shaped the nature of the music we so enjoy.[36] In other words, it leads those who find such resonance in sacred music to a better understanding of Christianity itself: and, perhaps, Christ's teachings reveal their divinity most clearly in the manner in which they address the deepest of human concerns, and show that Christian faith is one way in which the most contemplative and mature individuals throughout Western history have satisfied a longing for something greater than themselves and the society in which they live.

In the light of this, the distinction between the 'sacred' and 'secular' in an important sense loses its valence: whether the composer, performer or listener of great, serious and moving music chooses to recognize it or not, the attraction of beautiful and profound harmony echoes the message and ministry of Christ by appealing to much the same desires deep in human souls. Those desires, then, still clearly exist whether an age is considered to be secular or Christian; the popularity of sacred music today presents the opportunity to invite people back to faith who may have confused it with organized, institutional religion. Truly great music, then, whatever the intentions of the composer or context in which it is performed, is 'sacred' to the degree that it directs us away from the ego, and which brings a wide appeal because it speaks to a humanity united by shared frailty, doubt, and a desire to admire something transcendent; and in this regard it is a remarkably durable vehicle in which to convey the message of faith, or at least mystery. To be concerned that 'sacred' music has been dissolved in the 'secular', in this regard, is misplaced; rather the popularity of sacred music attests to the continued interest, whether merely affective or rational, in a music that developed as a means of admiration and reflection in worship, and might potentially lead back there.

---

[36] Such as the first BBC series of *Sacred Music*, featuring *The Sixteen* and presented by Simon Russell Beale, which was screened on BBC4 Easter 2007 and featured four programmes covering the history of sacred music from the beginnings of polyphony in twelfth-century France, through the Italian Renaissance, English Tudor music, and the sacred music of J.S. Bach. A subsequent series focussed upon later choral music by Bruckner, Mendelssohn, Tavener, Pärt and Górecki.

Outline

The book will be divided into two parts: (1) the practice of sacred music today, using evidence from personal experience and from interviews with composers and practitioners of music; and (2) the reception of sacred music, using further interview material from those who respond to, and think about, sacred music, how it relates to our culture and what its future might be.

Part I opens with an investigation of composers of sacred music. Their work is often shaped by the religious and cultural landscape in which they live, but, in turn, their work often helps to shape that landscape. Thus, Chapter 1 draws upon interviews with leading British composers, including James MacMillan, Sir John Tavener, Jonathan Harvey and Robert Saxton, who give their accounts of how they were led to write sacred music, and for what purpose. I ask them about the place of faith in musical composition, the influence of other composers on their work, and the context for which they write, as well as explore the compositional techniques they employ. These interviews reveal that a rich tradition of sacred music composition is still flourishing today. Chapters 2 and 3 examine the views of those involved in performing sacred music, both within the Church's liturgy and in concert settings. I draw upon interviews with musicians and conductors who have extensive experience of performing great sacred music in secular and religious/ liturgical contexts. I explore how they feel about the differences between those settings, and what they consider sacred music to offer in each separate context.

In Part II, I consider the reception of sacred music in society. Chapter 4 considers those who listen to sacred music, whether as a member of a congregation or audience, or in solitude. I ask the question: when sacred music is played, who is listening? Who is the real and intended listener to sacred music: congregation, audience, passer-by or God Himself? Indeed, what kind of sacred music appeals to different types of people, and what is the *best* sacred music and why? I also explore the relationship between music, emotion and meaning for the listener. In an interview with the former Archbishop of Canterbury, Rowan Williams, I consider the link between music and spirituality, discuss listening to sacred music intently and seriously, explore how to live with and before God through music and how sacred music has meaning for those with no faith. This chapter offers some explanation as to how music can touch one's soul through its ineffability and its noetic quality, its transiency and its passivity. Here I draw upon William James's suggestion that music is 'the element through which we are best spoken to by mystical truth'.[37]

Chapter 5 examines the relationship between music and culture, and the degree to which both sacred music and religious belief run contrary to mainstream cultural mores. On the one hand, I explore the implications of MacMillan's assertion that 'embracing spirituality is now one of the most radical and counter-cultural moves a musician can make'. On the other, I consider Peter Phillips' thesis that great sacred

---

[37]   James, *Varieties of Religious Experience*, pp. 420–21.

choral music can be fully enjoyed as a 'secular' concert item, like a symphony or concerto, implying that sacred music is not counter-cultural because it occupies a central place within the cultural mainstream. Thus, the question arises whether most people consider sacred music to be completely detached from its religious heritage. I argue that society, as a whole, seems reluctant to accept theology as part of everyday life; and yet the intrinsic theological essence of a sacred work of art cannot be extracted. I conjecture that it is this theological and spiritual nature of the music that attracts most, if not all, listeners to the music. If a composer has theological intentions when composing a piece of music, they are essential to its meaning. This kind of sacred music is, by its very nature, inherently transcendental, and leads the listener beyond worldly considerations, precisely because this was what the composer set out to do: to lead the listener to the divine. At some level, whether great or small, the faith embedded in the music must be acknowledged. In exploring these ideas I include an extended extract from my interview with the philosopher Roger Scruton.

My final chapter asks simply: 'What is the future of sacred music?' Using interview material and analysis, I examine how musicians, theologians and philosophers see the future of sacred music in Western culture, both from within the Church and without. I explore the idea that music might assist in a restoration of the 'Spiritual Community' of past generations; ask why Renaissance polyphony still plays a particularly important role in culture; and consider how technology has altered the way we approach and consume sacred music today.

The Scope and Limitation of the Work

This is not a work of musicology, nor a treatise on musical aesthetics, nor is it a guide to sacred music in history. It merely aims to provide a snapshot of musical history, through first-hand interviews, with some composers, performers and scholars, some of faith and some of none, who have thought deeply about sacred music in our society. As such, I aim to glimpse something of the status of sacred Christian music in Western secular society at the beginning of the twenty-first century, why it is so popular amongst those of faith and those of none, and what theological implications may arise from these findings. Therefore the work intends to be distinctive in addressing the specific relationship of Western Christian sacred music to modern secular society, that is unique in bridging the gap between musical and theological scholarship and general readership. I hope that you find this book accessible, whether you are a Christian believer, musician or neither.

However, I cannot hope, in such a short space, to cover all religions or spiritual ideologies in this work, nor can I examine all varieties of sacred or worship music. I seek to write only of what, and whom, I know in this field, which means primarily the Christian faith and spirituality and classical choral music written for it in the Western tradition. Many other works have addressed music and spirituality in other faiths and I gladly defer to other scholars' expertise in these arenas. I also am aware of my own aesthetical inheritance from the Western Judeo-Christian religion and I do not claim that my findings have a universal value in every culture. I am aware that ethno-musicological scholarship in the last fifty years has demonstrated that music of the Western canon is not universal in its appeal and that our perception of music is deeply determined by cultural factors. I am all too aware of the many other great contemporary composers and performers of sacred music, as well as commentators, that I could have consulted for this book, but from which I have been prevented by limitations of time and space. For these omissions and lack of breadth I apologize. However, I hope that the conclusions drawn from this small study may find resonance and applicability in other areas of faith, in other faiths and cultures, and, indeed, in other fields of study, such as sociology.

Most importantly, despite all these limitations, this work is for you if you have ever been moved by a piece of music or felt your spirits raised by the sounds of harmony; if you have ever felt taken out of yourself by art and experienced the transcendent power of beauty to transform your outlook on the world; and if music has ever given you 'a glimpse of something beyond the horizons of our materialism or our contemporary values'.[38] In short, if music has ever been an important part of your life, I hope you will read on and explore with me what power is transmitted to us when we hear it.

---

[38]   Ibid.

PART I
The Practice of Sacred Music

Chapter 1
Composers – Midwives of Faith

In music, there seems to be an umbilical link with the sacred. Through the centuries, musicians have proved themselves to be the midwives of faith, bringing their gifts to the historic challenge of inspiring the faithful in worship.

James MacMillan[1]

Writing [music] for me is prayer, it's my umbilical cord, my reason for existing.

Sir John Tavener[2]

The artist, whether he knows it or not, is consulting God when he looks at things.

Jacques Maritian[3]

In this first part of the book, I address the practice of sacred music by adopting a personal and first-hand approach to the question of what it means to engage with sacred music today. This is centred upon the areas in which we encounter music: composition and performance, both within and outside of organized religion.

In order to assess the current state and status of sacred music within secular society I have undertaken a number of interviews with composers, performers, theologians and philosophers. I also make use of material from published interviews with Sir John Tavener, Jonathan Harvey, Sir John Eliot Gardiner and others. Thus, in the next three chapters, my own questions and views are mixed with those of various colleagues with whom I have worked in the world of music, academia and the Church.

First, I examine what it means to be a composer of Christian music today. Many composers' sacred music has been shaped by the religious and cultural challenges posed by the times in which they lived. In Europe, composers were forced to adapt to the shift from the Medieval to the Renaissance world, and indeed to the cultural, political and religious upheaval of the Reformation. Emerging from a Puritan Commonwealth with the Restoration of monarchy in 1660, England sought to rebuild culture, art, music and sacramental religion, along with social and political harmony. Tensions, however, remained well into the eighteenth

---

[1]   James MacMillan, Sandford St Martins Lecture delivered at the Royal Institute of British Architects to mark the thirtieth anniversary of the Sandford St Martins Trust, October 2008. See http://www.telegraph.co.uk/news/religion/3116598/Composer-James-MacMillan-warns-of-liberal-elites-ignorance-fuelled-hostility-to-religion.html. 2008.

[2]   Sir John Tavener, interview with Nigel Farndale, *Daily Telegraph*, 29 July 2004.

[3]   Jacques Maritian, *Art and Scholasticism* (New York: Sheed and Ward, 1933), p. 64.

century; and this was characterized by fears (well-founded, or otherwise) of the
uncertain denominational allegiance of many of its monarchs. From huge Church
growth in the nineteenth century to what is popularly believed to be a slow decline
of religious attendance in the twentieth, we now live in a new era of a so-called
'secular society' where 'much debate about religion in recent times has become
polarized and fractious'.[4]

So what does it mean to be a composer of sacred music today? Is the
task primarily defined by the subject matter treated – the words or text? Is it,
alternatively, concerned above all with the intention of the composer or their
personal faith? Do you have to be a believer at all, or can you be a believer of
another faith? How much does one's upbringing matter, and to what degree can it
influence their music? What compositional techniques are used in creating sacred
music and, if music sets a text, does it necessarily have to be a biblical or religious
one? For the composer, does it matter what context one is writing for – the church
or the concert hall? These are just some of the areas covered in my discussions.
The conclusions reached from these investigations, which reveal divergent yet
heart-felt and strongly-held beliefs, point in one very distinct direction: that,
for the contemporary composer of sacred Christian music, the religious liturgy
is by no means the only intended destiny for their music, nor is it necessarily a
significant motivation for composition. The concert hall is an equally valid, and
perhaps an even more appropriate place, for sacred music to be encountered as
a religious house of worship. Thus, in today's society, the sacred is no longer
confined to the 'insiders' of the church-going few, but is now more available than
ever to the majority of people, through many different types of media, and in a
more accessible way than ever before.

This chapter will begin by assessing the significance of subject matter, whether
textual or thematic, in the composition process. The following section will ask
whether the composer's personal faith matters in producing good sacred music, or
whether sincerity of purpose is sufficient. Thereafter we consider how composers
of the past have had an influence on the sacred music composed today. This is
followed by an investigation into the importance, or otherwise, of the context
for which the composer is writing. Finally, I examine whether there are specific
compositional techniques that are particularly appropriate or powerful in the
creation of meaningful sacred music.

Subject Matter

Religious text is only one way in which music can be defined as sacred. There can
be a strong spiritual presence in purely instrumental music, such as J.S. Bach's
works for solo violin, cello or organ. So it was interesting to note that, when I

---

interviewed James MacMillan in October 2011, he was working on an instrumental piece that he described as 'theological':[5]

JA: Are you composing at the moment?

JM: I'm writing an orchestral piece for Marin Alsop, who's been a great champion of mine over the years and performed quite a lot of my music. It has a theological aspect to it but is purely instrumental – no text.

JA: Like *Veni Veni Emmanuel* for percussion – instrumental but with a text foremost in your mind?

JM: Yes. In fact, some of the more abstract works that I write do have a kind of extra musical dimension – a theological nature, sometimes text-based, sometimes image-based. The piece I'm writing now is both really. One of the pieces that Marin performed recently was my third piano concerto called *The Mysteries of Light*. It tries to revive an ancient practice of writing music based on the rosary. The Biber Rosary Sonatas came to mind but John Paul [II] introduced this new set of mysteries in the 1990s – the luminous mysteries – using five titles and reflections, so that was the basis. The work is in one movement but it has five sections: the Baptism of Jesus, The Miracle at Cana, and so on. So there's something both visual and textually reflective theologically.[6]

JA: Is that the case with all of your instrumental music or is some more abstract?

JM: Some of it has become more abstract. There are two piano sonatas, cello sonatas and a horn quintet where there's nothing extra – no theological context. I think, in the past, there have been more composers open to non-musical stimulus and that sometimes leads to a degree of suspicion. As you know, in the music world, amongst composers especially, there is a pride about music's abstract nature. There's a pride in the fact that music is complete in itself. It doesn't need anything other than its own material to communicate itself. That's fine and absolutely true and I quite enjoy a lot of abstract things. However, music does have this power of representation, connection and sometimes collaboration with the other arts – with words, with images and so on and it seems perverse to ignore that, especially for someone like me who's fascinated by these other things.

JA: There's no spiritual subtext or agenda to your Cello Concerto, but is your faith as a composer or the faith of the listener somehow involved in that?

JM: I think so. When lovers of music talk about the 'spirit' of the arts, they mean all music, not just music that's been inspired by liturgy or theology. It's the purely abstract works as well. It's the fact that the Bach Cello Suites can have that numinous effect on a listener even if they're not believers in

---

[5]   By the time this book is published no doubt the piece will have been completed, published and performed.

[6]   The five sections are: *Baptisma Iesu Christi, Miraculum in Cana, Proclamatio Regni Dei, Transfiguratio Domini Nostri, Institutio Eucharistiae*. See J. MacMillan, 'Why I Wrote a Piano Concerto Based Upon the Rosary', Blog, *Daily Telegraph*, 18 April, 2011.

any conventional sense. They will nevertheless, many of them, lapse into a terminology that implies a spiritual base to what the whole process is about. I'm certainly cognizant of that and there probably isn't anything substantially different in the effect of communication between the works that are purely abstract and non-theological and the ones that are theological.

JA: So, you can't take the faith out of the composer and whatever the listener perceives, the initial process of composition involves a spiritual aspect?

JM: I think so.[7]

This passage of conversation was very revealing: from this composer's point of view, the music could be sacred by virtue of its theological subtext, its power of connection, representation or collaboration, or its essential musical luminosity that can only be described by the language of the spirit. The liturgical context is not a prerequisite for any of these, and MacMillan perceives a sacred aspect to non-theological and theological works alike.

This leads me to my next question: does the devoutness, or sincerity, of the composer have a bearing on the quality of sacredness in the music?

Sincerity of Faith

Some composers are Christian and write from an explicitly faith-based perspective. Others produce wonderful sacred music almost as a by-product of their main intention of simply writing music. As Karl Barth wrote of Mozart:

> [He] does not intend to proclaim the praise of God. He just does so in fact; precisely in the humility in which he – himself to a certain extent only as an instrument – lets be heard what he apparently hears, that which impresses itself on him from God's creation, which rises up in him and demands to proceed out of him.[8]

For others, sincerity of faith is at the heart of the motivation for composing, something as true for some living composers as their Renaissance predecessors. For Harry Christophers, founder and conductor of *The Sixteen*, integrity of faith comes through in certain musical compositions:

---

[7]   Interview with James MacMillan, 18 October 2011, London.

[8]   K. Barth, *Wolfgang Amadeus Mozart 1756/1956* (Zurich, 1956), trans. C.K. Pott (Grand Rapids: Eerdmans, 1986), p. 27, quoted in Söhngen, 'Music and Theology' A Systematic Approach' in J. Irwin (ed.), *Sacred Sound: Music in Religious Thought and Practice*, Journal of the American Academy of Religion Studies, Vol. 50, no. 1 (Chico, CA: Scholars Press, 1983), pp. 1–19. Here at p. 8.

The music of the Renaissance is so incredibly special and composers like [John] Tavener and [Arvo] Pärt have brought things full circle, and are equally important – in particular Pärt, whose personal faith has made his music so exceptional. He uses silences to great effect – giving time to reflect … He says that people who perform his music must find their own way into it. If you look at his scores, there are very few markings – he does not dictate how you interpret his music.[9]

Harry is clear that, in today's society we take it for granted that Medieval and Renaissance composers from the West were, naturally, Christian and perhaps we relegate the significance of their religious belief to a past age. But one cannot ignore that some of the greatest composers of the twentieth century were also writing from a stance of faith:

More and more I find that sincerity [of faith] in their music sets those composers apart from others. We know that for most Renaissance composers their main employment was the Church; they were immersed in Church life all the time. Only a handful of the top composers in the twentieth and twenty-first centuries have made a real impact on Church music. If you compare [Francis] Poulenc with Michael Tippet … it's quite clear Tippet lacked faith. In the same way that Tomas Luis da Victoria's music is personal, Poulenc's music is personal. Particularly in the *Lenten Motets*, there's an intimate interpretation of the words, which only he could write – they are extraordinary and highly individual.[10]

The same is true of some of our greatest living composers, like James MacMillan:

James's music is constantly amazing because he is so imbued with the Catholic faith and is able to project that. He's a great composer, first and foremost, and that's why his music has such effect and we've found that, every time we perform a piece by James, we may find the audience a little bit nervous at the beginning [of the concert] because it has a modern piece of music in it, but come the end of the concert, that's the piece they go back and talk about. It's the same with his new setting of Psalm fifty-one, the *Miserere*, which is highly charged with emotion. There are one or two phrases where he's chosen to be absolutely joyous where another composer would probably follow a more reserved form. Other composers, who don't necessarily possess a faith, might, if they were to write a *Miserere*, think: 'This is a piece for Lent so we have to write it a traditionally penitential way.' Not James. It's the same with Arvo Pärt. Obviously he's much more introverted about his faith and his whole existence has been against political strife. He's coming at things from a different angle but nevertheless his music is deeply felt. [John] Tavener was a master at writing effective pieces.

---

[9]   Interview with Harry Christophers, Quadrant House, Fleet Street, London, 13 December 2011.

[10]   Ibid.

I sometimes question whether it's too formulaic. The *Song for Athene* and *The Lamb* are great pieces and very effective and they conjure up wonderful things. But I worry about many contemporary composers who copy him … In the world of choral music, there are three composers for me whose personalities come out of their music, so overtly in a really powerful way full of incredible faith, and that's Victoria, Poulenc and MacMillan. They happen all to be Catholic.[11]

For Harry Christophers, good sacred choral composition is not just about high art classical music:

In more recent times, Taizé music and chants have become very evocative. Margaret Rizza has written similar chants … She's a late convert Catholic and it's interesting to see how her music works in a different way from that of James MacMillan, for instance. They're perhaps easier on the ear than some other music and they don't challenge you in the way that James MacMillan will challenge. But they have an important part to play in sacred music today.[12]

For the conductor Peter Phillips, the choral music of the Renaissance is as great as any piece of large-scale Romantic repertoire:

When it comes to the craft of music, there have been composers of every period who have been masters of [it]. But I get the impression that in the Renaissance period an awful lot of people were very good … I used to go into the library and I'd think, let's do a piece by Mouton. So I'd get the Mouton volumes down and, literally, I could open any volume on any page and the pieces I found would be worth doing … There aren't very many Renaissance composers that fall below that litmus test … I've never understood why the average standard was so high in the Renaissance. Line up Strauss, Beethoven and Josquin, they're on the same level! Josquin and Beethoven are a very interesting comparison. These two have the technique and the brain to tower over their contemporaries and do absolutely anything they wanted with music as they found it.[13]

Likewise, Harry Christophers sees quality throughout Renaissance choral music that has endured:

How many pieces from the Renaissance would you call rubbish? There aren't many … Maybe it's the form in which they were written. They weren't all going by the textbook at the time. You think of Sheppard and all those false relations in

---

[11]   Ibid.

[12]   Ibid.

[13]   Interview with Peter Phillips, Merton College, Oxford, 21 February, 2012.

his music – what were they there for?[14] They're there for a creative purpose. All the Victorian editors took them out because they thought they were so gross but actually, the subtleties of that marvellous form were lovely.[15]

So much for comparisons between dead composers of the past. But what about living Christian composers, of whom there are many: how has their background influenced the means by which they approach their art? James MacMillan shares his experience again:

> JA: From your upbringing, what's your background as a believer and how has it influenced you?
>
> JM: I think a lot actually. I grew up in semi-rural Ayrshire in the Sixties. Catholic communities in places like that were big but also well integrated. Extended family all lived close together – school, parish, community – so that the reception of the sacrament was a communal activity, something we learned in a class of thirty kids: communion classes, first confession, and first communion were greatly celebrated by the wider community, which was very large. I was aware that there were hundreds of people around for one's first communion. So it was an intense, sometimes perhaps an introverted community, because it was a part of the country which perhaps felt that it was slightly under threat. But it was shared public Catholicism. The idea of making religion a private thing would have seemed nonsense to those people, to my parents and grandparents and so on.
>
> JA: I know other cradle Catholic musicians who have lost their faith, but not you?
>
> JM: I've tried to think of times when I might have, but I just didn't, not even when I joined the Communist Party when I was fifteen and didn't stop going to Mass. At conferences I would miss the Sunday morning session and go to Mass, and in those days, in the 1970s, the Communist Party was profoundly Stalinist, so they just wondered what on earth I was doing. It was a good experience for me. I learned a lot about politics. I'm not on the left anymore (I am not on the right) … So that would have been the time to stop, but I didn't and I think, especially now, there are people who are offended by so much in religion that makes them recoil. They're just disgusted with it. But you and I know that that isn't the big story and it's a continual rearguard action to try to explain to people that there's something better.

---

[14] A false relation 'is the name of a type of dissonance that sometimes occurs in polyphonic music, most commonly in vocal music of the Renaissance. The term describes a "chromatic" contradiction' between two notes sounding simultaneously, (or in close proximity), in two different voice parts. For example, the clash between an E♮ and an E♭. See G. Dyson, 'False Relation' in L. Macy (ed.), *Grove Music Online*, http://www.oxfordmusiconline.com/public/book/omo_gmo (accessed 16 February 2007).

[15] Interview with Harry Christophers.

JA: I suppose your inspiration came from that bigger story, which is a narrative centred around Christ the historical figure and the risen reality?

JM: Exactly. I was very lucky in that, when I left home at eighteen and went to university, I think that's the time when things disintegrate for lots of Catholics. For them, Catholicism remains mummified or infantilized, and they never let it develop. There's more catechesis that allows it to develop. However, I fell under the spell (if that's the right word) of the Dominicans at Edinburgh; and coming under their scholarly way of thinking, my Catholicism developed. It became an adult Catholicism. It became a thinking Catholicism.

JA: Of course the Dominicans place an emphasis upon preaching and teaching. Is that part of your agenda?

JM: I get asked about this because the O.P. after the names of the Dominicans. It means 'Order of Preachers'. I get a lot of hostile secular interviewers saying, 'Oh, so you see your work as preaching do you?', which just confirms their view that I'm a religious fanatic using my music as an instrumentalist tool to convince and convert, and that isn't the case. Although, when you want to explore what preaching means, beyond the merely generalistic, you are getting into an area of giving witness to the truth and, to be honest, I can't say that that's not what I'm doing. I've got to own up to that. Everything I do is a kind of witness; it's not Bible bashing in the populist sense, but I am very much aware that everything I write posits something in the secular culture that some will find offensive, some won't, and some will be neutral about it. It's just a given; it can't be any other way now.

JA: Is this role of witness something you have unwittingly fallen into?

JM: Yes, in a way. I'm just responding to what's there in me and the music is an outcome of all these things we've just talked about, from my family background to the Dominicans, and my reading, my own study, my own development intellectually and musically. So it's inevitable that the music would be the way it is, even non-text based things. So I don't know if I could do it any other way.[16]

In this section of the interview, having shared some insight into his religious upbringing, James goes on to suggest that his life, and therefore his music, is a kind of Christian witness. Whether he particularly intends to write a piece of 'sacred' music or not, because of the nature of his faith and his life experience, his music will inevitably contain a trace of his background, reading, study and faith, even in an abstract piece of instrumental music. Again, we are reminded of how composers such as MacMillan, as well as Arvo Pärt, John Tavener, Jonathan Harvey, Jonathan Dove, Gabriel Jackson and many others, have written music that will have a witness within secular society well beyond the confines of the church doors.

The contemporary Jewish composer, Robert Saxton, composes from the faith perspective of his own religious tradition, but also enjoys writing sacred Christian music. When I interviewed him in Oxford, he told me the story of how he was

---

[16]   Interview with James MacMillan.

clearing out some boxes in the attic and found compositions that he had scribbled as a child:

> I found, and this was genuinely to my surprise, because I don't remember it, the beginnings of pieces that were written when I was about eleven or twelve … There are literally hundreds with twenty bars and then they stop! … A lot of them are about two things and two things only: they are either about Norfolk and the beach and the countryside or they're religious. They're [the religious ones] either about Moses or Abraham or they're carols … My Hebrew lessons as a child about the Old Testament stories and characters must somehow have gone very deep because all these pieces seem to be about it![17]

I am fascinated by this religious background and how it has influenced him in his life as a composer:

> I was born eight years after the Second World War, and a lot of people in my synagogue were German refugees. The war wasn't a historical thing for me. I had a German aunt whose parents had been murdered by the Nazis; my mother's family are Dutch Jews with French relatives; my mother's father was Polish; Dad's family are Russian and Lithuanian but my father's mother was Yorkshire Protestant – a butcher's daughter from Hull. It is an extraordinary mixture.[18]

Moreover, Robert's education in a Christian school and at Cambridge University, studying with Benjamin Britten and Elisabeth Lutyens, had a tremendous cultural influence upon him. In the end his musical influences are a blend of cultures:

> It's a very odd mixture of cultures and I think it has affected me musically. And then of course knowing [Benjamin] Britten, there's another connection with East Anglia. I just think that it's gratitude too, on a very deep level, for the country and the culture … When I was at school I always loved it when we sang [music by] Vaughan Williams.

So is Robert Saxton's music in some way influenced by the English Christian tradition?

> Yes, English Christianity from Iona and Augustine … I always feel tremendously at home in English churches and cathedrals. The point about the tradition is whether it's a cultural or a spiritual thing. For me it is a spiritual thing but it's not specifically Christian … I agree with Schoenberg who said that Jesus is the greatest human being that ever lived.[19]

---

[17]　Interview with Robert Saxton, Worcester College, Oxford, November 2011.
[18]　Ibid.
[19]　Ibid.

Thus, from Robert's Jewish perspective, there seems to be an element of religious humanism in his work, by which I mean that, as human beings, our greatest potential is unlocked by means of following the example of the greatest religious teachers. Robert has written extensively for religious liturgy, so I asked him exactly what he was expecting from each project and what he might be hoping to achieve:

> Well, if you want me to be high-minded it is that I'm contributing to something which has an enormous cultural, spiritual and religious heritage. The difference that it makes as a composer, the difference in psychology of writing for a service and not selling your wares in a concert, is that you're not so worried about the critics and what the audience think. In a sense you're released from that burden of having to be the focus. [Rather than asking] "Did I enjoy your piece of music or not?", people focus on the worship instead. Even if they aren't devoutly worshipping, they are focussing on the whole service.[20]

Nevertheless, Robert's most recent large-scale work is an opera, commissioned by the BBC for radio broadcast, entitled *The Wandering Jew*. The legend of the Wandering Jew inspired Robert to examine the phenomenon in music, using texts from several different religious traditions, including Psalms, Arabic literature, Goethe, Dante and the Bible.[21] But in general, Robert makes a clear distinction between the liturgical setting for compositions and the secular setting. For instance, in considering Wagner's *Parsifal*, he questions: 'Is the audience at [a performance of] *Parsifal* a congregation or an audience?' He makes the point that many Wagnerians would see the opera *Parsifal* as a work of Christian spirituality and perhaps has become music that is worshipped in itself, to the extent that Wagner the man has become an object of worship for some. Robert Saxton has no time for such sentiments and answers his own question: 'If it is a congregation then, in my book, it's a fake congregation.' What makes a *real* congregation is sacred music employed within the liturgy. On the one hand, even liturgical music eventually ends up being performed in the concert hall and retains its sacred nature. On the other hand, writing for the liturgy perhaps releases the composer from a concern with the self, and the audience's criticisms; and instead focuses the composer, performers and listeners on the task of enacting the religious service. Both of these two scenarios, the concert and the church service, have legitimacy.

However, according to some critics, not all contemporary classical choral music, however popular, is sacred in the sense that James' and Robert's music is, and not all is composed to the same rigorous compositional standards. In an article entitled, 'Religious Music for the Commitment-Phobe', Ivan Hewitt took

---

20   Ibid.

21   Robert Saxton, *The Wandering Jew*, Roderick Williams in the title role, BBC Singers and Symphony Orchestra, conducted by André de Ridder (London: NMC, 2011).

exception to the 'quasi-religious' music of one composer, whose music was performed at the 2012 BBC Proms at the Royal Albert Hall:[22]

> Eric Whitacre, current darling of the large audience that enjoys so-called 'spiritual' music ... This late-night Prom showed why. The music is suffused with a sense of easy spiritual uplift ... There were no blemishes anywhere, not a hint of darkness in Whitacre's Day-Glo world. Everything had a peculiar weightless and unreal quality, like the musical equivalent of a stage set.[23]

Without taking sides on whether Hewitt is correct in his criticism, he picks up on a vital point in discerning the quality of so-called 'spiritual' music. It is not sincerity that is proof of its spirituality, but content. Hewitt goes on to make an interesting comparison with composers who have demonstrated a more serious engagement with the sacred:

> The man positively oozes sincerity. Whitacre is so sincere I suspect he would glow in the dark. And that's the problem. As Stravinsky so wisely put it, 'in art, sincerity is the *sine qua non* which at the same time guarantees nothing'. Sincerity needs content, otherwise it shrinks to the bogus sound of the politician on the hustings who ends every statement with the phrase, 'and I mean that sincerely'. In the case of Eric Whitacre, content of any kind is exactly what's missing. To begin with, he avoids anything that might smack of belief. 'I'm not an atheist, but I'm not a Christian either,' is about as close as he gets to a credo.
>
> In itself this isn't a problem. Plenty of agnostics have written fine religious music. And who's to say the overtly religious composers such as Bach didn't have their moments of doubt? What counts isn't possessing certainties. It's the serious engagement with the substance of belief, rather than the easy evocation of feelings. In music, this tussling with something difficult and problematic is symbolised by the composer's tussle with a musical language.
>
> For a great religious composer such as Bach, the musical language he was born into had the force of law, as unavoidable and exacting as religion itself. It wasn't something he could just pick up and put down at will. The language had tough rules, and yet Bach never dropped any hint that he found them irksome. He actually relished the difficulty of writing counterpoint, and liked to make things even harder for himself. He would have agreed with Edmund Burke that 'difficulty is our true friend'. The severity of strict rules is one thing that enabled Bach to 'keep it real'. Another was the fact that his music sprang from a particular time and place.
>
> We forget this, because we like to praise Bach for his 'timeless' beauty. But there's nothing timeless about Bach's great Passions and cantatas. They are

---

[22] http://www.telegraph.co.uk/culture/music/proms/9528897/Religious-music-for-the-commitment-phobe.html.

[23] Ibid.

absolutely rooted in their own time. They are full of chorale melodies, those sturdy affirmations of the Protestant faith that Martin Luther designed to be sung by the ordinary man and woman. The counterpoint is in the tremendous North German tradition that stretches back through Bach's great forebears such as Buxtehude.

Look at other great religious composers, and they all have that quality of being rooted in a coherent style, and in a definite time and place. Palestrina's Masses breathe the air of Counter-Reformation Rome. Thomas Tallis's English anthems show the stresses and strains of England's break with Rome. Modern religious composers are deprived of this context, but the better ones try to find substitutes. Some, like James MacMillan, weave a sense of the dark conflicts in human nature into their music. Arvo Pärt has invented his own musical language, as tough and rule-bound as Palestrina's.

Compare Whitacre, who doesn't dirty his hands with such things. He and the many composers like him offer instant uplift with no emotional cost. Their radiant gestures feel weightless, because they have nothing to affirm, or deny. His is the perfect religious music for the commitment-phobe, which is surely why it is so popular. One can only hope that, in time, it meets with the commitment-phobe's usual fate.[24]

Hewitt may be unduly harsh, but his point makes an important contribution to our discussion: namely that, if we are to discern what is truly sacred, then we must resist confusing genuinely great religious music with instantly gratifying 'feel-good' music. The great sacred composers of the past (Tallis, Palestrina, Bach) have stood the test of time. Many of today's composers of sacred music have substantial claims to greatness by the weight of their serious engagement with both faith *and* society, and their refusal to shy away from the realities of both belief and doubt. To deny either of these positions is a denial of the fundamental issues we deal with as human beings. We now turn to consider what other influences impact upon the modern composer.

Influences of Other Composers

Thus far, we have been able to deduce from these interviews that cultural and religious background form a natural starting point for these contemporary composers. But what about musical influences from previous generations? What music, and which composers, have inspired James MacMillan?

I've always been interested in music of our own time, so that I consider the last century to be a huge influence on what I have done, but I think I've had to learn first principles from great figures of history and it's no accident that composers

---

24   Ibid.

need to absorb the mindset and working approach of people like Bach and Palestrina and the great contrapuntalists. That's why we study counterpoint so intensely as students, and some might find that a chore, but to be honest, as a composer, it's absolutely essential … The way they build complex structures, although the material might be different in our time, the basic principles of multi-linked strands are a fundamental lesson. But the interesting thing is that the great contrapuntalists from history, the abstract figures, the ones that really made counterpoint, they must have made their listeners feel like they were in heaven, so there might be a connection between complexity and the mind of God – the window onto the divine.

JA: Like Victoria, from Avila in Spain, where the mystical tradition of Teresa seems to have been imparted into his soul and is perhaps conveyed in his music?

JM: I think so. His work is imbued so much by his context and his culture. There's something in Victoria that even Palestrina doesn't have – a kind of red-bloodedness that comes from that experience of Spain at that time.

JA: Do you think Victoria gained from what he learned in Rome from Palestrina?

JM: Yes, I was thinking that when I heard *The Sixteen* the other day.[25] After the Council of Trent and the importance of getting the text over, sure enough I could hear the text, and that came from Palestrina in a way that you wouldn't have heard in earlier composers.[26] There's a lot of music from just before then where that certainly would not have been the case, so that must have been a Palestrina impact to an extent that composers were dwelling more on the text.

But what about more recent composers who have been an influence?

I feel that I'm absolutely rooted in something that has lasted for thousands of years but, even in modernity, in my branch of the arts, if you think about it, all the great composers of the past hundred years have been religious one way or another – Stravinsky, who set Masses, set the Psalms and was a believer with his orthodoxy and various interest in Western Catholicism. He was conservative in his religion, as conservative as he was revolutionary in his music making. But he was a believer. Schoenberg reconverted to a practising Judaism after the Holocaust and all his late works reflect the Jewish tradition. Messiaen: another great giant of the twentieth century – profoundly Catholic. Every note of his works is shaped by a theology. All the composers that came after Shostakovich from behind the Iron Curtain were profoundly religious people. Schnittke,

---

[25] *The Sixteen*, Choral Pilgrimage Tour, featuring the music of Tomas Luis de Victoria (1548–1611), a Spanish composer, singer, scholar and later priest who spent many years in Italy before returning to Spain to live out his days as a chaplain and musician; Giovanni Pierluigi de Palestrina (1525–94) was the greatest Italian polyphonist of his day and taught Victoria in Rome.

[26] The Council of Trent (1545–63).

Ustvolskaya, Kancheli, Arvo Pärt.[27] Even in this country, Benjamin Britten
possessed a kind of social questioning Anglicanism. To try and disassociate that
from Christianity is perverse. So I feel part of a mainstream. But if you start to
point that out to people they say 'Oh no!'. I'm not peripheral – people like me,
John Tavener, Jonathan Harvey, it's not peripheral at all. It's not just plugged
into the Christian traditions but the very experience of modernism in music so
I'm imbued with a confidence and I don't feel out on a limb.[28]

In mentioning Jonathan Harvey (1939–2013) and John Tavener (1944–2013),
MacMillan points to other British composers whose faith comes through in their
work. Harvey, however, started out as a Christian and became a Buddhist, as he
revealed in an interview with Daniel Jaffé: 'I like to unify, not into an easy unity,
but a unity which is rich and complex. I'd like music to speak of, to herald and to
prophesy a better world, less entangled with personal egoistic emotions'.[29]

Like Robert Saxton, Harvey instinctively wrote music as a child. He sang as a
chorister at St Michael's College, Tenbury (an institution which no longer sustains
a choir).[30] Harvey has written several small sacred choral works (most notably
perhaps *Come, Holy Ghost* (1984) and *I Love the Lord* (1976)); but one concert
piece particularly evokes a strong sense of the religious. His first electronic
composition was *Mortuos Plango, Vivos Voco* (1980), composed in Paris while
he was working with Pierre Boulez. In the work Harvey used recordings of the
great bell of Winchester Cathedral – on which is engraved the Latin words *HORA
AVOLANTES NUMERO, MORTUOS PLANGO, VIVOS AD PRECES VOCO*
('I count the fleeting hours, I lament the dead, I call the living to prayer'). The
music also included the recorded singing of his son Dominic, at that time a
chorister at Winchester. At the heart of Harvey's compositional outlook is a faith
in which 'emptiness' is a key concept:

> Emptiness is ... a Buddhist word which is very hard to understand and for
> people to explain: it really means 'lack of inherent existence'. Nothing that
> we call an individual object – whether it's a table or a person – really has any
> individual existence: we give it a label, but in fact it's changing all the time,
> and it's composed of parts, the parts are composed of parts. Everything is an
> imputation of a kind of continuum. So in the Buddhist view of things, nothing
> has inherent existence, but a kind of shifting existence of impermanence ... It's
> particularly a concept to do with the self, in that [the] person that we think we are
> is a kind of an illusory tacking together of static things, and the self is something

---

[27]   Alfred Schnittke (1934–98); Galina Ulstvolskaya (1919–2006); Giya Kancheli
(b. 1935); Arvo Pärt (b. 1935).

[28]   Interview with James MacMillan.

[29]   Jonathan Harvey (1939–2012), interview with Daniel Jaffé, *Classic CD*, July 2009.

[30]   Ibid.

we grasp at, which we try to desperately establish. And this is the root of all our suffering.[31]

So how does this religious philosophy feed into Harvey's music?

I think music [is] a very profound wisdom which shows, with these notes, or a few notes which are always changing, must make different shapes and 'forms'. If you call 'ba-ba-ba Bah!' [sings the opening notes of Beethoven's *Fifth Symphony*] the 'first subject' or whatever – you think 'gosh, what a strong character that has!'. But you know G and E flat – the next moment those notes mean something totally different. So music develops to us this sense of the shift of nature, of reality; we believe in things but they're constantly dissolved before our eyes.[32]

John Tavener was one of the most successful composers of Christian sacred music of modern times and, in an interview with David McCleery, he made it clear that he had a universalist vision for the world and hoped that his music might contribute to the healing of the world's problems:

The fact that I've been given this universalist vision of the world makes it a possibility that I might be able to contribute, just fractionally, toward the healing of a planet that's torn to pieces at the moment, by strife, by war, by different religions warring with each other. Now through the universalist language of music perhaps there is a possibility to bring about a healing process and, after all, music originally had this function. If one listens or looks on the rituals of the American Indian or African tribes one sees that all ritual ceremonies and all music was either addressed to the creator or it was music of healing … Music in the West has become so sophisticated … that I think we've lost sight of this dimension in music.[33]

Thus, Tavener moved away from particular forms of institutional religion in favour of a more harmonized approach to all religions where music plays a central role in healing divisions. Tavener's account of the evolution of music in the West corresponds to McGilchrist's thesis concerning the domination in contemporary society of the left hemisphere of our brains.[34]

---

[31] Ibid.

[32] Ibid.

[33] Sir John Tavener, interview with David McCleery, transcribed from 'John Tavener Reflects … A Recorded Interview' on the CD recording *John Tavener: A Portrait* (Naxos, 2004).

[34] McGilchrist, *The Master and his Emissary*, pp. 94–132.

I know that I'm very intuitive and sometimes I know what people are needing to hear ... I just feel that the Western tradition, the highly sophisticated, the highly complex ways in which art has gone has exhausted itself and we need to sit back and we need to contemplate and we need to meditate a bit more and we need to think about the feminine and we need to go back into the heart.[35]

But Tavener's notion of the 'sacred' in music, as in his universalist approach to religion, leads ultimately to silence: 'Any kind of music that is dealing with higher realities in the end must go towards a kind of sacred nothingness so, therefore, possibly one day I shall just stop'.[36] Until his death, Sir John continued to be inspired by something divine, which he referred to as the 'Jesus imagination' and the 'angel of inspiration':

Increasingly, I understand Blake who referred to the 'Jesus imagination' ... The imagination is a divine thing and is not capable, in its true, pure sense, of having a profane idea. These ideas that come like that put me in a state of semi-ecstasy and leave me feeling revitalised. There is no way I can forget them because they seem to emerge from deep down in the subconscious. I can't get an idea out of my head because it's part of me, in a way. Sometimes I have the sensation that I've known it already. Like *déjà vu*. Not that it was another piece of music, but that one has known it before. I think Yeats experienced something similar in writing poetry ... I see myself as a conduit. It has to be effortless. Effort for me means existential angst and ego and I don't want any of that in the music. Music must be about transcending the ego rather than being imprisoned by it ... Once you start seeing the ego of Beethoven, his music can seem self-conscious, particularly in the late quartets. But then you look at the late Bagatelles and there he seems to ... give up the effort and it is sublime.[37]

Like Karl Barth, Tavener considered Mozart to have perfected an effortless sound in music, one that left Tavener baffled: 'Mozart is inexplicable. Everything in his music is ecstatic. If you just change the position of a single chord, the whole thing falls to pieces. It's so perfectly poised. That's why it moves me. And if music doesn't move one, if it doesn't inwardly reduce you to your knees, what's the point of it?'[38] So, Nigel Farndale asked, what for John Tavener was the distinction between a religious experience and an aesthetic one?

You almost have to become childlike in relation to a religious experience. I never have doubts when I'm writing music. I may well have quite strong atheist thoughts the rest of the time but that is perhaps irrelevant because when I'm

---

[35]   John Tavener, interview with David McCleery.
[36]   Ibid.; John Tavener died in November 2013.
[37]   Sir John Tavener, interview with Nigel Farndale.
[38]   Ibid.

actually composing I have my proof. I have a certitude ... writing for me is prayer, it's my umbilical cord, my reason for existing.[39]

I'm not sure Sir John could have been any clearer than that about his motivation for composing. Thus the Judeo-Christian religions, Buddhism, the Eastern traditions and a universalist vision have all been important influences upon these musicians, who have composed, like many others not mentioned here, for both liturgical and concert settings. So now we turn to ask: how much does context of performance space matter in the compositional process?

Context

We have seen that, in the Renaissance, Reformation and Restoration periods, sacred music was mostly confined to performances either within churches and cathedrals as part of the liturgy, or in more domestic settings as part of religious devotion. The eighteenth century brought a European-wide change with the rise of the large, purpose-built and luxurious concert halls, enabling the expansion of sacred music to a wider public arena. So for today's composers of sacred music, does context matter anymore? I asked James MacMillan, who is familiar with both ecclesiastical and secular settings for his work, whether composing concert music is like writing for those who don't wish to go to church, but are happy to hear sacred music in another setting:

> There are a lot of people like that, but I think there's an overlapping section of that audience who are church-going still. I was thinking of that when I attended a packed *Sixteen* concert in Edinburgh.[40] A lot of the audience weren't church-going, but many were. My *St John Passion* [2007] was performed in Glasgow a few weeks ago, and I think I knew about half the audience and a lot of them were Christians. There is also a kind of 'new age' element who find this music so 'pure' and 'disembodied'.
>
> JA: Is there a difference between what you do in a liturgical context and what you do in a concert setting?
>
> JM: Well, there is an adjustment that the music can be used for different purposes. A lot of my music is not written for liturgy, even the *St John Passion* is not written for liturgy, although it's imbued by liturgy and a lot of these orchestral pieces that we've been talking about are written knowing they would be performed in secular spaces for a secular audience and I'm aware that that secular audience have this thirst and a knowledge, a deep knowledge, of the connections between music and the spirit. They talk a lot about 'spirituality' and it can mean a lot of things, and it's unfocussed a lot of the time but, nevertheless,

---

[39]   Ibid.
[40]   Greyfriars Kirk, 2011.

a lot of people are aware that there's something about that world that connects them with something more than themselves, more than the sum of their parts. There is other music that I write, which is geared totally for the liturgy and written according to liturgical principles, but even then I'm aware that that music will find a secular audience and that people will clap at it. I'm at ease with that.

JA: Is it a kind of witness do you think?

JM: Yes, it is happening, but it doesn't seem to be part of that conscious part of my brain where I'm setting out to be instrumentally insinuating an idea, an agenda. It just happens because I'm part of that tradition. I'm mired in it, rooted in it. It's just there whether I want it or not.

JA: Do you see sacred music of the past (e.g. Renaissance), originally written entirely for the liturgy, now enjoyed purely on an abstract level?

JM: I've thought about this a lot in connection to the *Passion*, having written one, and the fact that people will come, especially in Holy Week, to hear the Bach *Passions*, and they'll hear them in churches but they will be performed as concerts a lot of the time and people especially in those situations, even though they're not believers, know there's something else going on. It's not just a kind of lowest common denominator musical abstraction. There's an acknowledgement, if the listener is intelligent, of the civilization that gave rise to it. But I think also, if they're sensitive, they're aware of something much, much deeper than that. That they may not be able to relate to in a confessional way anymore but they acknowledge … that there's something profoundly religious going on in these concert encounters with Bach (for instance) and that the audience who go to hear Bach's *Passions* at that time of year, go to hear the whole range of different perceptions of the numinous. I don't think it is as entirely atheistic as some would want.[41]

Thus, as a confessing Christian, James is at ease with the notion that his music, even if it is specifically composed for the liturgy, will almost certainly also be performed in a concert setting. James sees this as an opportunity for many who cannot confess to a faith nevertheless to engage with something deep, spiritual and numinous. Following on from these assertions, I wanted to explore more, with James, what musical heritage was at the heart of good sacred music. His answer was unambiguous – plainchant:

JA: Is there something fundamental in plainchant and the rhythm of prayer and life? Has chant always been of interest to you?

JM: Yes it has, because I've always found it beautiful but it seems to be the most paradigmatic form of sung prayer through Christendom, especially Catholicism. It's the sound of Catholicism as far as I'm concerned. Its timelessness takes you into that kind of cosmic liturgy that's on-going and gives a different sense of place and process and prayer and it just seems so natural.

---

[41]   Interview with James MacMillan.

I always feel that it's a great shame that it's got knocked on the head a little bit and knocked out of the ordinary experience of most Catholics.

JA: Is it not used in most Catholic churches?

JM: Not so much. It seems to have fallen away. There are lots of reasons for that and it's all mostly disputed. It's all to do with well-meaning and good people trying to think of practical ways of renewal of Church with the Holy Spirit and sometimes the wrong turn they took was trying to make it more relevant with popular culture and secular culture even, and that meant taking the music from the secular world. I think that has been a big miscalculation that many denominations have made and it's made many liturgies just banal. If we go back to the great paradigmatic song fare we would ennoble the liturgy once again and make it Godward in its orientation.

JA: Is there much of that going on in churches?

JM: Well, we've been given this big new opportunity (some see it as an opportunity, I certainly do anyway) of the new translation of the Mass, which has allowed us a way to catechize again about the meaning of the liturgy and the better priests have done it and it has involved a return to chant in English as well as in Latin. And also looking to what we should be doing. The hymn sandwich we adopted from other traditions doesn't really work for us and other people get used to it and think there's no other way. Whereas these Propers and entrance Gradual antiphons, which [in the past] were never sung, or only perfunctorily mumbled, and nobody really knows what they're there for, but they should be sung. So we've started looking – there's a move to get people in the pew to start singing these again. There's different ways of doing it, but there's a marvellous American book, which is a translation of the *Gradualia Simplex*, for use in small churches. It's in English but the British are getting their own soon. Basically, the *schola* would sing a very simple monastic chant – Psalm verses with a simple Psalm line or verse from the New Testament sung as a response by the congregation, so immediately the congregation are involved intrinsically in the work relating to that day's liturgy, not just some sort of half-accurate add on. We sing a lot of unaccompanied [music], so immediately there's a more Gregorian feel to liturgy – a bit more asceticism, which worries some people. It certainly doesn't worry me. It just roots the heart and the mind. It's all to do with character. If you can change the character of the liturgy into that more authentic feel, then I think you're doing the Church a great service.

James puts his own opinions regarding chant into practice by employing plainsong and his ideas in the parish church choir he runs in Glasgow:

It's a Dominican church, St Columba's, and no one else was doing it [the music], so I just started doing it. There's no money involved or anything but I absolutely love it. It's one of the poorest parishes in the whole of the Archdiocese and people are reticent, a sort of quietism, and Catholics are generally not good singers compared to Anglicans and Protestants … It's a constant struggle to try and engage the congregation but it's not impossible. But if it's simple enough, and Gregorian chant can be very simple, and those little refrains are just a couple of alternating notes, it's possible.

JA: It's fascinating. Your choir are not musically trained?

JM: Not at all. Even my choir to begin with is made up of people who've hardly sung let alone read music. A lot of them don't read music so anything complex requires a lot of note-bashing. But generally people get to know what was going on and students started to arrive, so standards rose. I've lost a lot of them because they've all gone off to university and so on. So the last few weeks I've started going back to chant with them.

JA: It's very interesting for people like me to know that you're musically involved at a parish level. What is the best way of incorporating music within the liturgy in a parish church?

JM: There have to be different ways. I think those places with high professional standards should be encouraged. The problem was that a kind of anti-professionalism entered the Catholic Church and I think the Anglicans have had their own issues about the nature of liturgy. But the 1960s saw a kind of 'bonfire of the choirs' throughout the Catholic Church because they were regarded as elitist. And at one time Westminster Cathedral was under threat. The school nearly closed and they just managed to hold on by the skin of their teeth really. And all of that was kind of well-meaning ideology really – A skewed ideology taken from the sign of the times – the *Zeitgeist* – rather than the *Heiligegeist*. It took on 1960s egalitarian values and with that goes an anti-elitism, and sometimes an anti-professionalism even amongst clergy. So you don't spend a lot of time and energy focussing on the liturgy, but be creative – can it be better? – the kind of 'spur of the moment' rather than the pre-planned, pre-prepared, which just leads to slovenliness in a lot of cases. So we've got a lot of 'unprofessional' clergy a lot of the time and they preside over increasingly banal liturgies. A new questioning of that has entered the Church. Unfortunately it means that people like me are unfairly characterized as reactionaries. It's not the case. But there is that old background context of liberals and traditionalists battling away at these things and the pro-music, pro-Gregorian and pro-choral tends to be on the traditionalist side and that can sometimes get mired into irrelevant, political dealings.[42]

Thus, for James, there are challenges ahead for the Catholic Church in terms of professional and amateur liturgical music alike, and Gregorian chant may be one way to encourage high standards of sacred music back into the churches. Likewise, for the Anglican Church, it is essential to value and invest in those professional choirs who sing in our cathedrals and colleges, where congregational attendance is rising; but also to nurture the tradition of sacred choral music at a parish level, and maybe plainchant has a role here, too. The next area for discussion, therefore,

---

[42]   Interview with James MacMillan.

is what kind of compositional techniques are particularly employed when writing sacred music.

Compositional Techniques

Can music, by nature of the form in which it is composed, intimate to us something of the sacred? For Harry Christophers, some Renaissance composers were able to use techniques that perfectly expressed their intentions. One such composer was Victoria:

> He's very special, there's no doubt about it. (a) he knew exactly how to write for voices but (b) he knew just when to highlight a particular [vocal] part. He knew exactly when to bring out a little nuance when there was a particular word that was special to him. You can hear it, whether it be *O Vos Omnes* or the *Lamentations* or the *Requiem* and it's dynamic stuff.[43]

Jonathan Harvey emphasized a combination of basic musical ideas and preparation: 'I'm excited by the materiality of the sound itself, by the "suchness" – to use a Buddhist term – the "thing in itself": the grain, the richness, the quality of the sound.'[44] As Daniel Jaffé points out, a good example of this technique can be found in Harvey's piece *One Evening* (1994) where rhythm speeds up along with a rising pitch until it is transformed into a single tone. Harvey also considered this to be a good example:

> That is a kind of concept of dance rhythm turning into a static thing which has all sorts of levels [of meaning]; there's the body, and there's the spirit. I don't particularly like to draw a distinction between these two things as you end up with a dualistic philosophy; but that is the seamless transition from dance and the continuous shimmer or colour, static sound; once you've speeded up the first it becomes the second and you can't put a sword in between them.[45]

Another characteristic of Harvey's compositional technique is a blending of different electronic and live sounds: 'there's no divide between electronics and acoustic instruments; you can't tell where one starts and the other finishes'.[46] His piece *One Evening* is an experimental concert work, but also contains texts relating to the Buddhist faith:

---

[43] Interview with Harry Christophers.

[44] Jonathan Harvey interview with Daniel Jaffé.

[45] Ibid.

[46] Ibid.

At the core of the work is the idea of emptiness, where it's approached from four different viewpoints. First is a Chinese Buddhist's experience of emptiness, like moonlight on snow; second is a vision of unity in which Rabindranath Tagore experiences a sensation that the people and objects he sees from his balcony become rhythmic light; third is a woman's sudden fearful loss of self – the sense that she only exists in relation to her history and context; the final movement is a trance-like blend of bliss and emptiness, expressed by floating voices over a dancing tabla accompaniment.[47]

Thus the sacred element of the music comes directly from Harvey's own experience of the Buddhist faith, and his concert works reflect that faith, just as his earlier works for choral services reflect the Christian faith. I asked James MacMillan if he deliberately used particular techniques in order to express theological concepts in his work:

> JA: In your piece *O Bone Jesu*, for instance, there is a repetition of the word 'Jesu', set to block chords, which slightly change throughout the piece, and it has an extremely high soprano part which ends with a high soprano solo note. Do you try and push the boundaries of performers' abilities in order to express something of 'the Other'?
>
> JM: I think so and it depends who I'm writing for. *Christus Vincit* was written for Westminster Abbey, Westminster Cathedral and St Paul's Cathedral Choirs, three of the best [cathedral] choirs in the world really, so I could write to their strengths. I have found, as my music's become more known, that a lot of other choirs have found certain pieces very difficult to do. A lot of them would love to do *Christus Vincit*, which is very exposed, and not every choir could sing with that kind of tidiness and precision. So what I've done, which is a practical thing in recent years, I've tried to drop the level of difficulty. There's a whole set of motets called the *Strathclyde Motets*, all written for the liturgy, which means that more ordinary church choirs and amateur choirs can tackle the music. It still pushes them though. I wouldn't say they were too easy, but there has to be a sense of physical graft involved in the most spiritual of music, because it's a kind of wrench or reaching for something which has to take a physical kind of corporeal incarnation for me. It has to be physically intense. That again is a kind of incarnational theology that goes right back to a deep reflection I had when I was writing *Veni, Veni Emmanuel*, which is about the incarnation. I always remember getting the material for that piece, for percussion and orchestra, and realizing I was taken by this chant: '*Veni, Veni Emmanuel*', but how do I turn that into a rhythm? Because it had to be a rhythmic piece and I realized that with the refrain from that chant '*Gaude, Gaude*', so I spent a lot of time improvising and thinking about it and after a while you realize that there's a kind of pulse there: a didactic short – long, short – long. It's like a human heart beat and I

---

[47]   Ibid.

realized – what better way of representing the incarnation in music than the iconic use of the human heartbeat in music and rhythmic form? So the human heartbeat, the human Christ, as it were, is omnipresent as a leitmotif in almost every bar of the piece. It's that that becomes the DNA of the whole piece.[48]

Thus, for MacMillan, the objective of pushing the boundaries of the singers' or players' range and skill is to set a challenge for the performer. In the piece *Veni, Veni Emmanuel* the plainsong upon which it is based is expressed in purely instrumental music for an elaborate and very difficult percussion solo, written for Evelyn Glennie. This extremely advanced and technically complex music is nevertheless based upon a simple chant melody which becomes, as James relates, the heart of the music, representing the incarnate human Christ.

Conclusion

In this chapter I have been exploring what it means for someone to be a composer of sacred music in the twenty-first century by analysing interviews as well as comparing today's composers with those of the past. Sacred music is not confined to the liturgical context and, indeed, in many cases the liturgy is no longer the intended context for sacred musical compositions.

We have discovered that the interest in and quality of compositions of sacred music in the West are as strong as they have ever been, and remain part of a tradition stretching back over a thousand years of musical and religious development. For those interviewed the music of the Renaissance was a golden era of composition, producing consistently high-quality music, which has been influential ever since and the role of plainchant was also identified as central to the sacred music tradition. Moreover, music from the twentieth century was also singled out as a rich period for sacred music.

It was suggested that the composition of good or great sacred music does not simply require sincerity but also conviction, rigour and engagement with the difficulties and ambiguities of faith and with the influence of past composers. We have seen that sacred music, both in its ideology and compositional form, is part of a long tradition of believing and, for some composers at least, a witness to their faith is an inevitable consequence of anything they write (as in the case of MacMillan), even if it no longer relates to any particular institutional religion (such as John Tavener). But music also relates to doubt (as demonstrated by those agnostic composers who grapple with the notion of the divine). The context in which the music is performed is not necessarily a defining factor, nor a constraint; and in the next two chapters I shall be examining the thoughts and viewpoints of performers both within and outside of the religious context.

---

[48]   Interview with James MacMillan.

Chapter 2

The Performers I:
Within the Context of Religious Worship

So how do we explain to someone what understanding music means? ... Sometimes it will just be a matter of how one plays, or hums, the piece, now and again of the comparisons one draws and the images with which one as it were illustrates the music ... Understanding music is a manifestation of the life of humankind.

Ludwig Wittgenstein [1]

In the previous chapter I considered how contemporary composers have approached the subject of creating sacred music and how they relate to composers of the past. In this chapter we begin to consider the practitioners of sacred music today. I explore the views of musical directors who have experience of performing classical sacred music. I aim to discover how they feel about the music, what motivates them in their profession, and what differences are involved in performing within a purely liturgical religious context and a secular one. The chapter will relate the views of some of the best church musicians of our time through original interview material. It will, however, first consider the essential connection between musical performance and society, and particularly explore how music has its most fundamental expression through the human voice.

Music's Connection with Society

For many years there has been a strong strand in music scholarship emphasizing the autonomy of music, stating that music can be listened to in a self-contained, pure, aesthetic way without the need for any reference to any other aspect of existence for its meaning.[2] The meaning is simply the sound alone, with no further need of

---

[1] L. Wittgenstein, *Culture and Value* (Chicago: University of Chicago Press, 1980), p. 70, quoted in P. Stoltzfus, *Theology as Performance: Music, Aesthetics, and God in Western Thought* (New York: T&T Clark, 2006), pp. 167 and 249.

[2] Dahlhuas, *Absolute Music*; Bonds, *Music as Thought*; P. Kivy, *Music Alone: Philosophical Reflections on the Purely Musical Experience* (Ithaca: Cornell University Press, 1990); N. Cook, *Music: A Very Short Introduction* (Oxford: OUP, 1998); K.M. Higgins, *The Music of Our Lives* (Philadelphia: Temple University Press, 1991); C. Norris, *Music and the Politics of Culture* (London: Lawrence and Wishart, 1989); D. Hargreaves and A.C. North, *The Social Psychology of Music* (Oxford: OUP, 1997).

explanation or connection with wider society, the arts or aspects of our humanity. This contention is succinctly expressed in D.A. Thomas's suggestion that 'genuine art must forgo all attachments to language, meaning, and content in order to enjoy autonomous self-referentiality'.[3] However, the idea of absolute music has been, for many generations, 'problematic for any philosopher willing to take it seriously'.[4] I wish to argue, before we go on to consider the views of contemporary performers, that the self-referentiality of music is a notion that cannot be sustained, as music is always interconnected with other temporal phenomena in our society. In order to do this, I draw upon the arguments of Jeremy Begbie in his work *Theology, Music and Time*, who offers a helpful introduction to the subject of how music becomes meaningful through its performance:

> One way in which music becomes meaningful for us is through the interplay between its temporal processes and a vast range of temporal processes which shape our lives in the world – from the rhythm of breathing to the coming and going of day and night.[5]

Begbie offers four examples of how music is connected with the extra-musical in our society. First, music is embedded in social and cultural practices; it 'embodies social and cultural reality – no matter how individualistically produced'.[6] These links are not always easy to discern, and when considering music one must be careful not to reduce the meaning of music to purely social conditioning. Nevertheless Begbie emphasizes, along with Nicholas Cook, that music cannot claim to be 'autonomous of the world around it', because there is no such thing as unmediated access, as all music is related to our social beliefs and experiences.[7] Second, 'music-making and hearing arise from *an engagement with the distinctive configurations of the physical world we inhabit*', by which Begbie means that we must take into account our physical surroundings, which have a direct influence upon how the music is performed and sounds.[8] This point relates directly to my study of the difference between liturgical and non-liturgical settings. Begbie's third and fourth points are that one cannot escape from the truth that the performance of music is both bodily (physiological and neurological) as well as emotional (in that, as performers, we

---

³   D.A. Thomas, *Music and the Origins of Language: Theories from the French Enlightenment* (Cambridge: CUP, 1995), p. 6, quoted in Begbie, *Theology, Music and Time*, p. 13; see also J. Begbie, *Voicing Creation's Praise: Towards a Theology of the Arts* (Edinburgh: T&T Clark, 1991), pp. 193ff. and pp. 215ff.

⁴   J.L.H. Thomas, 'The Idea of Absolute Music by Carl Dahlhaus: Roger Lustig. Review by J.L.H. Thomas', *Music and Letters*, 72 (1991), pp. 89–92. Here at p. 89.

⁵   Begbie, *Theology, Music and Time*, p. 13.

⁶   Ibid.

⁷   Cook, *Music: A Very Short Introduction*, p. 117; Begbie, *Theology, Music and Time*, p. 13 n. 16.

⁸   Begbie, *Theology, Music and Time*, p. 15.

are attempting to feel the way the music should be communicated). In relation to musical performance, Roger Scruton has convincingly argued that emotions are not merely subjective, individual feelings, but are essentially public intentional states of thought in that they relate to others. Moreover, in music 'the expression of an emotion is also to some extent the creating of an emotion'.[9] Scruton argues that the performer externalizes emotions in relation to both the music and the listener, which evokes a 'sympathetic response' from the hearer, who is encouraged to 'dance' or move with the sounds:

> The great triumph of music ... involves this synthesis. Whereby a musical structure, moving according to its own logic, compels our feelings to move along with it, and so leads us to rehearse a feeling at which we would not otherwise arrive.[10]

Begbie's four examples lead to the plausible conclusion that music is an 'embodied' art form, distinctive in itself, and yet always, in performance, inhabits the body, mind, and emotions as well as the immediate physical surroundings, and indeed the wider context of our personal experiences, beliefs and society. Much of the music I will consider in this chapter will be choral and vocal, and draws from discussions with those who perform it. Thus, in relation to the embodied nature of music, I begin by asserting that in all assessments of how, why and where sacred music is performed, we must recognize that at the heart of any healthy society is the act of singing. Making music with the voice is one of the oldest, and deepest, expressions of humanity and civilization.

The Singing Society

In the story of evolution, I sometimes wonder about the precise moment when *homo erectus* became *homo sapiens*. That is, the emergence of the first human being as far as we are able to conjecture. In their primitive attempts to communicate, sounds must have been much more important than any kind of developed language. Their voices would have been essential for their survival; and, over the course of their historical development, the voice, and singing in particular, became a central characteristic of every culture: from the ancient world, to Biblical times, to the present day. Wilfrid Mellors described singing as one of two fundamental expressions of our innate musicality: 'In any healthy society there are two main channels for musical expression. One is that the individual will himself sing, using the musical instrument which is provided for him by

---

[9]   Ibid., p. 17; R. Scruton, *The Aesthetics of Music* (Oxford: Clarendon: 1997), pp. 346–64.

[10]   Begbie, *Theology, Music and Time*, p. 18 quoting Scruton, *The Aesthetics of Music*, p. 359.

nature; the other is that music will be used to accompany dancing feet'.[11] Indeed our voices, especially our singing voices, are a fundamental part of what defines both our civilization and ourselves. The prospect, indeed, of a society that does not put vocal expression at the heart of every intellectual, physical, cultural or spiritual pursuit seems inconceivable. Whether in politics, journalism, the media, religion, sport or education, singing has played a part, from protest songs, to self-expression, to cultural movements, to national sentiment, or prayer and praise.

In the film *Into Great Silence*, the daily lives and movements of Carthusian monks living a religious life in the French Mother House of *Chartreuse* are documented over the course of several months. Of course, their vows do not allow for conversation, as the film title suggests; and the majority of the footage is silent, apart from the odd sounds of doors or books opening and closing. However, the major exception to this rule is the singing of the sacred office in their large and beautiful chapel. At allotted times from the early hours of the morning and throughout the day, the monks respond to the bell calling them to prayer and to sing the Gregorian plainchant settings of psalms, canticles and prayers. In a world of vocal silence, the singing, even the monophony of the plainsong, becomes a resonant and glorious contrast to the contemplative silence that surrounds it as the monks perform their daily chores. The use of the singing voice in the worship music highlights the seriousness, the reverence and the sacredness of the texts being sung, the melodic lines expressing the beauty of creation, and the solidarity of the brothers in the purpose of prayer and in lives solemnly dedicated to the service of God. It would be possible for the monks communally to gather to say their prayers in silence or just to say them together, but there is good reason for the act of singing them instead, as Saliers comprehends:

> The act of singing is a deeply human act, found in every culture. This is so because singing activates things that seem so central to human life itself: bodily, emotional, intellectual, and moral animation. To sing requires breath, physical production of sounds, emotional resonance, uses of the mind, and characteristically collaborative patterns of listening and participation ... If these things are so, then the act of singing to God is a deeply theological act ... Singing *enacts* the praise, thanksgiving, and blessing. Singing also *enacts* sorrow, anger, lament, and the questioning of God.[12]

Singing is not, therefore, merely a physical act. It is also a mental, emotional and collaborative process and, in the context of monastic prayer or any gathered worship, it becomes a theological act in itself, bringing sound, words and resonance to the silent praise of the heart. Singing can enable a release of emotion from within through the physical act.

---

[11]   W. Mellers, *Music and Society: England and the European Tradition* (London: Faber, 1946), second edition, ed. K.P. Etzkorn (1950) (New York: Wiley, 1973), p. 29.

[12]   D. Saliers, *Music and Theology* (Nashville: Abingdon Press, 2007), p. 63.

In Manning and Payne's recent article, 'Vocal Performance in the Twentieth Century and Beyond' there is remarkably little reference to sacred choral music at all, despite its worldwide popularity. However, one small passage recognizes the increasingly popular and significant role of sacred choral music in our society:

> Recent works by John Tavener and James MacMillan (b. 1959) have re-established the sacred and churchly aspect of choral performance, for long the mainstay of the tradition in contexts such as the Three Choirs festival.[13] Conductor Gareth Malone's inspiring work with unskilled and initially unpromising choral forces, shown on television late in the first decade of the twenty-first century, provides a telling example of what can be achieved with a combination of vision and persuasive energy. The vital importance of recreational singing for our spiritual, physical and social well-being is perhaps being rediscovered.[14]

Singing is indeed important for our spiritual, physical and social well-being. As I have already argued, music is an 'embodied' art form. However, to reduce these characteristics purely to 'recreational' singing, and by implication relegating sacred music to the realm of the amateur choral society, is a misinterpretation of the blossoming of sacred music in the latter part of the twentieth century and an even worse description of the state of sacred music today. My own experience of singing with professional choirs and directors who specialize in performing sacred repertoire reflects this. It is just one testament to the fact that sacred music today, at its best, is in the hands of specialists who over the past few decades have been responsible for its growth in popularity, which is itself quite possibly a contributing factor to the rise in cathedral attendance.[15]

I devote the rest of this chapter to interviews with several of these professionals and consider their insights into the relationship between sacred music and secular society. Singing is at the centre of the lives of all those interviewed below. Although all the musicians to whom I spoke, and those I quote from other sources, all work in various musical media, sacred choral music in some way unites them all.

The Nature of Performance – within Worship

What is the best way to perform sacred music within the liturgy? Indeed, when a choir sings for a service, is it valid to call this a 'performance' at all? James

---

[13]   They cite Taveners' *Celtic Requiem* (1971), the all-night vigil, the *Veil of the Temple* (2003), and MacMillan's *Seven Last Words from the Cross* (1993) and *St John Passion* (2008).

[14]   J. Manning and A. Payne. 'Vocal performance in the Twentieth Century and Beyond' in C. Lawson and R. Stowell (eds), *The Cambridge History of Musical Performance* (Cambridge: CUP, 2012), pp. 776–7.

[15]   http://www.churchofengland.org/media-centre/news/2012/03/cathedral-attendance-statistics-enjoy-over-a-decade-of-growth.aspx.

O'Donnell, Organist and Master of the Choristers at Westminster Abbey, thinks that it is a perfectly acceptable term, and advocates the professionalism of practising liturgical music:

> The word performer, or the concept of performance, is sometimes used in a pejorative sense in the context of worship but if you just strip it down to what it means, one could argue that, just as a surgeon performs an operation, a musician performs a piece of music. You could use other words, but it's as good a word as any for what musicians do. They can't not perform. There are hundreds of different ways of doing that, but I don't have a problem with the term itself.
>
> JA: So you are performing within the liturgy just as much as you are performing in a concert setting?
>
> JO'D: You are performing your role or your function just as much as a priest is. The priest's proper role in, for example, the Eucharist, is to celebrate. By extension the director of the choir has a particular role, as does each singer and each member of the congregation if you look at it that way. Everybody is performing their proper role. The word 'performing', as applied to musicians, can be used to imply that there is something slightly dodgy about performing music within a sacred context ('too much of a performance'). I really think we have to get away from that and my contribution as a church musician, in worship, is doing what I do as well as I can, which means drawing on all of my experience, all my musical professionalism, training and art, so far as I have it. So I'm definitely performing a professional role. I don't think that the word 'professional' is wrong here because it is our profession; that doesn't in any way get rid of the vocational, personal and spiritual commitment that may or may not be involved: it doesn't exclude it. So I'm quite happy with that word 'perform'.[16]

James's ease with the notion of professional performance within the liturgy led me to explore with him notions of vocation and role within service:

> JA: Do you see people as having their clearly defined roles within the liturgy and an expectation that they are performing to their best?
>
> JO'D: I wouldn't want to be too absolute about the separation of roles and to claim there is no overlap, for example, between the role of the priest and the role of a church musician or even a member of the congregation or a reader or a preacher. Part of the great privilege of being involved in liturgy and worship is that it is multidisciplinary and there are so many facets to it ... To be professional means doing something well and drawing on one's training and skill in order to do it well, partly for our own satisfaction. There is a great sense of satisfaction in doing your job well ... I think it would be very strange for a priest to deliver what they knew was a really good sermon, that they worked hard on, that went over well, with lots of good comments about it, and yet not to feel a certain

---

[16]   Interview with James O'Donnell, Westminster Abbey, 18 October 2011.

amount of satisfaction about that. It's similar to how a musician feels when you've chosen the music well and it has gone well: you have the knowledge that it has worked.

Standard of performance really matters to James, and I certainly perceived that there was a sense of satisfaction in his vocation of producing high-quality music for worship. But on what levels is that performance working? Does it matter what the music is intended for as to how it is performed?

When you try to define the levels, that's when you get in trouble ... How do you know what levels you're working at? So many people come to services, for example in Westminster Abbey, but who knows what their background is? Who knows what they're taking from it and on what level? They might come in just to hear a particularly unusual piece of music and they might end up having their lives changed. And I know stories about that. You can't possibly legislate for people's experiences and therefore I don't think one can really legislate too prescriptively one's own functions. I think that would be to miss the point. I personally may not get much from a clergy person who preaches badly, or a reader who isn't very good at reading, and I suspect everybody finds that difficult. So there's a certain amount of training and application involved in being better at those things in order to benefit those who are due to benefit from those functions and I have no problem with that. I do have a problem with the people who say: 'Oh well, the heart's in the right place and they like to read so we let them read every so often'. I can see a certain pastoral dimension to that but I think there's a wider pastoral dimension.

For James, the point about performance standards in the service of the liturgy is that the worshipper should be not distracted by the mechanics of how the music is being produced, but be drawn instead towards the devotion that the music ideally encourages:

I always tell the choir here that if you're processing well, nobody will notice and that's the right thing. Nobody notices it's good, and nobody notices it's bad, it just happens. To an extent that's true of music making, or preaching or reading, you just listen to what's being said you don't direct your attention to how it's being read or whether the person is doing this or that or whether the choir are singing in this way or that way. It's inevitable that those who are involved in these things do think about that aspect, but for the congregation, who are there to experience the totality of the liturgy, they don't terribly want to get bogged down in the mechanics of the individual items and the way that they're delivered specifically. I think they want to derive the benefit from the sum of the parts, from something greater than the sum of the parts. That's when you're really in business. That's what I find exciting, that possibility of 'releasing' the music, that I hope is excellent and that enormous trouble has been taken over, into something which is bigger than itself. I find that very liberating and stimulating.

So, when performing sacred music as part of worship, it is essential that the object of worship remains more important than the practicalities of the worship itself. In this case who is the music for: the congregation or God?

> JA: This gets to the heart of really what I'm thinking about here, which is when you are performing a piece of liturgical or sacred music, who do you imagine is on the receiving end? Is it just that it's worth doing for its own sake? Is it for God? Is it for somebody who might just be popping into the Abbey?
>
> JO'D: I think it's all of the above and probably many others that you haven't mentioned! There is a sense in which expensive cathedral choirs, and in my experience they have been expensive, are making music partly because it is a valuable tradition in itself. Human cultural activity at a higher level has inherent value. Whose benefit is it for? Is it for God? I think yes, partly, but it's more complex than that. In my experience as a musician, I believe that God has given us music as a gift, as well as musical talent, skills and culture, which is definitely of God ... But it's also for the edification of those who go. For instance, I find that the musical elements of the liturgies that I attend can be very uplifting for me personally, as I find are the skills involved in composing good music or listening to things like Gregorian chant ... When I hear a Gregorian chant Mass sung quite well, I find it takes me away from here and now and points me in another direction entirely. I think that's the whole point of sacred music, I think it does direct the human heart and the mind and the soul away from itself and outwards into other areas.

To offer sacred music in worship, then, is to offer a direction to the soul, away from itself and towards something greater. But how is this achieved? Is it by manipulation of the emotions? For James, this is not the answer:

> You can't say: 'This is what you feel when you hear this piece and this is what you're supposed to think when you go to church ... on Ash Wednesday you're supposed to feel a bit miserable.' There are some people who try to manufacture things in order to manipulate that kind of reaction and that's a rather crass thing to do. There's a large sense in which sacred music is for human consumption and nourishment. I find it a problem when people say it doesn't really matter if people come or not ... if you're doing something for years and years and nobody's ever coming I think that does open up a question ... why are you going to all that trouble? Because it is for people to listen to, even if it does have an intrinsic value.

So performance standards are important and so is the purpose of enabling devotion in the listener and pointing their attention towards the divine. But what distinguishes good liturgical music from bad?

I feel that one has to draw one's own line here, and where I draw that line might be different from where a colleague draws it ... Music is a very powerful liturgical entity and it worries me that people might occasionally want to harness that power in a way that oversteps the mark in a liturgical or a sacred context. There are certain composers of choral music whose musical idiom I sometimes find to be slightly manipulative: to me it feels as though they're deliberately manufacturing a certain atmosphere. I wouldn't say that one has to avoid that music at all costs, but one has to handle it with care. I find quite a lot of the chorus music of the evangelical tradition is transparently manipulative and is designed to tug at the heart strings, using semantic referential musical language that offers both performer and listener a package of ready-made feelings, emotions and associations ... Some people like that music, and that's fine, but I'm worried about the processes involved in producing it. One has to assume that people have integrity. It's very easy to assume that people who do things differently from oneself are wrong!

So what does lie at the heart of good sacred liturgical music? For James O'Donnell, as we have seen with James MacMillan, somewhere at the heart of sacred music is plainchant:

Even at the height of the Anglican cathedral choral tradition, the chant lies there in the foundations. If you imagine that Church music or liturgical music is basically chromatography and at the centre of that is the chant: melodic, monophonic, monotonous, at its very simplest the singing of one note ... it is essentially a vehicle for text and brings with it a certain humility before the text – in a sense, taking the text and germinating it with music.

But what has old fashioned plainchant got to do with the performance of polyphonic, Baroque, Classical, Romantic or Modern repertoire? Is there a connection? James suggests that, where a connection can be found, it is to be cherished:

I might not hear any Gregorian chant or plainsong ... within the music itself, but I might feel that there is a connection to it that can be [found in] the most elaborate, innovative and complicated art music, but it still has that [Gregorian] quality and I look for that. Whereas I will tend to shy away from music where I sense there has been some kind of interruption there.

So is the performance of Gregorian chant still important for sacred music today?

The new [English] edition of the Latin *Missal* contains chants for the priest and the congregation ... printed out in musical notation in the body of the text ... not confined to the appendix, as it used to be. So there's very much a feeling now that the music is part of what is meant to be involved in liturgical celebration. In other words, singing is not some kind of optional adjunct to it but is a fundamental element of worship. Some of that chanting is very straightforward: singing a prayer or an *Amen* on one note or a simple alleluia before the gospel or the *Lord's Prayer* that everybody can sing together ... It doesn't have to be particularly complicated, but what it does is to involve everybody at every level; it doesn't exclude a highly trained musician nor a totally untrained person because it's so close to that heightened speaking that one would naturally have in the formal or public space.

So, in the Roman Catholic liturgy, is chant at the heart of a sacred music revival? James O'Donnell thinks the answer is yes.

The chant is probably the best starting place for any kind of desire to re-establish a singing tradition ... Many present-day cathedrals and collegiate foundations represent a continuity of the monastic tradition and of course Westminster Abbey was a monastery, as were many of our cathedral and collegiate foundations, and we're aware of that thread here. It's an evolved application. Many aspects of monasticism are alive and well in our society, if you look at the way Parliament is arranged for example. This collegiate-style layout for so many of our organizations and our public institutions derives a lot, it seems to me, from the monastic pattern but [has] evolved into something else.

How does this monastic heritage feed into the practice of sacred music today? James suggests that it is to do with a rhythm of life:

The practice of sacred music, of choral music, does imply a certain rhythm, as any music making does. You can't, for example, really get very far on the piano unless you practise regularly, there has to be rhythm to your work and your preparations ... If you're a professional musician it would be difficult to maintain your standards if you were not only not practising regularly but also not performing regularly. So there has to be a rhythm. What that rhythm is doesn't really matter, but it has to be a rhythm that you perceive and interiorize and the same is true for any choir.

How then does James see that rhythm of sacred music over the past few centuries and his place within it now?

You mentioned the millennium-long tradition of sacred music and that's absolutely right but of course it's hugely evolved and been the subject of much legislation: at the Reformation, Counter Reformation and the Council of Trent, suddenly incredibly elaborate Masses ... and those based on rather dubious songs, were no longer allowed ... and all the music had to be very transparent and the texts had to be made clear; then there's the very chequered history of the nineteenth-century Anglican choral tradition, with various parts hanging on by their fingernails; it's been an up and down story. It's possibly too romantic to think that there's been wonderful, uninterrupted progress of evolution and development, but despite the peaks and troughs, the trajectory is very clear. It's quite exciting to feel that one is part of that trajectory and also to know that long after one's disappeared from the face of the earth that it's going to continue.

JA: I suppose you're responsible for your particular bit in history now?

JO'D: If you work in a place like this [Westminster Abbey], or any institution which has a history and, one hopes and trusts, a future, you become very aware that you are only there for a bit of a blip and you are looking after it for the moment and you are doing what you can with it. You're not the bee's knees, you're a steward and you're handing it on to the future and while you're there, you're the custodian of it, in whatever sense you're working. I know from conversations with colleagues elsewhere that a lot of people feel that very strongly and they're not territorial or possessive about it. They feel very much that they're like a gardener, pruning, deadheading and pulling up the weeds and even, you know, completely clearing it, you sometimes do have to do that. That's probably quite a good metaphor for what's involved really.

So what, I ask, is the difference between performing a piece by *Victoria*, for instance, within a church service and in a concert? Is the concert an inferior setting?

I think, in many ways, it's fine to do liturgical music in concert. If it directs attention to that repertoire, if it broadens the awareness of that music, if it wins people over to it, to that style of musical utterance and if people perceive in it something of its inner character, who knows what they're going to make of it? You can't say it's wrong to pay 'X' amount of money to go to the concert hall to hear that when you should really be going to church. You might get nothing from it in church and a lot from it in the concert hall, or vice versa, and you can't legislate for that.

I am quite clear when one would get the most out of a Victoria Mass, for example … If you came to Westminster Cathedral to hear the choir singing in a Latin liturgy, with Gregorian chant Propers and so forth, I think you'd find that you would inevitably experience the musical elements of that Victoria in a completely different, complex [way] and with far greater and more proximate associations than from an excellent performance of it in, say, a concert hall given by an expert group such as *The Tallis Scholars* or *The Sixteen*. You have to decide how you want to experience these things. You could experience it one way one day and the other way the next day … I feel that, as a church musician, given the visual and sensory aspects of an amazing building, the beauty of the ceremonial, the liturgy, with perhaps a really good sermon, all the elements are really clicking tightly together and therefore taking you away from the immediacy of any one element and into something far bigger and pointing beyond. That's where I think the excitement is. It would be difficult to find that in a concert hall because you would be deliberately taking one element out and saying, '*just* listen to this', and you would be inviting people to experience it in a particular way and at a particular level. There's absolutely nothing wrong with that, but you have to be aware that there are other, perhaps better, ways of experiencing it.

Thus, for James, performing sacred music in a concert hall is distinctively different from performing it as part of liturgy in a religious building. I put to him Peter Phillips' point that great sacred choral music can be enjoyed on the same level as a Mozart piano concerto or a Beethoven sonata. Can it purely be enjoyed on an abstract level and, if so, is something missing?

> I would say that you are missing something if you purely enjoy it on that level … If you go to see an altar piece, let's say a *Tryptic* from in a Florentine church, in the National Gallery, can you say it's the same [kind of art] as a portrait of a Tudor monarch, or a Stuart politician, just because it is in the same medium? … It was intended to sit on top of an altar in a church, and it comes from a particular tradition and context of making art for a particular reason. Whereas the portrait of your Stuart politician or your whiskered Gladstonian politician is from a totally different world, although it's in the same medium. So you could say that [William] Byrd's *Infelix ego* is a piece of music and so is a Mozart piano concerto, but I think that it would be very difficult just to say that they're therefore the same and I'm going to listen to them in exactly the same way. You have to have some context I think … So I think that you can't be reductive about these things and you can't control how your audience hears. What I think Peter's trying to point to is the fact that it's not just church music, it's brilliant music, and you need to know that it's fine and you need to give it that respect and attention. I've got no problem with that attitude at all, but I would say that a perception of the context … is going to put you in a different relationship to it.
>
> JA: Is there a danger that we become antiquarian about 'old' sacred music performed in concert halls and see the context as something that was once important but which we have grown out of now?
>
> JO'D: It's almost like saying, here's a 3D object but we're only going to look at one dimension. I do perceive antiquarianism to be a danger. I also perceive that there are some specialized choirs, *The Tallis Scholars* is an example, who tend to limit their repertoire, on the whole but not exclusively, to music of one period and one *genre*, [whereas] a liturgical choir would be very unlikely to do that. The nearest probably is Westminster Cathedral Choir … where the music is focussed very much, but by no means exclusively, on polyphony and chant. We [at Westminster Abbey] have no particular focus. We would turn our hand to Tudor Anglican music one day, Latin polyphony the next day, Gregorian chant the next day and something contemporary the day after that … I absolutely love that.

There is a significant notion of place in James's argument. Freelance professional choirs are free to perform, more or less, whatever repertoire they wish in whatever context, without relation to a particular place. This is not the case for many musicians:

Even some of our orchestras have a place that they are associated with, the London Symphony Orchestra is associated very strongly with the Barbican [Centre in London], for example, or the Hallé Orchestera with Bridgewater Hall [in Manchester] ... We're the Choir of Westminster Abbey – we have a *locus*. So our existence has a multi-dimensional geographical, situational, context that a freelance group of musicians, lovely concept though that is, doesn't have ... If the choir of Westminster Abbey goes and sings in a Japanese concert hall, in a sense we are taking Westminster Abbey and all that it embodies there. *The Tallis Scholars*, for instance, are taking the music with them and their reputation. So it's kind of a different animal, I'd say.

Given this distinction, I ask James one last question. Could he imagine himself as a pure concert musician, without any professional musical involvement in liturgy or the Church?

It would be very odd. I've been involved in Church music since I was twelve, or possibly even longer. I can't imagine not being involved in it in some way. That's not to say I'll necessarily spend the rest of my working life entirely in Church music, which is basically what I'm doing at the moment, although I am extremely fulfilled and happy in that way. I find it's very interesting because it's so broad and I'm very fortunate because on the whole I don't find I have to narrow my field of vision, and I don't feel the horizon is crowding in on me ... When I go to church, I like going as a member of the congregation but it feels as if I'm playing truant. I feel like I ought to be doing something musical, even singing in the choir, which I don't notably do but I would be very happy to do that. In fact I'd love to do that and I'd have a taste of my own medicine which would probably be very good for my soul!

For James, performing as a musician at Westminster Abbey is not just a profession:

I think I would describe it is as a vocation – a coming together of various things in a compelling way and my life has led me in this way ... I would never have imagined, when I was beginning on my professional life, that I would end up as Director of Music at Westminster Cathedral or here [at Westmister Abbey] and I feel really, really, fortunate and privileged about that. I suppose I've been open to that ... partly through opportunities that have opened and partly decisions that I have made. So that's what I find is vocational, a coming together in a consistent way and focussing towards one thing that feels right.[17]

Having talked to James O'Donnell and been fascinated by his commitment, vocation and passion for his endeavours at Westminster Abbey, I turned to a singer who has performed sacred choral music for many years in both liturgical and

---

[17]   Ibid.

secular settings: I asked Francis Steele whether, in his experience, the context in which he had sung (such as cathedral liturgy or concert hall) made any difference to his approach? In his reply, he makes a distinction between vocal and mental approaches:

> In terms of vocal technique – none at all. In either case that technique is mediated (though not altered) by considerations such as acoustic or the type of music, but for a singer employment of that technique remains a 'non-negotiable'. After all, in the sixteenth century when the Church was a leading patron of music, for whom would Pavarotti or Fischer-Dieskau have sung, if not Palestrina or Lassus?
>
> In terms of mental approach – intellectual or intuitive – my response is entirely personal. I have always accepted that music sung in a liturgical context is subservient to that liturgy and its larger purposes, whereas a Mass performed in concert is an end in itself, and is potentially the poorer because deprived of those larger purposes. In passing, I would add that concert performance requires of the performer an outward and visible advocacy of the music, which is largely redundant in a liturgical context, for the very act of congregation and witness supplies the need for such advocacy. For entirely personal reasons, I was more at home on the concert platform than in the [choir] stalls, acting as advocate for the music, rather than the larger causes which the music itself might advocate. My point of departure is agnosticism, the journey leads me to approach the numinous (albeit dimly apprehended). For me, it is best made alone. I approach more closely through abstract music – *The Art of Fugue* or a Bartok quartet – and I don't feel the lack of either a theocentric context, or the company of fellow travellers. At the inconclusive conclusion of *The Art of Fugue* when the scratching of Bach's pen ceases and it falls from his fingers, when the triumphantly assembled lines evaporate into silence, there I approach closest to both mortality and the divine.[18]

Francis movingly captures how the agnostic performer, as well as solitary listener, can approach the issues of mortality, the numinous and the divine. His honesty is illuminating and demonstrates how an increasingly agnostic society might approach music, all meaningful music, whether abstract or with text. The question arises whether we need community at all in our consumption of sacred music, but we shall leave this issue to a later chapter.[19]

For now, I turn to another musician often engaged in providing music for the liturgy, as well as having a busy concert career as a conductor and organist: Stephen Farr. I began by asking him for an example of what he considers great sacred music to be:

---

[18]   Interview with Francis Steele, *La Maison Verte*, Roujan, France, March 2013.

[19]   See below, Chapter 4.

My concept of what musical perfection is, is best expressed in [J.S.] Bach ... I find in it an expression of something that I don't find so readily in other composers. But how an analyst or historian or theorist could pin that down I don't know. If we could write about these things we wouldn't have music would we? It's because we don't know that we play music, which is probably a very glib response to the problem.[20]

However, when pressed, Stephen was willing to offer a partial explanation for the music's power:

Of all the great composers ... Bach is the one that people are drawn to because it does have an elusive quality of something that invites contemplation ... I'm sure there are lots of very clever analyses of [Bach's music] ... both musical and psychological and biological probably ... but even atheists find something in it which is uniquely expressive ... [reminiscent of] T. S. Eliot's 'still point at the turning world'.[21]

Bach wrote music that is now performed in concert halls. I asked Stephen whether the liturgical or secular context made a difference to the performance:

The ideal is that you are bringing the same processes to bear in the preparation and the performance for both. As a craftsman and musician there are certain things you aspire to in any performance ... From the purely mechanical point of view, you are more concerned about those things in a concert. Not because the liturgical aspect doesn't matter, it matters a lot, it's part of the *Gesamtkunstwerk* (design of the concert).
    JA: What's that?
    SF: It's the concept that Wagner used to describe his operas as a complete art work. So it wasn't that you just had the music and the words; the *Gesamtkunstwerk* was in control of the whole thing: the space [and] design of the theatre, the libretti, the music. Maybe it didn't go as far as the costumes and the details of the staging, but this idea [was] that every aspect of the operatic production was part of a bigger whole and that all of those parts impinged on each other. I can remember going to hear a very well-known Renaissance ensemble of some repute in Cambridge Guildhall and it was just the most arid experience, not because they weren't all superb singers and they'd taken a lot of care, it was the setting that just didn't work at all. But if you'd taken that same performance and put it in the middle of a dimly lit cathedral it would have been spectacular.

For Stephen, then, the physical context can make a difference to how the music is received, and an evocative programme of sacred music works best in suitable

---

20   Interview with Stephen Farr, Worcester College, Oxford, 27 November, 2011.
21   Ibid.

surroundings. As for the liturgy itself, Stephen shares James's ambition for the standards of excellence in worship music, but is also realistic about some religious institutions:

> From a purely practical point of view you often can't always aspire to the same quality in the day-to-day liturgy as you can in a concert performance, with so many other factors impinging on it. There is a difference, of course, in dealing with kids [rather] than dealing with adults and professionals. There are choirs and foundations that show that a great deal of [musical] subtlety is possible, but they are the ones by and large that are a little bit insulated, in some ways, from the reality that other places are dealing with either financially or otherwise.

JA: You talk about the context, about the aesthetics of the building, of the setting, so maybe, thinking about Sheppard's *In Media Vita*, a piece that's all about 'in the midst of life we are in death', would it have more power at a funeral than it would at a concert, even if it was a beautifully candle-lit concert in a cathedral with a fantastic acoustic?

SF: I suppose it's in the ear of the beholder to some extent. Yes, another example is the Purcell *Funeral Sentences*. In a concert that's just fantastic music, but you put that in the context of a funeral or memorial and they are overwhelming. But whether that's a spiritual reaction or whether it's purely an aesthetic overload, I don't know. An analogy from the visual arts would be the exhibition that was on at the National [Gallery] two or three years ago of Spanish Baroque art – very gruesome, life-like depictions of the crucifixion or the martyred saints: effigies and statues [executed with] the most extraordinary care. In that setting you admire the craft but if you were of a mind to be venerating while in a Catholic cathedral in Spain or Italy, I think you would have a completely different dimension.

JA: If we are venerating in a liturgical context, are we supposed to see through the music, like a window, and actually be concentrating on an end result that is beyond the music?

SF: It can work both ways. In the Renaissance repertoire there are pieces of polyphony that are purely abstract and don't make any attempt at all to induce one particular kind of reaction and then there's, for example, the Victoria *Tenebrae Responseries* [for Maundy Thursday] that are not in the least bit dramatic or pictorial, they're more austere. Not much happens, there's no great contrapuntal display, they are not richly scored particularly, a lot of them are in three or four parts, little trios and quartets, but they produce the most powerful reaction because of that austerity and the purity of it.[22] One can hear, in a powerful [Thomas] Tallis setting, a much more direct, not pictorial depiction, but a more overt emotional reaction to the text. Speaking purely personally I tend to find the austere things more appealing. They're not asking for a reaction, they're just there, that's what they are ... For instance, the Tallis *Lamentations* ... The whole

---

[22]   See Harry Christophers on the Victoria *Tenebrae Responseries*, below, pp. 70–71.

thing is a masterpiece, of course, but the most exquisite music is the *Aleph, Beth* bits,[23] because it's just absolutely pure, perfect, austere, it's not trying to express anything it's just saying 'A' or 'One'; and in a way that's more beautiful than the bits that are about the weeping and the wailing and the gnashing.

JA: And they're just alphabetical headings.

SF: A, B, C, D, absolutely.

Stephen reminds me that what is sacred to one performer may not be so sacred to another, and it leads me to think about whether we can talk about 'sacred' when we are thinking of, say, the late string quartets of Beethoven:

I think you'd have to be quite a special kind of listener not to find something transcendent in late Beethoven, although there are people I know that have a very violent reaction against it. But I think it's very hard to hear the slow movements of the final quartets or the end of the C major sonata … without thinking that it's about something. It may not matter that the listener's idea of what it's about is the same as Beethoven's … Beethoven's idea may have been just simply that it was about the manipulation of the material and about the style itself rather than trying to express a theological, moral or emotional concept or abstract idea. Maybe sometimes the thing that music is about is itself. Bach, however, is part of that great long tradition that says that all music is an expression of God. You can't distinguish between a cantata and a harpsichord piece. The whole thing was about God.

So, can any concert music lead to a 'transcendent experience? If so, what is the cause?

A misadventure …? Over the summer at The Proms, for the Colin Matthews piece, *No Man's Land*, I did a bit of coaching and preparing songs, and so on. But I remember that there was a scenario in one of the poems that he set, where one of the two soldiers sings about somebody taking out this mouth organ and playing a tune and everybody stops in the trenches to listen to this little ditty, which is in itself just a scrap of a pub song or something but in the context, it just makes everybody absolutely still. I remember the line that I was very struck by was 'As if listening was a kind of music', which I thought was quite an interesting concept.

One of the most extraordinary musical experiences I've ever had was going to hear *St Francis of Assisi*, the opera, at the Proms in 2008.

---

[23]   In the setting of Jeremiah's Lamentations, the text is divided by the Hebrew *Aleph, Beth*, and so on, equivalent to an English A, B, C heading. The mundane words of the headings are, paradoxically, set to the most beautiful music.

Messiaen had a mission to be a witness to Christianity in a secular age; and one of the pieces in which he most successfully achieves this is his opera *St François d'Assise* (1975–83), a monumental work lasting over four hours long that is rarely staged. In the leitmotif representing Francis's 'interior progression of grace toward God, charted through the harmonic, melodic and timbral changes' in the music, we may also perceive that Messiaen was also trying to achieve the 'redemption of secular modernity and humanity through his opera'.[24] Stephen related to me his own experience of the opera and of a particularly powerful scene:

> In the middle of the piece, when Francis gets the stigmata, the angel says to him something like: 'I will show you the music of the spheres' and, for what felt like an hour, in a good way, the colossal orchestra plays just a C major triad: very, very soft, muted violins and this tune coming from miles, miles away. That night, I was with six or seven other people sitting in the box, all quite kind of hard bitten people, who'd been round the block, and nobody could look at anybody else for the whole of that musical performance; everyone was on the verge of tears and people couldn't talk about it. Once or twice you could hear each other breathe in and someone was just about to lose it. There was something incredibly powerful about that. ... There was something so profound about that simple moment in the middle of this great complex wealth of sound that just got everybody. I thought that was extraordinary. I still don't quite know what it was or what it was about that moment or how it was done or the process of it happening but something about those marks being on the page and the way that they were produced was extraordinary! For fifteen or twenty minutes you could have heard a pin drop, nobody moved. I thought that was extraordinary.[25]

The moment for Stephen was a profound one, as it was for the audience at the Proms that night. Even listening to the story being related was moving. The scene is taken from the 5th tableau, *L'Ange Musicien*. St Francis asks the angel if he might be given a foretaste of heaven. The Angel answers with a paraphrase of Thomas Aquinas (1225–74): 'God dazzles us by an excess of truth; music transports us to God by an absence of truth'.[26] But to try and analyse why that musical moment was so powerful is very difficult to express. Stephen explains it partially in terms of Messiaen's genius and ability to transmit an idea of transcendence in the most effective way within the context of a vast and complex opera:

---

[24]   Sholl, R., 'The Shock of the Positive: Olivier Messiaen, St Francis, and Redemption through Modernity' in J.S. Begbie and S.R. Guthrie (eds.), *Resonant Witness: Conversations between Music and Theology* (Grand Rapids, MI: Eerdmans, 2011), pp. 162–89, at p. 166. A leitmotif is a particular musical phrase or harmony related to an individual character or subject within the opera.

[25]   Interview with Stephen Farr.

[26]   T. Aquinas, *Summa Theologica*, q 101, a 2, ad 2, quoted in C.P. Dingle and N. Simone, *Olivier Messiaen: Music, Art and Literature* (Aldershot: Ashgate, 2007), pp. 309–10.

I think that it is a prime example of somebody, a genius really, thinking about transcendence and doing the simplest thing. I suppose, you could say, well it's the obvious thing, what could be simpler and more transcendent than C major? But I think it takes a very particular compositional insight to do that. Especially if your style in general is a much more highly coloured, exotic one. So I thought that was very interesting.[27]

For many scholars, conductors and performers, Messiaen was a theologian as much as he was a musician.[28] It was his explicit purpose to bear witness to his faith through music. Theologically, he related himself closely to Thomas Aquinas:

For both Messiaen and Aquinas, God is the ultimate reality, possessing a dazzling superabundance of truth that lies behind the comprehension of human beings. As a part of his compositional aesthetics, Messiaen strove to illuminate the theological truths of his Catholic faith through music.[29]

Given the nature of his music and the response it has evoked in people over the years, it is becoming increasingly clear that Messiaen succeeded, at least in part, in his vocation to be a theological illuminator. As Francis Steele related to me:

In considering the work of Olivier Messiaen, one cannot fail to be struck by the deeply orthodox Catholic faith that it evinces, any more than one can miss its startling modernity in rhythmic and harmonic terms. He founded *Jeune France* (a group of young composers) and went on to teach Boulez, Stockhausen and Xenakis, to name but three. Were bequests to the Church such as Messiaen's common, we would not be questioning the future of sacred music in our culture. But they are not. Furthermore, words like young or modern do not necessarily spring to mind when considering the pre-Vatican II Catholic Church for which much of his music was conceived. In fact, there almost seems to be a contradiction in terms: a radical Catholic composer.[30]

Stephen Farr's experience of the extraordinary operatic work of Olivier Messiaen is a good example of a spiritual encounter in a secular setting, so I wonder, did

---

[27] Interview with Stephen Farr.

[28] A. Shenton (ed.), *Messiaen the Theologian* (Farnham: Ashgate, 2010) contains compelling chapters on the subject by Yves Balmer, Peter Bannister, Sander van Maas, Karin Heller, Douglas Shadle, Vincent Benitez, Robert Fallon, Stephen Schloesser, Nigel Simeone, Luke Berryman and Cheong Wai Ling. See also Sholl, 'The Shock of the Positive', pp. 162–89.

[29] V.P. Benitez, 'Messiaen and Aquinas' in Shenton (ed.), *Messiaen the Theologian*, pp. 101–25, here at p. 121.

[30] Interview with Francis Steele.

the secular setting *enable* that experience more than a religious setting might have done?

JA: I'm interested in the engagement of the listener and on what level they choose to engage. Whether there's in fact a freedom in a concert hall that allows us to just simply be human, and respond to whatever is put in front of us. We don't have to go to Evensong, we don't have to stand up, sit down, say the Lord's Prayer, turn east ...

SF: That's interesting because ... I've heard it expressed by several people that one of the reasons why Choral Evensong and cathedrals are, in a sense, thriving is because they allow people to choose the degree in which they want to engage with the worship and if they do want to just sit in the back and listen to it then it's a framework in which they can just be, have some space ... I think that's why a lot people are drawn to cathedral, formal, worship more than they might be to other forms. That idea of being able to keep at an arm's length but being able to approach as close as you want to is, for some people, what they need and who's to say that that's better or worse? And maybe, also, it is just that the aesthetics are better. If it comes to it, I'd rather sit in Winchester Cathedral listening to a piece than the Guildhall in Cambridge because it's more peaceful. I think there is, in some quarters, a vague sense that you ought to feel a little bit guilty about enjoying the aesthetics of liturgy and church architecture and that somehow it's not wholesome to enjoy listening to polyphony in a fifteenth-century Gothic church – that it is somehow a bit indulgent.

JA: Which leads me to the functionality of music. In terms of cathedral music, there's always a lot of music in a Church year and not all of it is sublime. Is it all, nevertheless, equally valid?

SF: I think in the context, yes. I can certainly remember doing services at Guildford Cathedral, the archetypal foggy Tuesday in November when the music wouldn't be perhaps top calibre but once in a while something would creep up on everyone. It might be something like Tallis' *Fauxbourdons* or one thing I still find very powerful is the *Good Friday Reproaches* by Victoria, which are very simple with the most rudimentary progressions but they have a force in context which is very extraordinary. You admire the Byrd *Great Service* more than you admire Gibbon's *Short Service* and I think, in their place, those pieces can have a very powerful effect. It is how they fit into the rhythm and the style of the liturgy. I've certainly been to services at St John's College Cambridge, with the choir conducted by George Guest, and the most exquisite part in the service (although the whole thing is beautifully sung) were the responses – the way they would just sing a single response was so remarkable and they weren't on the face of it great music, they were just perfectly functional, but they were beautifully done.

JA: So there's an element of professionalism that enables ordinary music to be wonderful?

SF: Yes, I think so.

JA: What is the difference between music as sacred and transcendent and music as manipulation?

SF: There's that line isn't there, I remember, in one of the *Four Quartets* [by T.S. Eliot]: 'you are not here to reason or make argument'.

JA: Is there a sense in which, when you go to a concert or if you go to a service, and you're moved by a piece, you are responding to the humanity of that composer and relating to, or empathizing with, their response to God or just to life?

SF: I think worship songs are expressive of nothing universal, whereas I think a great piece of music is expressive of something very universal. Now how you would pin that down in terms of procedure, I have no idea. It's another one of those mysteries about music. It's all 'me me me me me' in worship songs ... It's as if they are singing: 'Listen to me loving Jesus!'. But I think if you hear a Brahms motet or a Victoria mass, it's about something bigger which is, for me, the whole point. If you're going to do religious music at all, it has to be about something big, hasn't it? That's not necessarily to do with dimensions in durational scoring or ambition or anything, it's just that sometimes people manage to put marks on a page that are expressive of something enormous and sometimes people can put very similar marks on a page that are expressive of nothing at all; and how we get from a few lines and squiggles that have evolved in the way that they have through centuries to being moved to tears by Palestrina is just, well ... I'll never understand it. I don't think anyone ever will. That's what makes the whole thing endlessly fascinating: the unpredictability, and that sometimes you can hear exactly the same piece, in the same setting, and it's great, you think: 'that was lovely'. Other days you hear it and you're suddenly surprised by it.

Conclusion

Sacred music within the liturgy is thriving in certain areas of Church life. Good quality performances of choral music may not be as common in rural parish churches as they once were; but in the cathedrals of the Anglican Church there has been a dramatic increase in the popularity of choral music within the liturgy, and standards have remained high in many cathedrals, city parishes and college chapels of universities such as Oxford and Cambridge. The notion of 'performance' is embraced by Church musicians today, emphasizing the duty and service offered by professionals to an overall excellence of liturgy, in which music plays its role amongst the words, preaching and sacraments. There still appears to be a thirst for this kind of religious offering and, from the musical point of view, the human voice continues to play a significant role in how such music is communicated. The voice is our fundamental expression of emotion and spirituality, and thus vocal music remains at the heart of sacred performance. James O'Donnell, Stephen Farr and Francis Steele spoke expressively about their experiences – the importance of performance and the role of music in worship as part of a bigger entity, greater than the sum of its parts or the *Gesamtkunstwerk* as Stephen put it. James O'Donnell and James MacMillan's opinion of placing Gregorian chant at the heart of the musical tradition reflects a broader rhythm of life and a musical development, through the centuries, that has not been an interrupted evolution or progress but one in which the contemporary Church performer stands in their part of history, as custodian of that tradition, particularly when working within the *locus* of a historic building. Both James O'Donnell and Stephen Farr related religious music's context to that of religious visual art: it can be seen in a gallery but its original context is clear. We must also be aware of the danger of antiquarianism, of relating religious context to a past age. For Stephen and for Francis one composer who was a genius at creating sacred music was Olivier Messiaen and his monumental opera *St François d'Assise* was one example. However, for Stephen at least, the sacred is also to be found in the functionality of the ordinary service, in a well-sung response or anthem. Likewise, all the contributors were keen to distance themselves from genres of music that were too emotionally manipulative and more directed towards the performer's own ego, rather than to something greater.

We now turn to consider how classical sacred music has been translated from the church setting to the wider arena of the secular concert hall, with profound and far-reaching effects.

Chapter 3
The Performers II:
Outside the Context of Religious Worship

Music is the mediator between the spiritual and the sensual life. Although the spirit be not master of that which is created through music, yet it is blessed in this creation, which, like every creation of art, is mightier than the artist.

Ludwig van Beethoven[1]

In the introduction to this book we found that some scholars defined sacred music as that which performs a sacramental role within the liturgy, and in the previous chapter we explored that same idea through conversations with practitioners of liturgical music today.[2] Talking to James O'Donnell at Westminster Abbey, for instance, one gets the impression that performing sacred music within the liturgy is an action that intertwines with several different and complementary elements, such as the architecture, words, prayers, sermon, ceremony and ritual that combine to create an experience that is more than the sum of the parts. Even when the Abbey choir perform in a foreign concert hall, they take something of the heritage and purpose of the Abbey church with them.

But, for other performers today, the multi-dimensional nature of the religious setting for sacred music is a distraction from the main point of performing sacred music: that it is purely great music by any standards and can therefore be performed virtually anywhere. This chapter consists of interview material with performers of sacred music within the concert hall or other secular settings and ends with a summary of what the purpose of sacred music might be in this context. Thus, I begin by examining the motivations of those who perform sacred music in concerts.

The Motivation to Perform Sacred Music

Tom Service, in a blog for the *Guardian* written in March 2010, asked this question: 'How is it possible to love this repertoire as deeply … and to conduct it as fervently as [Harry] Christophers, or to hear the essential message of the music as a listener, if you don't share the same intense faith of a MacMillan, a Bruckner, or a Tavener?' Harry Christopher's answer to this dilemma is both simple and enlightening:

---

[1] Ludwig van Beethoven, quoted in L. Bachelder, *The Gift of Music* (Mt. Vernon, NY: Peter Pauper Press, 1975), p. 36.

[2] See the Introduction above, pp. 4–6 and Chapter 2, pp. 45–62.

> You don't have to have any faith or any religion at all to get something out of
> this music. If the music is good, it will do something to your soul. Hundreds of
> people come to hear us sing this music, and very few are believers as such. It's
> just staggering, the effect that this music can have on an audience. You feel with
> James MacMillan, for example, that he knows the biblical texts inside out, and
> there is something extra that comes through that engagement. And then there's
> Brahms, who wasn't a practising Christian, but who knew his Bible intimately,
> and knew what he wanted to express with the texts he used in a piece like the
> German Requiem.[3]

Simon Russell Beale, who presented the *Sacred Music* documentaries for BBC
television, is also agnostic about the subject matter of sacred choral music (i.e. God);
and yet, he has another criteria for the value of this music: authenticity or honesty.
Russell Beale commented: 'I think James MacMillan's *Strathclyde Motets* are
written honestly, and I think John Tavener's *The Lamb* is written honestly'.[4] The lack
of a specific, intense, denominational Christian faith does not, therefore, invalidate
this music for the performer; but it is crucial that, even when performing to a secular
audience, it retain its core element of truth or honesty. If sacred choral music, and
particularly that of Tavener, Pärt, Górecki and their emulators, becomes merely
mood music, then that is the day for the performer to retire, says Christophers:

> There's a big danger that this repertoire can be classed as mood music, used by
> record companies to soften the soul. But the people who come to our concerts
> don't say that it's wallpaper music. They say it's doing something to them. They
> feel the power of the music. And for us as performers, the day it becomes mood
> music is the day we give up.[5]

Tom service ends his blog article with these words:

> As Russell Beale says at the end of the series, these pieces by everyone from
> Brahms to MacMillan are 'experiences: deep, deep spiritual experiences'. All
> music, according to MacMillan, is a means of 'searching out the sacred'. If
> Russell Beale and Christophers haven't got the final answers to how this music
> manages that spiritual alchemy, they share its mysteries and beauties, and show
> us why sacred music still matters.[6]

Whilst I obviously agree that sacred music still matters, I cannot help but be
intrigued by the term 'deep, deep, spiritual experiences' when faith seems to be

---

[3]   Tom Service, 'On the Trail of the Sacred', *Guardian* blog, 11 March 2010: http://
www.guardian.co.uk/music/2010/mar/11/sacred-music-simon-russell-beale.

[4]   Ibid.

[5]   Ibid.

[6]   Ibid.

absent. What does 'spiritual' mean once the sacred, confessional nature of the music, as intended by the composer, is watered down or ignored? I am interested therefore in how, as a performer, one 'searches out the sacred' and, if one finds it, how it is best communicated in the context of a concert.

Peter Phillips is one of the musical directors who, from the 1970s onwards, brought Renaissance polyphony of Masses and motets out of the chapels, cathedrals and churches, for which it was written, and onto the concert platform. When I interviewed him he explained why this was such an important achievement and why he chose the kind of repertoire he did:

> Right from the start I wanted to treat this music as great music by any standard. It happened to have sacred words (I don't think madrigals are as interesting as the church music, so it wasn't a problem). I wanted to do Renaissance music because I saw a gap in the market but I didn't want to do very much secular music and indeed haven't. So I was dealing with what I considered to be absolutely top material and it was my ambition, not being a particularly religious person and not wanting to have to work with priests, to be frank, to present this great music in concerts and concert series in international concert venues, in international artist series, in symphony halls or churches, wherever the people wanted to put it on. I wasn't going to make a fuss about what sort of a venue we were singing in unless the acoustics were dire. Even then I didn't make much of a fuss.
>
> JA: So the music has always been the primary driving force? The greatness of the music?
>
> PP: And my love of it. My reaction to it as music, yes. Because I wanted to put it alongside the best that any other period of music could offer, like string quartets, it seemed to me that sacred choral music was ideal for those series where there were lieder recitals, piano recitals, chamber music and orchestras playing in thousand-seater halls. We had to shape up. It was quite clear to me, and is still clear to me, that the singing tradition has lagged very much behind the orchestral playing tradition (I'm not talking about opera singers here). You get an orchestra together, and you expect it to make a good sound right from the start and wrong notes are not tolerated – it's elementary. Whereas in singing, it wasn't quite like that when we started and the public didn't expect so much. I thought, we've got to shape up and the average has to be very high. The average of what we do across a year of concert giving has to be very high. There are going to be bad nights but the average has to be good otherwise we wouldn't go anywhere.
>
> JA: So what was the situation like when you began your career? Was there a lack of professionalism in choral singing?
>
> PP: It was just that the expectations were lower. The cathedral singing tradition and the good choral society tradition had come from the nineteenth century and had evolved much more slowly than the orchestral playing tradition, which had shaped up around the year 1900 when people started to write really difficult music, [Richard] Strauss in particular, and orchestras couldn't play it. The Tchaikovsky violin concerto, when it was written, was said to be impossible,

but nowadays everyone expects to be able to play it. Well I don't think we've had that same kick up the bum in the singing world.

JA: Do you think we've had it now?

PP: Well, I'm hoping that *The Tallis Scholars* might have done something for that.

JA: So that the new choral groups emerging have a new generation of singer who can immediately slot into a very high professional standard?

PP: It's recordings that have done that. That was true all along: the moment that there was a recording out, everybody was shown up if they weren't as good as that recording so they all had to shape up to that. Recording voices was also fairly primitive for a long time so it didn't grow up as fast as it could have. I have been trying to put this into words, that the training of singing in this country, and I think by definition abroad, as we seem to lead the way, has been slower than it might have been.[7]

Recordings, concerts, the Internet and more radio coverage than ever before for sacred music mean that standards are also higher than they have ever been and that is certainly one reason for the popularity of sacred music. But, for Peter, there is another great advantage of performing this music in secular settings – it isn't compromised by religion:

> A concert isn't interrupted endlessly by the religion. I plan a concert programme very carefully so that I lead people through a series of events. I almost never interrupt that series by speaking myself: as you'll remember, I don't like doing it and I don't want other people to do it either. The experience of listening to polyphony is a completely engrossing one. People often say it acts on them like a drug and they go in a trance-like state and they don't want it to stop. Well, the moment some guy gets up and starts yacking on, the whole thing is broken. There you have the fundamental point, that in a church service the music is helping the priest do what he has to do and creating a different sort of trance, if you like, or however you want to describe the mood in a church service, so that's completely legitimate, it just wasn't what I want to do and I think that the music also can be put into the form that I put it in and presented in the way I present it. Of course, we sing to people who are not Christian at all. I think we're singing to a much more basic human need that people pick up worldwide.

JA: Is this purely an aesthetic situation or is there something else going on there?

PP: Well, I leave it to them [the audience] to make of it what they will. I'm very un-prescriptive. We give them the words, the texts [in the programme booklet]. It's essential that everyone can see what we're singing about because we're singing Latin almost all the time ... So they can take from it what they want. I'm not presenting it as a God-centred event, though I might, in the course

---

7   Interview with Peter Phillips, Merton College, Oxford, 21 February, 2012.

of the music, feel something very powerful in that way. If you go through a service and do it, you're roped in right from the start and there's no doubt about what you're supposed to do. I don't do that in our concerts. I also think that some of this music that we sing ... gets very close to being abstract.

JA: Does the fact that a lot of this music is in Latin assist with the abstract nature of it?

PP: Yes it does. I love singing Latin, because I do know what it means, more or less, and it's such a great language to sing. The Latin makes it more impersonal than English or German ... The chorales of Luther, and that side of German religion, I find more moving that anything really. I love the old Book of Common Prayer language. Latin is sort of parallel with that.

JA: So you programme very carefully and you take the audience through a journey. How do you organize a concert programme?

PP: I find it very difficult to describe. Every programme has its own starting point and logic. Often it's determined by the promoter, who says what they want ... I always assume there's an interval. If there's no interval, then everything's scuppered. You build up to the interval, you have your interval and usually the piece after the interval is quite a sensitive moment. The sensitive moments are the first piece, where you're introducing yourself, and the last piece, where you're going to leave an impression. Usually people talk about the last piece more than anything, especially if they've liked it. And that's the aim and object, that they go away thinking 'wow'; so the last piece is very important. Then if you want to do something experimental, it's usually after the interval where people are still there – they have decided to come back! ... We've been singing quite a lot of Arvo Pärt recently. He's the only modern composer that we've been singing ... the sound that he suggests to me goes very well with what we do ... I'm not putting on concerts in order to mimic church services, something the BBC failed to understand for a long time. They always thought we were trying to create Matins on St Ambrose day or something. We're not doing any of that. I've just chosen this piece because I like it. This is the piece I want to do and I will not feel obliged to do some other piece just because someone else thinks it has a greater liturgical relevance.

However, despite his long-term commitment to performing sacred music in concert settings, Peter now finds himself helping to nurture a choral foundation in Oxford at Merton College, where, along with chapel music director Benjamin Nicholas, he directs music within the liturgy in the college chapel. How does he relate to performing this music within a religious context now?

It's completely different. I love it too. I love sitting in chapel, surrounded by beautiful things: the building, the liturgy, contributing to something to the overall experience through music. I feel particularly at home in this chapel – as you know I've worked here since 1974.[8] It's a privilege to conduct Dyson in D in a service, but I wouldn't conduct Dyson in D in a concert.[9]

JA: In a service, does the music take on a meaning which is theological in some sense, as an aid to prayer?

PP: Not for me. The problem, which is a local one, is making that performance as good as a concert performance. In a concert the singers stand where they need to stand; in a church service, it may not be possible to do that and in fact it's not in this building [Merton Chapel] – the choir-stalls, for example, are very far apart, imposing difficulties which I would not tolerate in a concert hall. It has always been my intention that we [*The Tallis Scholars*] should be the best and we create the circumstances that enable us to be the best ... [In church] you can't turn away young people (singers) who are doing their utmost but have much to learn, whereas [with *The Tallis Scholars*] I wasn't answerable to any religious or educational element. I started off from the point of view that this was a secular activity and I was going to get the best and if I didn't get the best I would remove those I thought unsatisfactory and get other people. I wasn't doing a very God-like thing. But in the end I think you could say I got the kind of concerts I wanted, whereas in chapel we set out to sing the best we can, within the situation, which may not be entirely satisfactory.

JA: And what are the limitations of this situation for instance?

PP: Well, the organ is a long way away, which creates serious problems of co-ordination. But the Merton choir represents much more of an educational programme than anything I've done in the professional context, and it will run for years. You take someone in at eighteen and you train them up. We take this very seriously because the end result benefits from careful training, tuition and nurturing of these people. I conduct them in concerts quite often. One of my better roles is working with them in a concert.

JA: Do you prefer that?

PP: Well, that is my training. I simply think the music is stronger theologically when it's being sung well, and that is more likely in a concert. Perhaps people should come to our concerts as much as to our services. But the Christian Church wouldn't agree with that ... In a church service, the words that the priest says are very descriptive and set a precise theological scene. A concert of music that contains these lovely words is so much vaguer. Nothing is being demanded of you, you're not being told to think of anything in a concert, and yet you may well have a fantastic experience of a religious nature, it's just that no priest is trying to control it.

I find these last few sentences fascinating – that sacred music is 'stronger' when it is performed well, and that it is sung or played best in a concert, where there

---

[8]   Merton College has frequently been used by *The Tallis Scholars* as their recording venue.

[9]   George Dyson's setting of the Evensong Canticles in D Major.

is no priest or liturgy prescribing and controlling its meaning and our experience of it. There is a remarkable contrast between the way James O'Donnell talks about his work within the multi-dimensional liturgy of Westminster Abbey, with the way Peter expresses his ambiguity to music performed within the liturgy. Peter emphasized the great advantages – musically, emotionally, professionally *and* theologically – of performing sacred music outside of the liturgical context, in order that its power and meaning may be more fully appreciated in a concert setting. He is captivated by Pythagoras' notion of the 'music of the spheres', which, he suggests, is the great appeal of much music for the audience, who:

> leave the busy world behind for a space of time. They are transported. The image that always moves me is that of the music of the spheres. It's the idea that this music is out there, and the spheres in their motions are producing something like this. It's wonderfully imaginative, as you know, as a starting point for polyphony.[10]

For Peter the concert provides a medium in which the music and words can be fully explored and experienced, which can lead the listener in many different directions without hampering them with the particular concerns of denomination, confessional religion:

> The moment you say 'I'm a Catholic', everyone says 'Well, I'm something else', and they won't take any notice any more. But if you say, 'I'm going to sing a concert of music by Palestrina', who famously didn't write much secular music and it's never done anyway, people will come flocking. The evidence is there. We hardly ever sing to a hall that's not full and these are big halls. It certainly wasn't like that fifteen or thirty years ago. It can't just be the records. The records have been wonderful ambassadors all around the world and they are made to a very high spec., but in the end people want to hear the live article and when they say to me that it's as good on stage as it is on record, I'm really pleased because actually it probably isn't. We manicure, polish the records to the point where you can't do that live but they [the audience] are having a wonderful time ... the sheer excitement of hearing it right in front of you. I think the music must come across more powerfully like that.[11]

Peter Phillips is an unashamed promoter of sacred choral music in concert settings. He has dedicated his life to it, and he still considers it to be the most successful and uncompromising context in which to hear this kind of art.[12] The allowances one has to make in order to achieve regular choral music in the cathedral, chapel

---

[10]   Interview with Peter Phillips.

[11]   Ibid.

[12]   For a detailed account of *The Tallis Scholars'* history and work, see P. Phillips, *What We Really Do* (London: Musical Times, 2003; second edition, 2013).

or church, in terms of singers, repertoire, clergy, architecture, furniture, sermons, prayers and liturgy, are clearly unsatisfactory to Peter, compared to the well-prepared concert programme performed by hand-picked musicians with the single purpose of communicating the music without the clutter of a prescribed theological and moral subtext. But Peter also makes another very powerful point here: that music, simply performed at a high standard and without accompanying words or liturgy, breaks down denominational and doctrinal divides between people. Music brings harmony and shared experience, but one that is broad enough to encompass everybody's individual experience, religious or otherwise.

Is this, then, the way that other concert musicians view, and perform, sacred music in secular society? When I spoke to Harry Christophers, I began by asking him why sacred choral music is so popular with audiences today:

> Part and parcel is to do with the lives people lead ... particularly in the UK. We're not like a lot of other European countries where people seem to have the idea that there's time for everything. In Britain, it appears, there's never time. So, sacred music has a relaxing quality to it, particularly the music of the Renaissance, but we've found that it seems to affect everybody in a different way. Probably only 15 or 20 per cent of the audience that come to our concerts are regular church goers. The rest are not – so what do they hear in this music? Many people say to me, and it doesn't matter what the music is, be it pieces by Victoria, Byrd, Tallis, [Alfonso] Lobo or Josquin de Près (works they may have never heard of): 'I now know what paradise might be like', or 'I now know what heaven might be like because I've heard it in these voices.'

> JA: Interesting language!

> HC: Yes. Particularly when we're performing in beautiful cathedrals and abbeys, is that, through listening to the music, people really begin to realize that these buildings were built with this music in mind and the composers wrote with the building in mind and that simple hand-in-glove idea is significant. That is an incredible realization. For many people the music will be a soothing relief for them because there is something about the human voice that is incredibly soothing, especially when it is employed in a corporate way, in a choir that's singing to you. It is the inherent humility of the relationship between performer and listener, and a response to the fragility of the human voice, that makes the music so special. The response is, of course, personal and the better the group singing it, the more emotional that response is likely to become. There's no doubt about it, that any of this music will touch the emotions. Sacred music is such a broad genre. For instance, what effect do John Rutter's Christmas carol arrangements have on people? Perhaps they make them very happy and put a smile on their face. But what does a really serious piece of William Byrd do or Victoria? It makes people think and feel. One of the things I remember years ago when we used to tour Japan, where one has no Christian audience at all, is that the kind of pieces they related to were ones such as the Victoria *Tenebrae Responseries* [for Maundy Thursday]. They really engaged with the drama and

gripping nature of the story behind it and the music had a power to them that I found extraordinary. [In the UK] we'd probably much rather hear an *Agnus Dei* of a Mass or an *Ave Verum Corpus* because it's much more soothing.

JA: That's very interesting. I've also experienced the enthusiasm for this music in Japanese concert halls, as a performer. As a singer it's fascinating to be on the receiving end of that euphoria, given that we're so often used to a relatively reserved response in Europe. Does a more reserved response indicate a more internalized experience?

HC: It does, definitely. I've noticed a big difference in the UK. In Spain, for instance, the audiences soak up the music ... They have no [choral] tradition today ... Yet, of course, in the Renaissance they produced some the greatest music ever written. People are bereft of it and that is a big sadness in their culture. In Britain, we don't necessarily have the old fashioned fervent Catholicism that much of Spain still possesses. We have so many different faiths ... I'm increasingly finding that they don't look at the concert programme booklet and they'll sit and let the music do something to them.[13]

So sacred choral music has a worldwide power to affect audiences in different ways, whether in non-Christian Japan, or Catholic Spain, or multi-cultural Britain. But is there a danger that an audience who are 'soaking up' the beautiful sounds alone may be missing something fundamental in the music?

It is this power of the Renaissance that does that. I've always maintained that when I record a CD of Renaissance *a capella* music, I'll restrict it to sixty minutes in duration because that's all the brain can take in one go. Once you start exceeding that length, the recording is in danger of becoming wallpaper music. Moreover, if you're going to do things really well, then it's just the same in a concert, because the last thing I want this music to become is just music to soothe you after a hard day's work. That may be what some people find absolutely wonderful and it's great if they do, but I don't want that to be the only reason for this music. I want it to be soul searching, to find an emotion in it. When one performs some of this music, particularly [William] Byrd, and one considers what he went through [in his life][14] and the message that he conveyed through his work, it becomes very powerful music. So, if you perform it in a powerful and emotional way people do respond to that and find these hidden emotions.[15]

---

[13]   Interview with Harry Christophers, 2011.

[14]   William Byrd (1543–1623) was a secret Catholic living in Protestant England under, and working for, Elizabeth I for much of his career. His compositions conformed to the religious and political dictates of the time, but much of his music expresses the sense of his profound religious isolation.

[15]   Interview with Harry Christophers.

Harry makes the same point highlighted by James O'Donnell and Peter Phillips: that the standard of performance and careful selection of music and programming is vital in the effective communication of the music. The soothing sound is not the main purpose of this music whether in a religious *or* secular setting. There's also a sense, in common with other performers, that the highest standards of performance reveal a depth to the music that cannot be perceived by inferior renderings. So, I asked Harry, what was the key to a good performance, and have standards improved generally since the 1970s, when he began his professional career?

> Very much so; I can see the difference, over the years, in *The Sixteen*. Our approach is different from what it was in 1980. I've always tried to put the words, the text, on the same level as the music, or indeed in more recent years, superior to it. I've never been one to let the music speak for itself. I think that increasingly so in the last ten years – really to find a drama and emotion within the music and convey it. That's purely because of the simple fact that ninety per cent of that music is in Latin and nobody speaks Latin … So there's no point us standing up there in a glorious cathedral like York Minster and just putting notes to the words. We've got to inject something in it to convey the meaning of that text. That's not authentic in a way, the music was the accompaniment to the divine service, not to be the focal point and we're changing that.
>
> JA: So you put the drama in there, the expressive nature of the textual setting, in order to emphasize that this is music written for a particular purpose?
>
> HC: Most definitely, but also to convey its meaning, to try and get inside the music, and every composer is different in the way they write. If you listen to the works of John Sheppard, they'll almost always be based upon a *cantus firmus*, on the plainsong. It's not necessarily music that you can go out there and, as a conductor, interpret in the same way you can interpret Byrd. Nevertheless, there are nuances which can make very subtle differences and certain harmonic changes can be really wonderful. My approach is to make whatever we do sound natural. Even though rehearsal and a lot of work have gone into it to make it sound like that, to make it sound natural but not ordinary – that's the big difference, because this is great music. You constantly have to remind people that in the sixteenth century the best composers of the time were all in the service of the Church. In England, for instance, if you wanted to compose, the only job was to be a Gentleman of the Chapel Royal or in the service of the Church. They were the Beethovens and Mahlers of the sixteenth-century … So you shouldn't treat these composers with a faceless approach because they were injecting their own personalities into the music. It's easy to see the personality of Victoria coming through his music – every single piece. I've not come across a piece [of Victoria] which I, as a conductor, can't interpret. I can pull things around and make things special. It's completely unauthentic!
>
> JA: There's a passion in the music?
>
> HC: There is. Total passion. He's very special, there's no doubt about it. It's dynamic music.

Harry is passionate himself about his desire to communicate the depth of meaning of the music and the text. How then, I wondered, does the desire for this music not to become 'wallpaper' or background music square with *The Sixteen*'s role as 'The Voices of *Classic FM*': a radio station that brings classical music to a very wide and varied audience of millions a day, with an emphasis on relaxation and soothing calm. In a society that responds strongly to such a provision, can the music still be understood on different levels, or how does one stop it becoming background music on the radio?

> You're quite right about the chilled classics idea of *Classic FM*. It's definitely music that can be heard on different levels ... For some it will always be wallpaper music, it will be used for those relaxing times ... That's part and parcel of the modern day world: we have got the radio and CDs to listen to, and most people who listen to those aren't really aware that actually these things are bloody hard to do. They're lucky to be hearing nigh-on perfection when they hear many of these recordings. People don't witness the fragile nature of performance. It's very interesting when we made our [first] television series with the BBC how that opened a whole new world to people ... What that did for people was to open their eyes, not only to what was going on politically, in the Church and socially, but also to highlight various aspects of the style of this music, the way it all came from plainsong, how beautiful that original plainsong line is, that line that is so colourful, so evocative ... I find it fascinating that composers, from Renaissance times to the Modern day, still hark back to that plainsong line, that unison line that is so wonderfully human and evokes such feeling. That, of course, has been the wonderful basis of fantastic music since [Medieval times] to today.

Harry is in agreement with James O'Donnell and James MacMillan on the importance of plainsong in musical compositions, from the *Notre Dame* school of the twelfth and thirteenth centuries, with early polyphony by composers such as Perotin and Leonin, until the present day. Television documentaries have given Harry and his musicians the opportunity to demonstrate the process involved in a performer's approach to the music of the Renaissance, as well as to sacred music of the Romantic and Modern eras.[16] The programmes offer audiences the chance to see the creative, religious and political processes involved in the composition of the works and to learn something of the lives of the composers. But they also gave performers the forum in which to express how they felt about the music, and what they had to do in order to convey its power. I asked Harry what technical and personal qualities does a singer need to communicate sacred music well?

> You have to have all the basics of musicality; you need good ensemble, good tuning, good sight reading: a brain! You need to know the style of the group

---

[16]   Such as the BBC series *Sacred Music*.

(in *The Sixteen* we take [it] for granted). What I've always looked for is not just people who can sing the notes, it's about personalities. They don't all have to be the same ... It's about blending. In a group like *The Sixteen* what makes it such a joy to conduct the different singers is allowing them to breathe and for those personalities [to] come through, that's the thing, without stamping down a sort of dogma and doctrine and saying "You've got to sing like this" ... You don't have to be a fervent Christian of any kind to inject your personality into this great music ... It is about knowing what those words mean and interpreting them. If *The Sixteen* were to sing a Schubert lied they would inject the same passion and emotion into the words as when they perform a Mass ... It's going back to the basic principles about music which is all based on the pulse, on the heart beat ... Having that ebb and flow in the music and allowing the music never to stagnate, that's always the trick for me. One is constantly keeping the music alive so that it's going somewhere and it's not stopping.

With this performance practice in mind, I asked Harry to talk specifically about a concert given in York Minster at the start of the York Early Music Festival (mentioned in the preface to this book).[17] For Harry, the evening represented the fruition of years of endeavour:

That was a culmination of so many things. It was a culmination of the group's profile in the UK. Our main aim, through having associations with artists and orchestras and choirs, was to encourage people to like music. In the case of *The Sixteen* we have never ever dumbed down what we do. We've always kept our integrity through everything we've done. For a lot of the public, that integrity brings a realization that we believe in the music we're performing and that it's going to be good music. So we are lucky, people have seen us on the television, people listen to us on the radio, buy our CDs. All of that combined with the fact that, over thirty years from our beginnings, we're still there. I think that did do a lot for it but the main reason for that big rise was the start of our Choral Pilgrimage in 2000. It was this simple idea of performing music in the buildings for which it was written. We had that tag line didn't we? 'Music written for the glory of God' and people were able to relate to that and allow the music to do something for them. The amazing thing with York Minster, and the Choral Pilgrimages, is that all those people have come to those concerts because they *want* to come to them. Out of thirty-two Choral Pilgrimage concerts this year (2011/12) twenty-four are self-promotions, so you don't have the first ten or twenty rows full of Festival patrons, or the company who are sponsoring it ... All 1700 people in York were paying to come to that concert because they wanted to come, not because they're being dragged along to it. That is staggering! ... In a place like York, and other university cities, such as Durham, Oxford and Cambridge, the number of students that are coming to these concerts is rising.

---

[17]   See the Preface above, pp. xiii–xv.

I find that fascinating. People bring their teenage children, so there are young people coming to these concerts. There are fewer twenty-five to forty-year olds attending, perhaps, but there are good reasons for that: many are either established in demanding jobs that are keeping them at work in the evenings and many of them have young children, which reduces the opportunity of concert-going. But often, of course, once those demands recede, they come back to it, so I don't think it's a problem.[18]

Finally, I ask Harry if he can remember any particularly moving or powerful musical experiences in his life, and their context:

There are several things really. I remember when I was first a chorister at Canterbury Cathedral and just how special that was. I remember the anthem, *O Nata Lux* [by Thomas Tallis]. To sing that in Canterbury Cathedral as a ten or eleven year old, not realizing that we had all this pressure on us really, but to be in the cassock and surplice, singing glorious music in the fantastic acoustic was wonderful. That's remained with me forever.

As you mentioned earlier, one of the greatest moments for me was York Minster. It was the Early Music Festival and to see that full Nave and to have most of the choir coming up and saying 'What a privilege just to stand there.' You spend your whole life singing *Decani* to *Cantoris,* very intimate, but to sing to a full Nave, to sing to a glorious rose window, it was just marvellous! Fantastic!

Another occasion was when we went to Madrid and we did a concert in the *San Jerónimo el Real* Church associated with Philip II ... and we sang Alfonso Lobo's *Versa est in Luctum*, which was totally relevant to that building and indeed for the celebration for the anniversary of Philip II and the audience was in tears. I thought 'My goodness me, you don't have this music in your church services today', and yet here was this audience who are deprived of this music reduced to tears because they hear this piece live. That was a fantastic moment.[19]

Harry's memorable musical moments, at least the three mentioned above, all have a close connection between place and performance for their meaning: Canterbury Cathedral as a chorister, York Minster and Madrid's San Jerónimo el Real as a conductor. All of these powerful experiences were related to performing the music in the buildings for which it was originally intended. Indeed, since the Millennium, the aim of Choral Pilgrimage concerts has been to perform the music written for great ecclesiastical buildings in those buildings, but in concert form rather than divine service. Another choral pilgrimage set up at the Millennium was Sir John Eliot Gardiner's Bach Pilgrimage, which set out to perform all of Bach's 198 surviving cantatas, written for weekly worship in Weimar and Leipzig, in venues around the world. The project began on Christmas day 1999 but, as Sir John Eliot

---

[18]   Interview with Harry Christophers.

[19]   Ibid.

admits, although he had no idea how it would end, it was an ambition that had been growing for some time:

> It wasn't a spur of the moment decision but something that had been brewing inside me for many years. I suppose it was three things: the 250th anniversary of Bach's death and the millennium; a perplexity – that I still have – that this major tranche of his repertoire is partially known and rarely performed; and the state that I had arrived at with *The Monteverdi Choir* and *The English Baroque Soloists*.
>
> Having done the major oratorios, the Passions and some of the Cantatas, I felt that this was the biggest single slice of his whole repertoire that we really needed to come to grips with at some stage. This seemed the golden opportunity. [20]

The *Monteverdi Players and Choir* were to perform all the surviving cantatas in just one year. This posed a particular set of challenges:

> It was hugely challenging and ambitious to try and do all the cantatas in a single year. There were a lot of hurdles to surmount but what it gave us was an in-depth exposure to this repertoire on a weekly basis almost for a whole year. We had this bizarre phenomenon that on a Monday morning we'd be looking at three or four cantatas that we'd not done before, and we had to forget the ones we'd done the previous week.
>
> I'd spent the previous two years learning them but nonetheless, on a Sunday evening, I'd wonder what was coming up next. We had to be quite self-disciplined and put to one side all our memories of the cantatas we'd just been doing. [21]

Another of the practical problems was setting up a new record label in order to release CDs of the live concerts, eventually as a complete set. The new label was called 'SDG' after Bach's inscriptions at the end of each of his compositions, *Soli Deo Glora*, 'solely to the glory of God'. Sir John Eliot remembers the difficulties of such a venture:

> We did have a parting of the ways with DG [*Deutsche Gramaphon*] where money was transferred from them to us. This helped to tide us over and get the project under way. It didn't make up for the fact that we were left with a huge gap in the budget. Not that the project was ever driven by considerations of the recordings. It was conceived right from the word go as a concert pilgrimage. [22]

---

[20] Interview material taken from classic-music.com (BBC Music Magazine's website): http://www.classical-music.com/feature/meet-artists/sir-john-eliot-gardiner.

[21] Ibid.

[22] Sir John Eliot Gardiner interviewed by Geoffrey Norris, *Daily Telegraph*, 20 January 2005.

Thus, we see again, that sacred music in the concert format was being connected to buildings of ecclesiastical significance. The pilgrimage 'was a way of performing the cantatas in a coherent manner. It was also connected with buildings of special historical or architectural beauty and merit, because this music sits so much better in a sympathetic ecclesiastical setting than in the concert hall.[23]

Indeed the connection between place and music was extended to a liturgical connection in the Bach Pilgrimage, with each cantata performed on its relevant day in the liturgical calendar. But why is this music so great and why were they written? Sir John Eliot addresses these questions in the following terms:

> Emotions and preoccupations are woven into his cantatas – anything from grief at infant mortality to real apoplectic anger and frustration when he feels a lack of respect accorded to him for his abilities as a craftsman.
>
> He had a rigid deadline. They were sung twice on every Sunday. They rehearsed on a Saturday. He prepared the boys on a Thursday and a Friday. The chances are that the parts were completed by Wednesday evening or Thursday at the latest, though there may have been changes of mind – the sudden presence in town of a particularly good virtuoso who he wanted to draft in might change things. He wrote straight into score, so he probably started composing on a Monday and finished by Wednesday. That's my feeling but there's no way of proving it.
>
> There was no blotting paper in those days and each page of ink took twelve to fifteen minutes to dry. So he had to keep stopping, sometimes writing himself little mnemonics at the bottom of the page about how particular fugal exposition went on while he took a break. You can see this in the original part books.
>
> To keep that rhythm of output up for the length that he did was a simply prodigious feat. A lot of it was self-imposed. He could have performed the works of others. That's what most people did. He didn't have to compose pieces of such length and complexity. But it is wonderful music. The cantatas are the heart of him.[24]

Interestingly as Bach's music and even his cantatas (which have been under-performed until recently) increasingly enjoy worldwide recognition, Sir John Eliot believes that we are only now beginning to realize the importance of Bach's sacred music, written for parochial worship:

> My personal feeling is that it's only in the twenty-first century that Bach's going to come into a full recognition of this extraordinary – by any standards – breadth of musical creativity and inventiveness. There's a paradox that Bach was writing for such a parochial, specific, circumscribed liturgy, but that this music can lift

---

[23] Ibid.

[24] Sir John Eliot Gardiner interviewed by Alan Rusbridger, *The Guardian*, 12 December 2005.

off the page and speak to a far wider range of people today than lots of other composers. It's a phenomenon. I can't account for it but I can witness it and testify about it.

Is Sir John Eliot Gardiner 'witnessing' this music in the same way that James MacMillan is witnessing as a Christian when he composes music? Is he a Christian?

> At the moment I perform the music I am a Christian, yes. Culturally, yes. Doctrinally and theologically, no. I can't put it better than that. I have to subscribe, at the moment of performing, even preparing. And I'm acutely aware there's another realm of existence out there. But do I subscribe to the whole catechism? No, of course I don't. I can't ... But there's still a group of people out there who place a high value on classical music and, even if they're not card-carrying Christians, look to Christian-inspired music for solace or for diversion or for inspiration. Whether it's because of the failure of the Church or of the whole *zeitgeist* of contemporary culture is difficult to say.[25]

Sir John Eliot's comments, along with others who perform sacred music at professional concert level, resonate deeply with those who care for both the music and the faith aspect of its composition, performance and reception. Why does 'Christian-inspired' music bring solace or inspiration? It can be 'deeply spiritual' or speak to the 'soul' without any reference to any particular dogma. Sir John Eliot Gardiner, Harry Christophers and Peter Phillips, and the musicians with whom they have collaborated, have been responsible for a wider public engagement with sacred music in concert form than ever before, although often performed in ecclesiastical settings. Whether this has replaced an aspect of spirituality that the Church used to provide or whether it is part of a wider cultural shift, the religious language of 'pilgrimage' and the a-religious setting of 'concert' have now been joined.

Performance and the Purpose of Sacred Music

In this chapter and the previous one we have examined the practitioners' art of performing sacred music in different contexts, leaving us with a final question to consider: if sacred music is as powerful outside of the liturgical context as it is within it, what is its overall purpose? One performer who understands what it is like to perform as both a concert singer and a cathedral choir member for many years is Francis Steele, founder member of *The Sixteen*, a long-standing member of some of Britain's foremost choral ensembles, and former Vicar-Choral of St Paul's Cathedral, who now runs a specialist music school in the South of France. I asked him whether his many years as a professional singer of sacred choral music

---

[25] Ibid.

had brought him to a conclusion about the purpose of sacred music. The answer, he replied, lies in the performance:

> As a performer I often asked myself this question; as a performer of music within the liturgy the same question would lead me to examine my own rather dubious credentials as a performer. I should say at the outset that I think that the point of performing sacred music is to fulfil the purpose of that music, whatever that might be. Although music can be discussed, analysed and pondered *in absentia*, its true purpose is fulfilled only in performance. But what is that purpose? Faiths address many issues of fundamental importance to man by attempting to engage humanity at a variety of levels – intellectual, spiritual, moral or emotional. For as long as we remain at the level of the mundane, sacred music attempts to express – even to engender – the mundane; human emotions such as joy or sorrow, earthly pomp, even, where a Church is established, varieties of chauvinistic fervour. When skilfully written it can deepen the drama and help to formulate or elucidate ideas, and its formal structure can enhance that of the text, or even supply its lack, and song can be a more effective vehicle for the expression of human feelings than the spoken word.[26]

Music not only enhances text but also can supply meaning where text is absent. But music also provides depth of meaning and significance by dual temporal and timeless qualities:

> Furthermore, both music and language have an historical and social context, which fixes them in time, yet transcends time, in the same way as the sum of individual experience expands to embrace past and future when we ponder the human condition. Hence Spirituals, which we can place historically and socially, can be seen, like the Lutheran chorale *Jesu meine Freude*, as tributary streams flowing into the river whose source is the relative contempt for earthly life expressed by members of the early Church. Sacred music both sharpens the focus of its foreground, the present, yet deepens the focal plane to take in past and future, thereby underwriting a Church's claim to be universal and eternal. So much for the mundane.
>
> Liturgy is sometimes referred to as a form of drama, a word whose Greek root – *draō* –means 'to do', and so if it attempts to involve those present, it is as players (even if only spear-bearers), not groundlings. Since the *dramatis personae* includes God, this drama is cast not at a mundane, interpersonal, but a transcendent, level; and because the field of action is extended beyond mortal life to take in the eternal life of the soul, much of this drama is, from the point of view of human reason, ineffable.

---

[26]   Interview with Francis Steele, 2013.

But even outside of the dramatic liturgical context, music has the power to reveal mysteries beyond words through sound:

> I sense that music can communicate beyond words, outside of reason, and I can offer one experience from my performing life to which I can attest, but cannot explain. I frequently sang William Byrd's *Tribue, Domine*. It's a motet whose text deals both with the mundane, the fragility of man, and the numinous, the omnipotence and nature of God. In expressing the latter, it explores and expounds the nature of the Trinity with words more judiciously chosen than poetically inspired – in fact the text alone scarcely moved me on any level. But Byrd's music, when sung, articulated that text just as a great actor would his lines, and in doing so lent it an authority and persuasiveness that I could never discover in the text alone. It even seemed to inspire my colleagues. Singing that piece seemed to bring me as close to that mystery, of the Trinity, as I shall ever approach, and as close to (inarticulate, non-rational) acceptance of it as I shall ever come. Yet neither proximity nor consent were derived from any explicable source. I make no claims for this account – it probably indicates a deep, yet deeply muddled, response to music and the numinous – yet it does seem to suggest that music can engage with the numinous in a way that words and reason cannot, and in doing so, can involve singer or listener in those mysteries, making of him or her a player, not a groundling.[27]

We perform music because it takes us beyond both words and reason. For Francis, William Byrd's music was able to bring him and, seemingly, his colleagues, closer to understanding a deep theological mystery than words alone could ever have achieved. This affects not only the performer but the recipient of the performance. In his work with amateur singers today, I asked Francis how he approached performing sacred polyphony with them and whether he wished the singers to respond or relate to a piece of polyphony in a particular way? His reply related specifically to sacred polyphony as opposed to Romantic or post-Romantic music:

> When I look at a piece of sacred polyphony, I am often as struck by what appears to be lacking as I am conscious of what is given. Tempo indication, dynamic and expression marks, all are wanting; questions of scoring and pitch remain unresolved, and there is no indication of the composer's intentions as to use or performance – even the attribution can be wrong, or missing. We would search in vain for a 'lead' voice that might dominate or motivate the others with a display of power, virtuosity or sexuality, and the look of the thing on the page offers a similarly unvariegated aspect – no vast contrasts, or even pithy sound bites spun to our human attention span, no 'distraction from distraction'.

---

[27]   Ibid.

Are we to assume that the apparent lack of such elements evinces the composer's indifference?

> I personally do not think that such guidance, or direction, is lacking. In fact, I think that it is abundantly present in the music if one can accept the following assumptions:
>
> (a) that sacred polyphony is homogeneous; its musical grammar and syntax is respected by the composer, be he Palestrina or Gesualdo, and that the resultant musical language is demotic;
> (b) that the composers had no heterodoxical intent; and that they would expect in turn from the performer an utterly faithful and orthodox performance.

So how do these assumptions affect how you work with a group of singers on a piece of music?

> The effect of these assumptions, if valid, would be to place us alongside the music, in a position far removed from our current post-Nietzschian solipsism, and my first efforts in working with this repertoire are devoted to encouraging singers to adopt this state of mind and recommending the consequences of so doing. The integrity of each vocal line is only manifest when that line – that voice – duly defers to the integrity of other voices; even then, the integrity of the work as a whole transcends the sum total of its parts. I urge singers to sing in time, for the *tactus* is the heartbeat of creativity, and in tune (with each other; a relative skill, perhaps better expressed by the French *chanter avec justesse*, with its overtones of truth, correctness, precision and appropriateness). I encourage singers to use all of their vocal resources over which they have technical control, and try to discourage any idea that 'historical authenticity' demands less than full engagement of the voice, or requires anything other than solid 'modern' vocal technique.

So any sense of ego must be subservient to the music itself?

> At this point I defer to the composer. When I spoke of this musical language as demotic, I meant that it has catholic appeal, that it can deeply affect the 'average' listener, the 'good enough' singer; furthermore, it is as if hermetically sealed, requiring neither copious programme notes, nor the involvement of a musical giant, for its realization. So, if I 'direct' polyphony, it is only in the sense of directing the singers' attention to the composer's bidding: to derive tempo from the speed or tension of harmonic change, rhythmic activity, the verbal text; or dynamics and expression from vocal line and the interaction of melodic, harmonic and verbal inflection, in short, to discover all that we had thought to be wanting in a piece of polyphony buried deep within the score itself. So I try never to make any suggestion or observation that I cannot back up by direct reference

to the score, and ultimately, I suppose, I seek to render myself superfluous by teaching singers to read the scores for themselves. My highest aspiration would be to earn from Gombert or Byrd a commendation similar to that afforded to Pierre Monteux by Stravinsky after the first performance of *Le Sacre du Printemps*. 'the musical realization was ideal ... Monteux never cheapened the *Sacre* or looked for his own glory in it, and he was always scrupulously faithful to the music.' My talisman as a performer of polyphony was these few lines of Eliot; these days, I am content to offer them to my successors:

> You are not here to verify,
> Instruct yourself, or inform curiosity
> Or carry report. You are here to kneel
> Where prayer has been valid.[28]

Francis' attitude to performing and directing sacred choral polyphony is extremely well thought out and expressed and it offers an interesting snapshot of how at least one professional performer of this kind of music views performance practice in the twenty-first century, giving absolute priority to musical fidelity and little room for ego.

Conclusion

In this chapter we have witnessed significant variances in how performers approach the art of communicating great sacred music. Those who perform in concerts are focussed less on the liturgical context of how the music was originally performed or on how it might be performed liturgically today, and more on the music itself and the meaning of the text and what the whole piece might signify to an audience in a particular setting.

I would suggest that we can venture certain conclusions from the development of concert practice over the last few decades and from the words of the performers interviewed above. First, as Peter Phillips mentioned, music is theologically stronger when it is performed well. The link between theological meaning and musical standards is a phenomenon that has been, perhaps, difficult to establish in previous generations; but with the rise of the recording industry, digital technology and the Internet, standards have risen to such an extent that one can now expect a near perfect rendition of most sacred music in digital form, accessible by numerous means, and audiences expect a similar sonic experience in the concert hall. As the musicians above have intimated, this experience is best encountered without the encumbrance of interrupting monologue. Concert programming, therefore, has become the art of carefully arranging pieces together in order that the audience can best appreciate their aesthetic and spiritual qualities. Theologically, the biblical

---

[28]   From T.S. Eliot, *Four Quartets*, Little Gidding, I.

idea that we are bidden to praise God with our music and voices is most powerfully performed when it is done well. In offering the very best of art, we too, as human beings, receive the most from creation.

Second, we learned from Francis Steele the importance, in performance, of being utterly faithful to the music and that music has the potential to transform a relatively mundane text into one with authority and persuasiveness, that can inspire performer and listener alike and bring them closer to an understanding of the mystery of God, albeit inarticulate and non-rational, than we might ever achieve with words alone. Harry Christophers emphasized the need for blend among his singers, as well as individual character and responsibility held together by a conductor who helps to create meaning through the music and the text.

Third, music in itself is unfettered by denominational boundaries. Music by Palestrina, written by a Catholic Renaissance composer, is great music and accessible to anyone who has ears to hear. In music, people who are separated by divisions of faith are brought together in a harmonizing engagement with the sacred sound.

Indeed, fourth, one does not need to be a confessional believer to engage with good sacred music, but it must, nevertheless, *be* engaged with, rather than treated as 'wallpaper' music, if it is to have any power. But, as Peter Phillips suggested, the motivation for promoting the sacred music concert is that it is great music by any standards: Renaissance composers were the Mahlers and Beethovens of their day. For Sir John Eliot Gardiner he is 'Christian' in the moment of performance but no believer in the catechism otherwise.

Fifth, is the extraordinary phenomenon of the rise of interest in what has been labelled the 'concert pilgrimage', which takes terms from the secular and religious spheres and brings them together. The resulting concept fulfils a desire amongst people to rediscover the music afresh and something of the historical and ecclesiastical context, as well as find solace in Christian-inspired music performed in the buildings for which it was written. Whether this new phenomenon is filling a gap left by the failure in the Church's outreach, or whether it is part of the cultural *zeitgeist*, it is clear that audiences can find themselves, in such settings, lifted beyond the mundane to discover in music a response to the numinous, which is impossible in words and by the use of reason. This, says Francis, is what makes both the performer and listener 'players' – part of the whole drama and mystery, not a mere bystander or observer.

I believe it is this engagement that is to be celebrated, as it brings people to involvement in the divine mystery from which sacred music stems and that leads us back there. We may not know much about heaven, as most descriptions are vague, but common to most definitions is the inclusion of music. Sacred music is in the public domain today and is a powerful witness to an alternative reality, which is beyond materialism and secularism. It encourages us to consider the numinous and ineffable. In the second part of this book, I will consider at greater length how sacred music is received in society today by those who listen to it, explore its relationship to culture in general, and examine its future.

PART II
The Reception of Sacred Music

Chapter 4

Who is Listening?

When sacred music is performed, who is listening? Depending on your perspective, the answer can range from an accidental few – those passing along the street, perhaps, as a church choir rehearses for an evening service, lending their ears briefly, pleasurably, to fragments of song – to a paying audience in a concert hall, to the mightiest listener of all, the very One to whom so much sacred music is addressed. God is certainly, at the very least, the imagined listener of so many of these moving petitions and prayers in music.

Mark Kilfoyle[1]

To listen seriously to music and to perform it are among our most potent ways of learning what it is to live with and before God.

Rowan Williams[2]

Having considered the process of composition and performance via some practitioners of sacred music, we come now, in Part II, to examine the reception of sacred music in society by means of investigating (in Chapter 5) the relationship between modern culture and music, as well as conjecturing (in Chapter 6) the future role of sacred music in society. But first, in this chapter, we begin by asking what it means to listen to music.

When live music is performed, we can assume that those listening are those present (including the performer), or those to whom the music is being transmitted via a broadcast. When a recording is made the listener is, of course, anyone who purchases or happens to hear that recording. Since the broadening of sacred music beyond a purely religious function, be it liturgical or devotional, it is now less clear, than in earlier centuries, who is the intended recipient of a performance of sacred music: it may be a congregation, an audience, someone who happens to enter the building whilst the music is being performed, or maybe God himself. But this chapter examines more than mere hypothetical possibilities that may seem unhelpful categories in today's society, where barriers between the sacred and the secular in music are being broken down. In this chapter, I investigate the power

---

[1]   M. Kilfoyle, Programme Note for *The Sixteen*'s Choral Pilgrimage Concert Series, 2008.

[2]   R. Williams, 'Keeping Time' in *Open to Judgement: Sermons and Addresses* (London: Darton, Longman & Todd, 1994), p. 249, quoted in M. O'Connor, 'The Singing of Jesus' in J.S. Begbie and S.R. Guthrie (eds.), *Resonant Witness*, pp. 434–53, at p. 435.

of musical composition and performance on the recipient, whoever and wherever that person may be. Thus, when I interviewed Rowan Williams, I examined how he engaged with music and in what contexts, and explored what effect music had upon him. I also found that interviews with composers and performers gave useful insights into the process of receiving the gift of musical performance, particularly sacred music, and what they are attempting to achieve for the listener in creating the music. The conversation pointed towards a conclusion that, whilst the presence of sacred music in secular society presents opportunities for those who have faith to express their beliefs and practices through their art and communicate with a wide audience, nevertheless, the huge level of interest in sacred music in Western society is also an indicator of a society that is seeking a deeper understanding of reality than can be grasped with a purely materialistic view of the world. Sacred music, released from its liturgical and ecclesiastical walls is one of the main ways, if not *the* main way, in which spirituality is expressed in our society: not in words, but in sound. The most effective use of sacred music in our society, however, will be achieved if we can combine the dissemination of the sacred sounds with an educative approach to their derivation, intention and meaning; so that the listener not only engages with beautiful music, but also comes to understand more deeply its relevance to them.

To this end I examine the ways in which the listener engages with music, emotionally (connecting music with power) and spiritually, particularly Rowan Williams' explanation of what it means to listen 'seriously' and how that teaches us to live 'with and before God'. By contrast, I will also explore the notion that music is spiritually powerful to people of no faith in God. Thereafter, I investigate how music feeds the soul, relating the musical experience to the spiritual writings of Eastern apophatic theological traditions, as well as to the categories of 'mystical experience' defined in William James' *Varieties of Religious Experience*, which are ineffability, noetic quality, transiency and passivity. But I conclude that musical experience does not equate to mystical experience in James' sense, but is a way of 'searching out the sacred'.

Music, Emotion and Meaning

When Simon Russell Beale presented the second series of *Sacred Music* for the BBC, which explored Romantic and Contemporary sacred repertoire, he admitted that when he first heard Górecki's *Third Symphony* in 1992, which shot to fame partly because of extensive airplay on *Classic FM*, he considered it to be a relaxing piece of background music:

> I think it's a marvellous piece of music, but I was guilty when I first heard it of using it as a miraculous piece of meditative wallpaper. But the piece sets words written on the wall of a Nazi prison camp, so it's really a cry for help. And I didn't know that. This is emotionally complex music. And all of them – Pärt, Górecki, Tavener – are writing works that use the vocabulary of calm and stasis,

but actually they're about dynamism and movement, and ultimately, about redemption and death. That's the confusion in my head: I was using it as a kind of spiritual wash, and it's not.[3]

This is music that, on the surface, seems to be an aid to calm serenity, but which might become quite a different piece once the hearer learns more about the composer, the setting, the words, and the intention of the work. As Simon Russell Beale acknowledges, the most famous of our sacred music composers today share the musical characteristic of choosing harmonically and rhythmically soothing sounds that belie more profound and fundamentally existential notions of death and redemption. The three composers mentioned above possess a profound Christian faith that forms the basis of their compositional creativity. But more than that, each individual piece has its own particular genesis, character, text (or subtext) and, therefore, meaning. Any listener wishing seriously to engage with such music must, it follows, take the trouble to learn something about the music itself and where it comes from. Otherwise, the recipient of the music will to some extent miss the point; and the trouble taken by both composer and performer will be limited in its impact.

If this is so, why is it that most of our engagement with music, if we're honest, is not on an intellectual level, but on an emotional one?[4] Emotions of happiness, sadness, anger, fear and disgust can be demonstrated in the way we say we feel, the way we act, as well as the way our bodies behave.[5] Some theorists believe emotions to be a purely bodily (non-cognitive) phenomenon, separate from our intellectual capacity to reason; and others unite emotion with body and brain, allowing for an element of mental judgment in our emotional responses.[6] If the latter is the more convincing explanation, which many agree it is, we can also assume that emotions are directed towards people, situations or objects. Emotions are usually *about* something. As such, Begbie reminds us, they can be both well and ill founded: 'If it follows that emotions have this directional character, arising from beliefs about, and evaluations of, an object or objects, they can be *appropriate* or *inappropriate*.'[7] Thus, emotions become vital for how we perceive

---

[3]   Simon Russell Beale, *Sacred Music*, Series 2, Programme 2, quoted in Tom Service, 'On the Trail of the Sacred'.

[4]   See P.N. Juslin and J.A. Sloboda, 'Music and Emotion: Introduction' in *Music and Emotion: Theory and Research*, ed. P.N. Juslin and J.A. Sloboda (Oxford: OUP, 2001), p. 3, quoted in J.S. Begbie, 'Faithful Feelings: Music and Emotion in Worship' in *Resonant Witness*, p. 323.

[5]   P. Ekman and R.J. Davidson, *The Nature of Emotion: Fundamental Questions* (New York: OUP, 1994); D.G. Myers, *Psychology* (New York: Worth Publishers, 2004), Chapter 13, cited in Begbie, 'Faithful Feelings', p. 325.

[6]   Many such theories are footnoted in Begbie's chapter 'Faithful Feelings', pp. 329–31.

[7]   Begbie, 'Faithful Feelings' citing J. Macmurray, *Reason and Emotion* (London: Faber and Faber, 1935), page number not given in Begbie.

reality, how we see 'truth' and also how we make moral choices.[8] Emotions also provide motivations for our actions, whether we react out of a fear or out of joy and happiness.[9]

If emotion is object-led, how then can music bring about emotions when mere sound does not 'represent, denote, or convey objects for us to be emotional *about*?'[10] Music provokes emotion because no music is purely about itself:

> Music is perceived in a manifold environment. And this generates a fund of material for us to be emotional 'about'. Music swims in a sea of potential objects. The problem of how genuine emotion can be felt through music-without-objects only arises if we posit a sealed-off world of pure music. No such world exists.[11]

I recently experienced a very basic example of this when supervising my young children's piano practice. The piano primer denotes a C major scale with the word 'Happy and Sunny'; likewise the C minor scale with 'Sad and Cloudy'. Even if the children have not made these emotional associations for themselves with these differing harmonies, the tutorial book guides them into forging such connections, which they will no doubt make when they encounter major and minor harmonies in the future. But why on earth should major be associated with happiness and sunshine and minor denote sadness and rain? Even if these harmonies intrinsically bring about these emotions without being mentally guided, why do we value the emotional expressiveness of music? A convincing answer is that in a world where our emotions are often messy and difficult to discern, music allows us to concentrate on our emotions for a time, purified from irrelevancies and distractions.[12] Moreover, Begbie rightly argues that music can represent us, emotionally. For instance, at a funeral, mourners often respond to a piece of music that represents all of their disparate emotions and that can also 'connect them with their grief as it is and help them find new forms and depths of emotion, perhaps forms that help them to set their sorrow in a larger, more hopeful emotional context, and in this way begin to re-form them'.[13] This process might even be educative in that we may find emotions we did not know we had and be moved to feel emotions that we *should* be feeling.[14]

---

[8]   J. Dow, *Engaging Emotions: The Need for Emotions in Church* (Cambridge: Grove Books, 2005), p. 9; Begbie, 'Faithful Feelings', p. 333; M. Nussbaum, *Love's Knowledge: Essays on Philosophy and Literature* (New York: OUP, 1990), p. 40.

[9]   Begbie, 'Faithful Feelings', p. 335.

[10]   Ibid., pp. 338–9.

[11]   Ibid., p. 339.

[12]   Ibid., p. 349.

[13]   Ibid., p. 350.

[14]   Ibid.

All of which means that music is power and, if misused, it can become dangerous 'manipulation, sentimentality, and emotional self-indulgence'.[15] Begbie relates his findings of emotion and music specifically to Christian worship, but it seems to me that we can draw a much broader conclusion from these discoveries in considering how sacred music works in wider society. Taking Simon Russell Beale's two different reactions to Górecki's *Third Symphony* as an example, one can first notice that his initial response to the music was to enjoy the warm, relaxing glow of its harmonies. The emotional objects related to the music were limited to whatever he happened to associate with calm, soothing relaxation. However, once the emotional objectives had been broadened to encompass the fundamental human experience of death, and no less than mass murder in Nazi concentration camps, then the warm glow changes to a much more serious emotion with associations of the atrocities of the twentieth century. Knowledge has brought with it a maturity of understanding; and thereafter the music is listened to in an entirely different way. Each note, melody and harmony must now be examined and experienced with more respect, gravity and seriousness. The music now has emotional complexity and depth which, although more demanding upon the listener, is ultimately a more important educative experience. The music is no longer mere consonant sound; it is profoundly grave.

Emotion therefore forms a considerable part, and for some the entirety, of our experience of music. But I now wish to explore another way in which sacred music has been received by society, one that goes beyond the realm of emotion: spirituality.

Music and Spirituality

In a study as broad and wide-ranging as this, which embraces both confessional Christian and agnostic beliefs, there is the difficult task of reconciling two different points of view represented by these quotations: 'To listen seriously to music and to perform it are among our most potent ways of learning what it is to live with and before God'[16] and 'You don't have to have any faith or any religion at all to get something out of this music. If the music is good, it will do something to your soul'.[17] Can these statements, made by Rowan Williams and Harry Christophers respectively, both be true? I want to unpack the meaning within them and find out what truths they reveal about the way we engage with music in our society today. Brief as these statements may be, they are full of musical, theological and sociological insights that lie at the heart of this book and its thesis. In this section,

---

[15]   Ibid., p. 353.

[16]   R. Williams, 'Keeping Time', p. 249, quoted in O'Connor, 'Singing of Jesus', p. 435.

[17]   Harry Christophers, BBC *Sacred Music*, quoted by Tom Service, 'On the Trail of the Sacred'.

I will bring the strands of my investigation together in exploring James MacMillan's idea that music is a way of 'searching out the sacred'.[18]

To Listen Seriously

First, then, what does it mean to listen to music seriously? When I interviewed Rowan Williams in January 2012, I asked him what this meant and whether he indeed had any time to listen to music:

> Yes I do have time; I try to make time for it. I still listen to an enormous amount of Bach, given the chance. Also Tallis and Byrd ... [Henry] Purcell, occasional Mozart and some bits of the twentieth-century repertoire, VaughanWilliams particularly.
>
> JA: In what context would you be listening to these? Do you listen to that music with other people or do you like to listen alone?
>
> RW: When I think about it, I do quite often listen alone or virtually alone, though increasingly I find I listen quite a bit with my son who asked me last summer, 'Can we listen to some music together because I need to find out things about it?' He did sing in a rather good church choir so he has got a basic repertoire of liturgical music and decided he wanted to find out a bit more about it. Also, I like to make the occasion to go and listen to live music ... Just over a year ago, I went to the [Claudio] Monteverdi *Vespers* [of 1610] in the Sheldonian [Theatre, Oxford].[19]

The *Vespers* are a particularly interesting example: Monteverdi's work for choral forces, soloists and orchestra was originally for liturgical use, written on a grand scale for St Mark's, Venice at a time when Monteverdi was composing early dramatic operas, such as his *Orfeo*, for the concert hall. The *Vespers* could also be performed in the domestic setting of the nobility's palaces. They are long enough to fill a whole concert programme and are rarely performed liturgically today for reasons of length, scale and the musical resources it requires. I therefore asked Rowan Williams whether the context of this music made any difference to the way one perceives it, and whether it is difficult, now, to imagine it as a piece of music for religious worship at all:

> I think that's a very interesting question. It's a fascinating question about the context in which you listen anyway ... Both in Britain and on the Continent, from about 1590 onwards, liturgical music becomes something very different. It attracts a kind of theatrical surround to it, and Monteverdi's *Vespers* is one of the great examples of that. I'd say much the same of Purcell's proto-oratorios in some ways ... the writing is theatrical and virtuoso, in a way that, for Palestrina

---

[18]   Ibid.

[19]   Interview with Rowan Williams, Lambeth Palace, London, 16 January 2012.

and Byrd, would be unthinkable. These are show pieces and you may say that it is for the glory of God but it's not liturgical in the same way, it doesn't belong in the same action. That's why I suppose those are works that translate much more readily to the secular stage or the concert hall than Tallis and Byrd or, I was going to say, [John] Taverner [c. 1490–1545], but Taverner's already quite theatrical!

JA: In the eighteenth century a Mass setting by Mozart might be very charming.

RW: Charming's the word, yes.

JA: But is there something not quite so profound about it as a Palestrina Mass or a Byrd Mass?

RW: I think I'd have to say yes to that. I love a lot of the Mozart Masses and Haydn. I find them very difficult in a liturgical context because they are quite clearly dominated by an architecture that is musical, not liturgical. You can already see that at the end of the Middle Ages and the brief window if you like between the end of high Gothic around 1500 and the arrival of real Baroque 100 years later. But Protestants and Catholics are drawing back from theatre, whether it's Merbeck doing a one-word-one-note principle or Palestrina, working on very much the same principle [but using complex polyphony]. Tridentine reform goes hand in hand with that.[20] You look at the difference between Taverner and Byrd, between early and late Tallis, and you see how that trimming back is going on so that the architecture of what's being sung is moulded onto the architecture of the liturgy rather than, as already in Taverner, a few equal blocks of sound. So yes, when in a[n] [eighteenth-century classical] Mass that's what dominates the musical architecture, something's happened and the music ceases to be the unfolding of a single event quite in the way it was … In the Middle Ages, or the idealized Tridentine setting, the polyphony would be part of something in which plainsong would have a part and in which the spoken word would have a part … What's fascinating too is to see how that applies not just in Western but in Eastern Christianity … In the seventeenth century you can already find Russian liturgical music doing a Venetian polychoral development, which takes it right away from the chant and a tradition then unfolding, which reaches its absolute climax in the late-nineteenth century – music just as theatrical as you find in the West, if not more so, and then the gradual pulling back that you find in the twentieth century.

JA: Until we get to the minimalism of Arvo Pärt.

RW: Or the other Tavener [John, b. 1944].

JA: If we take the music of Pärt, for instance, is that trying to recapture something of earlier times?

RW: Definitely. Take Pärt's *St John Passion* for example. That's a deliberately undramatic, untheatrical rendering. It goes back well beyond Bach, even Schütz

---

[20] The musical and liturgical reforms for the Catholic Church that emerged from the Council of Trent (1545–63).

I'd say. And Schütz wrote a Passion like that and Schütz's *Seven Last Words* are, again, a highly theatrical bit of music, rather wonderful in a way. But Pärt is pushing you back in another way. It's the sort of thing you can only listen to if you have a certain amount of time and patience. Interesting, looking from that point of view, at Jamie MacMillan's *St John Passion*, which I think blends those two modes together rather doesn't it?

For Rowan, listening 'seriously' to music can mean a solitary experience, or a shared one with his family; or it may be within the context of liturgy and worship, or in a concert hall. What's fascinating about his response is that there is a clear distinction between music which is 'dominated by a musical architecture' and that which is dominated 'by a liturgical one'. Moreover, in the late-twentieth century there has been a return, in musical composition, to 'serious' religious music, by Tavener, Pärt, MacMillan and others, which seems to be coming back full circle to the religious fervour of the Renaissance. In this context, I wondered whether the 'serious', or profound nature of today's sacred music had its roots in plainchant:

JA: Something that's very important for MacMillan is … plainchant. It seems to be a thread that runs through much of his work. Is there something about plainchant that's still at the heart of Western sacred music or has it been lost?

RW: I don't think it has been lost entirely and its interesting when people try to find another idiom for it, they very often find they're drifting back towards the chant … Even a plainsong hymn is structured … but allows a loose organic development of a melodic line rather than a rigidly metrical one and yet keeps within an overall metrical pattern. That's a fascinating tension to work with. For singers, I think the challenge and the excitement of singing plainsong is that tightness of the overall structure and the sense that, within it, the line is a very loose and very organic thing. And then, secondly, if you look at the development of chant in the Gradual and the Ordinary Mass, then that organic line, from the Mass setting, the ways in which motifs can be played within different ways in that free-flowing line is another fascinating thing. I'm also very interested in the whole kind of melismatic side of plainsong, which we've rather lost sight of because it's another kind of virtuoso performance. You can see them in some of the codified melisma, such as the *Easter Hallelujahs*. You can see how that organic flow can be allowed its own logic, its own development, and how that corresponds to something very profound in people's sense of how music works … For example, the *Kyrie Orbis Factor* … and of course the solemn ending for the passion tone in the Palm Sunday/Good Friday Gospel, where, having stuck to a straight passion tone throughout, the end of the *John Passion* … you have a highly decorated version of the basic tone at the end. That's one of the areas where Eastern and Western sacred music of course still coincide: you can hear exactly that kind of melismatic collaboration on the basic tone in the Gospel sung in Byzantine Chant.

I find it very interesting that Rowan sees the roots of modern sacred music, in both Eastern and Western traditions, as being in chant, whether Gregorian or Byzantine. But the chant, whether sung as music in itself or as a *cantus firmus* in a larger network of polyphonic sound, seems to be at the heart of what it means for music to be one of the most 'potent ways of learning what it is to live with and before God'. In exploring this issue, I talked to Rowan about how music is best practised in our cathedrals, churches, and concert halls. In other words, how is it that music helps us to *learn* how to live with and before God?

Learning to Live With and Before God

In exploring how plainchant is still an essential element in today's quality sacred music, Williams touches upon the important point that good sacred music is not simply about moving the emotions. Plainchant does not make demands upon any particular emotions; it does not have emotionally manipulative climaxes. If music helps us to *learn* about something greater than ourselves, which we call 'God', then it is that encouragement to take attention away from ourselves and learn to take time to repeat the process of prayerful music-making, to listen, to be still, to be patient. Perhaps what we learn from good sacred music is what it means just to *be*:

> JA: James MacMillan, in his Glasgow church, makes use of a lot of plainsong with his choir. Do you think that plainsong might be a way of reigniting people's enthusiasm for singing Church music?
>
> RW: I think it's quite important, yes, because a couple of things matter here: one is that plainsong is not nearly as difficult as people think it is, for a start. I grew up singing in a village/suburban church in South Wales where we sang plainsong from time to time. We did the [John] Merbecke [c. 1510–c. 1585] and Martin Shaw Passions on Sundays and didn't give it a second thought. It was different but it wasn't impossibly difficult and choir and congregation seemed to cope with it. So, that's an important fact: that it's not as elitist and inaccessible, by any means, as people think. The second thing is, that there are (dangerous territory this!) certain values which plainsong embodies which are important aspects of sacred music. Plainsong doesn't expect you to come up with required emotions: you know, press a button and the emotions come. Because it's repetitive it assumes that you are prepared to take time, and that's significant. You don't necessarily think that everything has got a root or a climax and [expect] resolution instantly or almost instantly. And while I'm not ruling out or despising other kinds of music, there's something that plainsong does that other styles don't, which I think is important for understanding the role of liturgy as something that takes time, requires a measure of attention, physical settling, patience, etc.
>
> JA: A lot of European countries that used to have great traditions have lost their choral heritage, like Spain, France and Italy. How do you think we're doing in this country [Britain] at the moment in terms of sacred music?

RW: We still have a very good coverage on the ground at cathedral level and the older universities. Parishes seem to be very uneven here, very uneven. We've mortgaged our souls to the nineteenth century, organ and choir and all that that means, and where we've tried to get ourselves back we've often ended up mortgaging, in turn, to the worship band – to a style which is thought to be accessible, and in some ways is, but carries its own problems, its own different kind of specialism and elitism. Some modern choruses are very difficult to sing and depend heavily on strong direction from the front.

There's also a feeling I have, that in quite a lot of Anglican worship music, for example music for the Ordinary of the Mass, is seen as a bit of a decorative extra. Saying it is the normal thing and you sing [only] if you are feeling particularly adventurous. That is not a good place to be, in my mind. You don't get that sense, again, of the organic. Funnily enough, when in a charismatic service, somebody says, 'We're now going have a time of worship', they mean, 'You are now going to sing a lot of choruses'. Whilst some of them may be not so good, all credit to them for understanding that worshipping and singing are integrally bound together ... I think that's a good lesson to some of the more conventional churches to realize that this [music] is not just something bolted on.

Modern worship bands can produce an integrated notion of worship and music, but can also be highly emotional experiences, clouding the distinction between spirituality and mere feeling. So I asked Rowan how more traditional sacred music integrates worship and art:

Plainchant can be intensely emotional in one way. Certainly when I hear the *John Passion*, the start to the traditional chant on Good Friday, it is emotionally very intense. But it's not because the purpose of music is to introduce the emotions, it's because the music so carries the narrative that you're present in it and with it. It does touch things unexpectedly. That's why people sometimes burst into tears when they hear plainsong. But it means you haven't got the list of musical techniques and the list of emotions that correlate, which you sometimes have in modern music and again, I'm seriously trying to do justice to the good points of the modern choral world and there are many, but where I step back is the point at which I feel my emotions are being deliberately wrung by a set of rather obvious techniques. They may work or they may not, but you can see the workings. You can see it's gone slow or it's gone quiet, I'm meant to feel [this or that emotion] and I think that's something that good sacred music does not do.

Plainsong and its polyphonic descendants, at their best, enable access to a narrative, where emotions can be a part but are not being prescribed by the music. This leads us on to Harry Christophers' point that 'if the music is good, it will do something to your soul'. Therefore, I explored with Rowan Williams what is *good* sacred music:

Good sacred music says 'This is the stream into which you are invited to step'. It may carry you to some very disturbing emotional places, but that is because of the way it's going, because of its movement, its subject matter, its whole context. It's not because we have the technology to make you weep when we want you to weep and make you laugh when we want you to laugh. And I suppose that's how you can look at a series of different Mass settings, settings of Requiems or the settings of certain words and say 'I can imagine that in a liturgical setting, fully plugged in [to the worship] and I can imagine that sticking out like a sore thumb'. Requiems are a good case in point … Good liturgical plainsong or early polyphony [for instance] takes you steadily through something and you don't quite end where you began … I don't think anyone in their right mind would want to perform Verdi's *Requiem* in the context of liturgy; I have heard Mozart and Fauré's *Requiems* in the liturgical context but they don't seem really to work as liturgy. The [musical] architecture dominates everything else and architecture of the liturgy disappears. So what about plainsong and polyphony, and even quite a bit of Bach in the non-liturgical setting? I find myself quite challenged thinking about that because part of me says that there is something missing. Even with the Monteverdi *Vespers*, a very theatrical work, but it is vespers and it begins with simple plainsong versical[21] … I was watching on television, the other night, a repeat of that really rather lovely documentary about Vaughan Williams that was made a couple of years ago, I think before Ursula [Ralph Vaughan Williams' wife] died. There were reminiscences of R.V.W. conducting the [Bach] *St Matthew Passion* and how he would always get the audience to stand up and join in the Chorales as if to say, 'You are not going to understand what this work is about unless you are in it'. I have huge sympathy with that I must say.

This returns us to Harry Christophers' assertion that 'You don't have to have any faith or any religion at all to get something out of this music. If the music is good, it will do something to your soul'. Rowan Williams mentioned an element of participation, especially in the chorales of Bach's Easter *Passions*, which were intended to be sung by the congregation. Perhaps we also have this aspect of being plugged in when we attend a carol concert and sing the odd carol as the audience, or stand when we hear the 'Halleluiah Chorus' from Handel's *Messiah*. But is there another way of being participatory that involves a more mental, emotional and spiritual response to the faith of the composer who wrote the music? How much is it necessary that the audience understand the faith of the composer, and what they're trying to express? If they don't come from a perspective of faith, are they missing something? Rowan Williams thinks the answer is yes:

I think they are missing something. Although Vaughan Williams himself was an agnostic and it's a very loose matter what he thought was going on in the *St Matthew Passion*, but the point is that he thought something was going on,

---

[21]   '*Deus in adjutorium meum intende*' ('O God, come to my aid'): Psalm 70, verse 1.

which you did not capture simply by treating it as a concert piece. That's what's important. So I think anyone conducting or performing or listening to sacred music in the concert setting has, at least, to be aware that this is not concert stuff only, whatever is going on here, something perhaps in the presentation of it, in the performance of it, has to nudge [the listener] towards that [spiritual] dimension.

Another way of involving the audience in an experience that is more than just a concert of sacred music has been to re-label the concerts as 'Pilgrimage', as we have seen.[22] Sir John Eliot Gardiner's Bach Pilgrimage and Harry Christophers' Choral Pilgrimage have both been hugely successful. I asked Rowan Williams where the audience slot into that experience: are we pilgrims? Are we spectators? Are we watching the reconstruction of an historical event?

> I think all of these factors, at least, represent a registering of the fact that you can't just treat this as concert music. People may not quite know what to do with it, but even the context in which you choose to perform it, 'Bach Pilgrimage' says something which is not anything trivial. Obviously you can't expect that every motet written for the feast of the Assumption will never be performed except in church on August the 15th … Equally it would be rather strange if a motet written for the feast of the Assumption were never performed outside the concert hall or were never performed with any indication that this was the casing for the jewel.

The phrase 'casing for the jewel' trips off the Archbishop's tongue and I realize that much of what we are discussing is the search for the right 'casing for the jewel'. Is it on a 'pilgrimage' to Leipzig to sing in the church in which J.S. Bach worked? Is it to sing glorious polyphony to a thousand people in the cathedral for which it was written? Both of these examples presume that the 'jewel' in question is the music. But perhaps the 'casing of the jewel' has another connotation: the 'jewel' might also be our spiritual relationship with the numinous, the divine, the ineffable, the unknowable God; the 'casing' is the original context for which the music was composed and, wherever the music is performed, it allows us access to understand something of that ineffable, inexpressible being, which music can capture and words cannot. Rowan Williams recognizes that, even in a concert hall, sacred music will always mean more than just a concert, but he also sees the 'self' as taking a more prominent, and perhaps more obstructive, role in the concert than in the liturgy:

> People recognize, with sacred music, that there's something going on, more than just a concert and more than just the psyche as well … I'm saying that I can listen to Mozart's *Requiem* in a concert hall without too many qualms, not that Mozart

---

[22]   See Chapter 3 above, pp. 75–8.

is shallow, God forbid! But the struggle is very much a struggle of self. Whereas that doesn't belong in liturgy quite as much. People recognize something is going on and yet they don't want to be rushed into answering the question 'what's going on' or 'why'. They don't understand, they don't want to be put on oath as to whether they sing *Credo in unum Deum* or they hear it, they're committed to what it means, but the event quality of it still matters and people come searching for that. Something that goes outside the ego, outside the drama, outside the entertainment. I think all of those things are part of what's going on. There's drama in plainsong, there's drama in Medieval music, there's drama in Byrd and Tallis, goodness knows, but it's not the drama of the romantic soul.[23]

JA: And you hint that it's related to religious participation. If you've bought your concert ticket, you're not required to kneel down, face east, all sorts of things that you're obliged to do if you turn up to a service. Is that what people are paying for? Are they buying their (RW: opt out!) but keeping the cherry bit, the nice bit.

RW: A little of that I think. Although, because a lot of people won't even know what they're saying 'no' to, I wouldn't want to be too negative about that, too dismissive.

Every year in Canterbury, on the feat of St Thomas Becket, we have Latin plainsong vespers in the course of which I lead the congregation down to the martyrdom to commemorate the event. This year we had, I would guess, 500 people sitting on the steps of the altar. The drama was not the drama of a struggling ego; it was the drama of the event, the martyrdom itself. What we've evolved over the years is a sort of rhythm for the occasion which sticks to plainsong until finally the congregation and choir all go down to the crypt, which is almost absolutely packed solid, and the choir will then sing a short piece of polyphony, because we've got to the point where we can just flower out a tiny bit further. But it's come through that very austere presentation of the drama so far. And people come to it, in the sorts of numbers that they would come to concerts, because they recognize the event quality.

JA: Is the event quality related to the standard of the musical performance and power of the drama?

RW: Well yes, there's bound to be a bit of that isn't there?

JA: Is that a theological issue?

RW: I think the theological issue about any kind of music is what you do, you do well. That may be a sort of Thomas Hardy-esque 1810 band in a loft in Wiltshire, manfully fiddling and tooting its way through Sternhold and Hopkins.[24] Musically very good stuff, often, and doing it well. It may be Canterbury Cathedral Choir. But what it isn't, often, is second-rate stuff,

---

[23] This comment relates to composer Robert Saxton's view that in composing for the liturgy the 'self' is taken out of the process. See Chapter 1 above, pp. 25–6.

[24] Thomas Sternhold and John Hopkins, who produced the first book of English Psalms set to music in 1551.

half-heartedly done, whether it's plainsong or choruses or whatever. One of the toughest things in the Anglican context, I don't know whether you agree about this, is trying to persuade people that while Anglican chant well done is a wonderful thing, Anglican chant badly done is a curse. There are a lot of better and easier ways of singing the Psalms.

JA: We have been locked into that?

RW: Yes. When I first came across Gregory Murray's Psalm chants for Downside Abbey, I thought, 'This is wonderful! This is so accessible! All you need is the capacity to sing three notes at a time!' And I wished at the time that a good half of the parish churches I knew could simply see that this was a good way of doing it. Of course the New English Hymnal contains some of Gregory's stuff. But I don't think it ever really caught on.

In the context of liturgy and the words of the divine service, sacred music has a particular place and a particular meaning. When text is involved it is relatively easy to see the jewel of spiritual writing that needs to be encased by the ritual of worship or a finely crafted concert. But how is it that some non-verbal, non-texted, instrumental music can also provide a spiritual experience? I talked to Rowan Williams about his feelings on instrumental music, especially that of J.S Bach:

There's a phrase in Iris Murdoch's novel *The Bell* describing people listening to Bach, and Dora's looking through the window at this little group and 'resisting this music that so arrogantly demanded to be contemplated'. And that's what it does; it demands to be contemplated. Some of it demands that you shut up. The sacred quality people respond to in music like that is that sense of an authority or sacrament, just sit down and shut up. The only way of coping with it is to absorb it.

JA: Is it contemplative of itself or something else? Is it pointing towards something else?

RW: I don't think it points to something else because what it does is to create a particular kind of space in you which simultaneously is an opening to the givenness of the music ... What they're doing is not saying, 'I want you to feel x, y and z', but as with plainsong there are moments in the Bach Cello Suites where the emotions are intense and you can't say what emotion it is! 'Is this ... no, it's not grief; no, it's not happiness, it's not fear, but it's intense!' It's almost pure feeling, it's rawness, it's exposure to what's there ... What I suppose St John of the Cross would describe as 'the touch of the live coal on the nerves' ...[25]

Is there, I asked, a visual aspect to this raw emotion?

I don't know what other people find but, in so far as I ever have a visual sensation listening to the Cello Suites, it's of a kind of narrow white line scored on an

---

[25]   Interview with Rowan Williams.

immense blackness, curling and curving and dotting and weaving in the dark, it's just there – and has that commanding quality.[26]

Would it make any difference to our perception of the music, I asked, if we didn't know about Bach's religiosity?

> You can listen to the Cello Suites and have the responses that people have without knowing that Bach graduated in theology and if Bach had not been the diligent Christian he was ... There are other examples of the non-verbal that somehow touch these places, such as Britten's instrumental music, because he had such an unusual ear for scoring.[27]

So, for the theologian Rowan Williams, Bach's ability to communicate raw, pure feeling, which relates to St John of the Cross's experience of the divine remains a mysterious event, and one that defies ready explanation. After all, if it could be explained, there would be no need for the music! Dr Williams goes on:

> There are other examples of the non-verbal that somehow touch these places – Barber's *Adagio for Strings*: how and why does that work? But it works. Hugely powerfully for so many people and there are bits of Britten's instrumental music that function a bit like that.[28]

Rowan Williams' words are so rich in meaning that they continue to provide insight and provoke new thought when re-reading them. Having touched upon many areas in which music relates to spirituality and faith I now wish to turn to examine how music can touch the 'soul' when the listener has no faith.

'You Don't Have to Have any Religious Faith At All to Get Something Out of this Music ... '

I want to begin this section by quoting a blog that James MacMillan wrote for the *Daily Telegraph* in April 2011. As he mentioned to me in his interview, he wrote a piece called *Mysteries of Light*, based on the Rosary, and in his blog James wrote amusingly about a reviewer who was baffled by the religious references. The title of the blog was: 'MacMillan's concerto revives the tradition of rosary-inspired music'.

> I have been in Minneapolis for the premiere of my new piano concerto (my third) which was played by Jean-Yves Thibaudet and the Minnesota Orchestra under Osmo Vanska. It is entitled *The Mysteries of Light* and it attempts

---

[26] Ibid.

[27] Ibid.

[28] Ibid.

to revive, even for a one-off, the old practice of writing music based on the structure of the Rosary. In 2002 ... [a] set of meditations was introduced by John Paul II, the Luminous Mysteries. These are the basis of the five sections of my new concerto. The music is not liturgical or devotional in any accepted traditional form, but each image in the following titles becomes a springboard for reflection, and proceeds in quasi-dramatic fashion. The fusion of symphonic poem with concerto form has long been a favourite pursuit of mine. The five sections are: *Baptisma Iesu Christi, Miraculum in Cana, Proclamatio Regni Dei, Transfiguratio Domini Nostri, Institutio Eucharistiae.* An ongoing debate in music has revolved around the question of whether it is necessary or important for a listener to know, understand or recognize the extra-musical, or pre-musical associations that were obviously important for the composer's inspiration ... Personally, it doesn't matter to me if the general listener doesn't want to follow the connections, especially on first hearing. It is the musical outcome of the inspiration that matters after all, and only that will communicate any power, meaning, feeling or fluency. There are certain things that have drifted out of public consciousness anyway, such as the Rosary, for example. It is inevitable that many listeners would not be familiar with the references above, their symbolism and their potential for musical encapsulation.

One of the first reviews, in the Pioneer Press, a nice one, nevertheless seemed baffled by all the religious references. The reviewer heard nothing of their application, but this didn't seem to interfere with his facility for engaging with the music. Would his readers want him to be more knowledgeable on these matters? Would they have learned more about the music if he had been able to communicate the connections between the prayers and the resulting music? Who knows. But I was at the performance with a bunch of American friends who got every reference, number symbolism and transition, from all the Gregorian quotes and allusions, to the scriptural picture-painting to the reason why the fast coda was so brief (or as perfunctory as the *Guardian* or the *Scotsman* will no doubt say).

Who got more out of the concerto, then? The guys who knew their Rosary, or the musicologist who knew nothing about it?[29]

With James MacMillan's music there is often a subtext of Catholic piety or an overt structure of religious piety and practice as the basis of his art. As a musicologist and music critic, one should be wary of being unfamiliar with the Christian context from which this music comes. To do so makes one look foolish and ignorant, especially in the press. But more than this, James makes the powerful point that those who were familiar with the practice of using a Rosary and with its meaning will have gained more from the piece of music as a result. Not just as a result of their religious knowledge and Christian heritage, but also by virtue of their openness, and lack of cynicism, to the musical and theological ideas embedded

---

[29]　　J. MacMillan, 'Why I Wrote a Piano Concerto Based Upon the Rosary'.

within the music. James makes this point well, but I also wish to explore how music can be experienced as deeply meaningful, soulful and spiritual by those who have no faith.

'If the Music is Good ... It Will Do Something to Your Soul'

The interview with Rowan Williams, as with other contributors to this book, highlights the fact that not all sacred music is good and not all performances of good sacred music are worth listening to. It is impossible in a book such as this to adjudicate, *in absentia*, regarding any particular performance, ensemble or context, what exactly constitutes 'good' on any particular day. Certain musical ensembles, in the employment of the Church for the offering of music within worship, have proved themselves to be of the highest quality over many years. Likewise, the number of outstanding professional groups who perform sacred music in concerts is continuing to grow. But, given that it is possible to discern, albeit subjectively, what is 'good' in performance, what do we mean that it does something to our 'soul'?

Simon Russell Beale's comment that much of the sacred music written by composers from Brahms to Tavener is 'deep, deep, spiritual music' is a paradoxical one for someone who has, like many who love this music, no confessional religious belief. But it is far from being a contradiction in terms, for today's society is far from unique in history in comprising people who are searching for deeper meaning to existence. Even (or perhaps especially) in a secularized society, people crave music like this, not as 'wallpaper' music, but to engage with it on an intellectually serious and emotionally switched-on level. But the realm of 'spiritual' and 'soul' in this context goes beyond the psyche, as Rowan Williams said; we have also seen that it goes beyond the emotions. Indeed, really good sacred music is not emotionally manipulative. Good sacred music is that which leaves the listener open to the inexplicable, the ineffable, the unknowable. This idea relates to the theological ideas of previous centuries. The apophatic theological tradition, deriving from the Eastern Church, stresses only what cannot be known about God. Ideas in the works of the sixth-century Syrian writer Pseudo-Dionysius, such as his *Mystical Theology*, expressed the absolute truth of life only in negatives:

> The cause of all things is neither soul nor intellect; nor has it imagination, opinion, or reason, or intelligence; nor is it reason or intelligence; nor is it spoken or thought. It is neither number, nor order, nor magnitude, nor littleness, nor equality, nor inequality, nor similarity, nor dissimilarity. It neither stands, nor moves, nor rests ... It is neither essence, nor eternity, nor time. Even intellectual contact does not belong to it. It is neither science nor truth. It is not even royalty or wisdom; not one; not unity; not divinity or goodness; nor even spirit as we know it.[30]

---

[30] An extract from Dionysius the Areopagite (known now as Pseudo-Dionysius), *Mystical Theology*, trans. T. Davidson, *Journal of Speculative Philosophy*, 22 (1893), p. 399, quoted in James, *Varieties of Religious Experience*, pp. 416–17.

For Pseudo-Dionysius, the truth is not less than all of these qualifications, but superior in all respects. These ideas found their way to England in the fourteenth century in devotional and spiritual works such as *The Cloud of Unknowing*. This so-called 'mysticism' emphasized the individual's personal, spontaneous experience of divine, beyond-ordinary existence. As such, organized religion was often not the context in which the divine was to be encountered. I would go so far as to say that those who listen to sacred music, either in a religious context or in a concert hall, are opening themselves up to a 'mystical' experience in the sense that it was defined by William James, in his *Varieties of Religious Experience*. Those four 'marks' as he called them are: ineffability, noetic quality, transiency and passivity. I shall try and explain each one and how it relates to the experience of listening to sacred music.

Ineffability   In the sense that James makes every personal experience a religious one, regardless of any relation to organized religion, the idea of mysticism is too broad to have any meaning unless it is given some defining boundaries. The first is ineffability, by which James means that a 'mystical' experience 'defies expression ... no adequate report of it can be given in words'. Therefore, the experience must be personal – it cannot be explained to you by another, just as one cannot make someone else feel what you do. Regarding the listening of music in particular, James relates that:

> No one can make clear to another who has never had a certain feeling, in what the quality or worth of it consists. One must have musical ears to know the value of a symphony; one must have been in love one's self to understand a lover's state of mind. Lacking the heart or ear, we cannot interpret the musician or the lover justly, and are even likely to consider him weak-minded or absurd.[31]

Thus, James asserts that the quality of the musical experience of the listener is, to some extent, determined by their openness and receptivity to the power of the music.

Noetic Quality   The second mark of the mystical experience is that it imparts a depth of knowledge that is beyond that perceptible in ordinary, everyday intellectual life:

> They are states of insight into depths of truth unplumbed by the discursive intellect. They are illuminations, revelations, full of significance and importance, all inarticulate though they remain; and as a rule they carry with them a curious sense of authority for after-time.[32]

---

[31]   Ibid., p. 380.
[32]   Ibid., pp. 380–81.

Music, at its best, can bring this kind of understanding or revelation that goes beyond words and intellect. Indeed, the ultimate power and meaning of music is that it contains expressions of truths that cannot be expressed in any other way, cannot be clearly identified afterwards in words, and yet are irreducibly there. At the end of a really fine musical performance, we leave with a greater understanding of the depth of reality than when we arrived.

Transiency The transiency of any mystical experience is, perhaps, obvious enough. No one lives in a constant state of heightened experience. But, with regard to music, James' definition is particularly apposite, as it highlights the fact that the experience will be relatively short, and imperfectly recalled until it recurs:

> Mystical states cannot be sustained for long. Except in rare instances, half an hour, or at most an hour or two, seems to be the limit beyond which they fade into the light of common day. Often, when faded, their quality can but imperfectly be reproduced in memory; but when they recur it is recognized; and from one recurrence to another it is susceptible of continuous development in what is felt as inner richness and importance.[33]

Thus, music is by its nature temporal and can only be experienced in slices of time. If it is to be encountered at depth, then the relationship between music and listener must be limited, reminding us of Harry Christophers' words that a concert of Renaissance polyphony must last not much longer than an hour, for that is the right amount of time needed seriously to engage with the art.[34] Thereafter, the experience is treasured and remembered, albeit as an echo; but the return to another performance will recapture the initial experience but also add another layer of meaning and significance building up, over time, a rich series of encounters that relate to and inform each other.

As an example of transient, noetic perception of an ineffable truth, James quotes St Teresa of Avila:

> One day, being in orison [a mystical state] it was granted to me to perceive in one instant how all things are seen and contained within God. I did not perceive them in their proper form, and nevertheless the view I had of them was of a sovereign clearness, and has remained vividly impressed upon my soul ... The view was so subtle and delicate that the understanding cannot grasp it.[35]

The moment is fleeting and the understanding intense, but once it is over, the intellect cannot recapture the 'truth' of the experience in words.

---

[33] Ibid., p. 381.

[34] Interview with Harry Christophers, 2011. See Chapter 3 above, p. 71.

[35] James, *Varieties of Religious Experience*, p. 411.

Passivity   Finally, William James mentions that there may be an element of passivity in a mystical experience. The state may be prefaced by certain procedures such as 'fixing the attention'; but once the person is ready they may feel 'as if his own will were in abeyance, and indeed sometimes as if he were grasped and held by a superior power'. This reminds me, again, of Harry Christophers' words that his audiences often remark, after a concert, that they now know what heaven or paradise is like. Through the music they have experienced something ineffable that was previously hidden to them and could only be expressed through that means. They have gained that noetic quality of being able to understand, to perceive, a reality that is beyond normal intellect and, though the experience is transient, they have fixed their attention for a span of time that has allowed them to put their own egos to one side and allow the possibility of being influenced by a 'superior', or alternative power to their normal experience. Of course, this is a state that does not last in its intensity. Rarely, perhaps, will one be able to perceive the beatific vision of paradise throughout, say, the next day. But one may well be able to say how wonderful the experience was. As James puts it with regard to mystical states: 'Some memory of their content always remains, and a profound sense of their importance. They modify the inner life of the subject between the times of their recurrence'.[36]

Music not Mysticism – the Reality of the Unseen

Anticipating the criticism that the listener's experience of sacred music and the mystic's experience of the ineffable divine are not the same thing, let me say that I am not trying to prove that every experience of music is a mystical one, nor that we cannot appreciate music on intellectual, emotional, aesthetic and purely fun levels. What I am trying to draw out is that James' definitions of the most extreme forms of religious experience have a parallel to the definition of how we can experience the most profound music, given the right circumstances. All through this book, those who have been most authoritatively engaged with the pursuit of performing sacred music that is communicated well to a listener consider the music, not as 'wallpaper', but as 'serious'. In this context, the listener may experience something that is *like* James' definition of mystical experience: a sense of the inexpressible ineffable; of a new kind of depth of knowledge not possible with words or intellect; of a transient, yet profound experience that, through repetition of engagement, brings a richness and subtlety of experience over time.

But, most importantly, I wish to connect the religious audience, congregation or listener to their secular counterparts. In the context of apophatic theology, which emphasizes all that we do not know about God, cannot express or hope to define, and pins no definite attributes upon the ultimate truth, it seems to me that sacred music, wherever it is performed, is the language most apt to explore the unknowable and ineffable reality. Where words fail, music takes over. But the

---

[36]   Ibid., pp. 381–2.

music does not insist upon any particular creed or confession; it does not demand a process of initiation or catechesis; it does not judge or require confession and absolution; it has no argument except in its own beauty and no authority except in its irresistible power to transcend worldly values that are constantly bargained over in words. Music does no more than to *exist* in sounds created by composer and performer. The listener can choose to be prepared, to focus the attention, to open up to possibilities it can bring in the transience of time. Alternatively, the listener can choose to ignore. There is no compulsion, confinement or coercion, except in the sound itself.

William James refers to the work of Immanuael Kant in illustrating that words like 'soul' and 'God' and 'immortality' are not objects of knowledge at all: 'Our conceptions always require a sense-content to work with, and as the words ... cover no distinctive sense-content whatever, it follows that ... they are words devoid of any significance'. However, they do have meaning for our daily practise: 'We can act *as if* there were a God ... consider Nature *as if* she were full of special designs ...', and so on.[37] Whether you believe in these concepts or not, we nevertheless have some understanding of what they mean even though they cannot be seen. For James, it is the sub-conscious and non-rational that holds sway in the religious realm.

What then does Harry Christophers mean when he talks about music touching the soul, or Simon Russell Beale when he asserts the spirituality of music? The Christian and the non-Christian, the believer and the non-believer alike, use these words 'soul' and 'spiritual' to denote something that is not, and cannot, be seen, and yet the words are used *as if* we can give them tangible and clear meaning. Similarly with other words associated with sublime music: 'transcendent', 'heavenly', 'divine', and so on. All these have no concrete meaning in themselves, but are conceptual words that try to capture what cannot properly be understood in words; and therefore all of this vocabulary merely points to a place that is beyond our comprehension and, consequently, our language. Don Saliers puts it this way:

> As many philosophers and theologians have observed, music is close to 'spirit' – a non-material medium of receiving and conveying a sense of the world. In our deepest attentiveness and encounters with certain forms of music, we are opened to a depth of awareness; a feeling about life that words alone cannot give. This is why we must pay attention to what the music on its own elicits, conveys, and evokes about being alive. This is in part to call attention to how music is able to encode how life 'feels' as we live through time. Paying attention to what music elicits and evokes opens up two interrelated powers: music without words as having theological import, and the fusion of words and music forms to carry us beyond what the words alone signify. Both of these 'powers' of music are related human experiences of time and space.[38]

---

[37]   Ibid., p. 55.

[38]   Dan Saliers, *Music and Theology*, p. 66.

But the receptivity of the listener can vary, especially in a 'music-saturated' society.[39] Thus, 'the act of listening to music is crucial to the theological significance of the music, with or without sacred texts'.[40] The listener may or may not be receptive to the idea of music as revelatory, and indeed they may not even be paying attention: 'the deeper the mutuality of the musical patterns and qualities, the more complex are the capacities required for hearing'.[41] Thus, the sound of music through time is able to intertwine with and become part of the fabric of our lives:

> I am convinced that certain musical experiences give us the sense of the music transformed into the very melody and rhythm of how life is experienced. Such music can be very simple as in a child's lullaby or folk melody played on a dulcimer or song flute; but it may also be a great symphonic theme, or a complex polyphonic piece sung by a choir.[42]

Language is the key here and music is a language that unlocks for us so much more than words can do. Music that 'engages us with the suffering and the mystery, the joy and the glory of being human', but also music that goes beyond the human to evoke 'mystery and transcendence',[43] words that we cannot possibly hope fully to understand, but that seem only too appropriate to describe the deep listening of music. This is not just sacred music that is set to sacred texts, but can be music without any text whatsoever. It can be Christian, but it may not relate to any particular faith at all:

> Theology can sense the limits of language by virtue of the way music conveys a sense of time and pulse and pitch; reflecting the patterns of how we experience life in time, but also moving us 'out of time'. Here we may think of Bach's organ works, or movements of a Mahler Symphony or … Samuel Barber's 'Adagio for Strings' or Aaron Copland's *Fanfare for the Common Man*.[44]

I will end with some words of George Steiner and Don Saliers. Steiner writes that: 'It is in and through music that we are most immediately in the presence of the … verbally inexpressible but wholly palpable energy in being that communicates to our senses and to our reflection what little we can grasp of the naked wonder of life. I take music to be the naming of the naming of life. This is … a sacramental motion'.[45] Saliers, meanwhile, asks: 'What is the "more"? This mystery beyond telling in words? Perhaps we can only acknowledge that human beings may

---

[39]   Ibid., p. 67.

[40]   Ibid.

[41]   Ibid.

[42]   Ibid., p. 68.

[43]   Ibid., p. 69.

[44]   Ibid., pp. 71–2.

[45]   George Steiner, *Real Presences* (Chicago: University of Chicago Press, 1989), p. 217.

occasionally "hear" the morning stars singing, and the angel hosts, and the voice of God when the songs of earth and heaven converge'.[46]

Conclusion

In this chapter we have explored what it means to listen to music – emotionally, spiritually, in liturgy, concert or via recordings. The emotional power of music can be transmitted through the harmonies, which seem to imply calm and stasis, whilst knowledge of the music's text, context or subtext can bring a maturity of listening that can alter one's impression entirely. With Rowan Williams we have examined some of the spiritual depths of music, which can teach us to live with and before God. Rowan Williams differentiated between music that was primarily dominated by musical architecture and that which was conceived for a liturgical framework. The Romantic drama of the nineteenth century has given way to music in the twentieth, such as Pärt, which returns to the nature of chant, is often undramatic and embodies something of what it means to listen seriously – it takes time, attention, physical settling and patience. Good sacred music is not manipulative and does not indicate how the listener should feel at any given moment. If a large part of the Church's music in Britain has been mortgaged to the nineteenth-century dominance of choir and organ or to the modern worship band, then some sacred music been relegated to decoration for special occasions. But good music is that which takes us beyond ego, drama and entertainment. Thus, purely instrumental music can also provide an imperative to sit still, be silent, to listen and create a space in which an encounter with the ineffable is possible.

Thus, through the ideas of Christian apophatic theology and of William James, I have conjectured some ways in which music touches the soul, even to those who have no faith. A long tradition of spiritual writers suggests that God is unknowable, inexpressible, invisible, uncertain, only known by faith and by experience.[47] It is for this reason that a concert of sacred music can offer a perspective on faith, at least from the composer's point of view, and an experience of the ineffable, unknowable, non-materialist part of the universe, experienced personally and communally as music. No other art form comes close to opening up the pathways to experiencing the inexpressible divine. That is why words like soul and spirit, transcendent, divine, heavenly, paradise and transfiguration are legitimate because, whether a believer or not, they are the only vocabulary we have that gets even close to the reality that the music conveys. Emotional objectives and associations, such as using music as an educative tool and as a way of promoting communal harmony, are important. But for many in today's Western society, sacred music is a pathway to faith and to an experience of the ineffable, which we do not even need to name as God.

---

[46]   Saliers, *Music and Theology*, pp. 72–3.

[47]   Such as Walter Hilton, Julian of Norwich, Richard Rolle, Pseudo-Dionysius and the author of *The Cloud of Unknowing*.

Chapter 5

Sacred Music: Culture and Society

God is the natural appellation, for us Christians at least, for the supreme reality, so I will call this higher part of the universe by the name of God. We and God have business with each other; and in opening ourselves to his influence our deepest destiny is fulfilled.

William James[1]

This chapter explores how the civilization we have inherited is steeped in the traditions of both music and sacrality. We investigate how a society that seems to refuse to accept theology as part of everyday life still acknowledges and relates to the intrinsic theological essence of sacred works of art, from which the notion of God cannot be extracted. We also consider how those who create and perform sacred works of music are, in a sense, involved in a counter-cultural exercise; and, with the insights of the composer James MacMillan and philosopher Roger Scruton, we assess in detail the place of sacred music in today's culture, both within the Church and without. By these means I hope to engage with the idea that music is not just an art form that imparts pleasure but that, at its most profound, can lead us to an understanding of a greater truth to the world, beyond the material, which enhances the reality of existence and leads us to a greater sense of what it means to be a human being.

Sacred Music and Modern Society

Whilst it is true that 'the experience of music is irreducible, never fully explained by reflection or analysis', we can agree on some characteristics.[2] Begbie and Guthrie assert that music is threefold in nature: there is music making, musical language or form (organized into sounds), and music hearing. Therefore the creator and recipient of the sounds will always be in relationship with each other in some way:

These practices are *socially and culturally embedded*: the way we make and hear music is shaped by our relations to others – our social setting, all the way from one-to-one relationships to very large groupings. And because of this, making and hearing music are shaped by the meaningful patterns and predicates that we

---

[1]   James, *Varieties of Religious Experience*, p. 517.

[2]   J.D. Witvliet, 'Afterword: Mr. Holland's Advice: A Call to Immersive, Cross-Disciplinary Learning' in *Resonant Witness*, pp. 454–63, at p. 456.

fashion as we relate to others and the natural world – in other words, by 'culture' (social institutions, images, books, customs, etc.). Further, musical practices are *politically* entrenched: they are inevitably mixed up with the power relations that are necessary for social organization.[3]

Culture, politics, religion and the relationships integral to all three are bound up in music. As William Mellors suggested, music has an inextricable relationship with society by virtue of its influence: 'What do we mean by musical culture? What do we expect music to give us? The mere quality of music tells us nothing. We want to know what kind of relation the sound has to the society that produces it. We want to know what bearing it has on the way people live.'[4] The philosopher, Roger Scruton, puts it this way:

> Our civilization is bound up with music as no other that the world has known. In social gatherings, whether sacred or secular, formal or informal, ceremonial or friendly, music has played a dominant role … whether singing hymns in church, whistling a tune in the street, or sitting rapt in a concert hall, we are enjoying the expression of human life – but in an enhanced and perfected form, which offers a mirror to our own understanding.[5]

For Scruton, a musical culture introduces its participants to 'three important experiences, and three forms of knowledge': melody, harmony and rhythm. But music has, for many, lost some of its 'sacred' essence, which was considered to be intrinsic in music for Pythagoras, Palestrina or Pärt, in an age of postmodernism:

> The postmodern world is not merely democratic; it is essentially irreligious since that is what 'life in the present moment' requires. It has become deaf to the voice of absent generations, and lives in the thin time-slice of the now, calling over and over the same timeless utterance – 'the loud lament of the disconsolate chimera' … In such a condition it is inevitable that people should lose all sense of a sacral community, so as to become locked in the isolation of their own desires.[6]

Similarly, Lois Ibsen al Faruqi identified a trend in modern, and postmodern, society that runs contrary to any notion of transcendence and a distinction between the sacred and secular:

> The influence of relativism and logical positivism has created a sense of fear and insecurity in man that is revealed in scepticism along with a proclaimed doctrine of anti-transcendence. For many of our contemporaries in the twentieth

---

3   J. Begbie and S.R. Guthrie, 'Introduction', *Resonant Witness*, pp. 1–24, at p. 6.

4   Mellers, *Music and Society*, p .17.

5   Scruton, *Aesthetics of Music*, p. 500.

6   Ibid., p. 506.

century the discovery of the nature of the transcendent realm is no longer a valid quest; they in fact recognize no transcendent aspect to existence ... Even the contemporary denial of divinity has its expression in the religious music of our own time. We see this evidenced in the abolition of any hint of boundary between the sacred and the secular, a development which has taken place in recent decades in many religious contexts in the Western world.[7]

Scruton's and al Faruqi's pessimism about modern, or postmodern, society is tempered by Chua's assertion that a society that tries to do away with God, ironically, puts God centre stage and ends up replicating theological methods of thought:

Theology persists in secular thought for two reasons. First, intrinsic to the historical development of modernity is the progressive marginalization of God as the source of explanation. On the one hand, this allows humanity to take center [*sic*] stage as the autonomous agent that shapes the world; yet on the other hand, in defining itself against God, the modern world finds its identity bound to him, albeit as a negative image or anti-theology. Second, despite its rebellion, modernity ends up replicating the old, theological structures as its new modes of thought; its 'grand narratives' are often a rehearsal of the biblical ones – creation, fall, redemption, apocalypse – all revised without God, of course ... Music, acting as a kind of divine surrogate, is elected to exemplify both the possibility and the ultimate futility of these human projects. Thus music can be heard as a mode of 'secular theology' that exposes some of the major theological issues of our times.[8]

As Mellors opined, whether one is religious or not, the theology of music will come through in society, because the theological themes are the ones that speak most profoundly of the human experience – love, suffering and death: 'Music is something that should happen whenever people feel a need to speak through sounds, to thank God they are on the earth or to curse him for what they are suffering'.[9] James Herbert suggests that one of the reason why we cannot separate the sacred from the secular in our society is due to an historical saturation of religious culture within the arts. The 'sacred' is simply part of the artistic language: 'Religious issues arise even in seemingly secular works [of art and music] where we might not expect them, because Christian mysticism and metaphysics thoroughly permeate the rhetoric and sensibility of western cultural production'.[10]

---

[7]   Faruqi, Ibsen al, 'What Makes "Religious Music" Religious?' in J. Irwin (ed.), *Sacred Sound*, pp. 21–34, at p. 29.

[8]   D.K.L. Chua, 'Music as the Mouthpiece of Theology' in *Resonant Witness*, pp. 137–61, at p. 138.

[9]   Mellers, *Music and Society*, p. 18.

[10]   J.D. Herbert, *Our Distance from God: Studies of the Divine and the Mundane in Western Art and Music* (Berkeley, CA: University of California Press, 2008), p. 3.

Herbert is echoing the words of the Italian scholar Cianni Vattimo, in this respect: 'While our civilization no longer explicitly professes itself Christian but rather considers itself by and large a de-Christianized, post-Christian, lay civilization, it is nevertheless, profoundly shaped by that heritage at its source'.[11]

Thus, in this line of thought, in order to appreciate the sacred in art, it is not a pre-requisite to be a believer in God. In contrast to Scruton's desperate assertion that individuals have lost their sense of 'sacral community, as to become locked in the isolation of their own desires',[12] Herbert believes that we have assimilated presuppositions concerning the sacred to which we all relate, regardless of any religious belief:

> Whatever our own religious (or irreligious) tendencies, and irrespective of the manifest content of the artworks we encounter, we look at images, listen to music, and proceed through ritualized space with that sacred legacy forcefully moulding our experiences ... art and music address audiences presupposed to possess characteristics such as omnipresence, linguistic transparency, and ethical certainty that are attributable only to entities greater than humans. Such qualities in the Western cultural heritage are associated most often with the first or second 'persons' of the Trinity.[13]

Thus, Herbert's argument that a meaningful concept of sacred does not depend upon a certain belief in God leaves him sitting on the fence. God can be absent from reality but present as a concept in sacred music. However, the music is not just a representation of human creation, it somehow means more than that, even if God does not exist.

> We need not contend that God actually descends to analyse how his presence might be felt in art and music; neither need we assert that such feelings must be nothing more than human sentiment.[14]

This assessment of the nature of the sacred in art and music leaves a set of questions unanswered. If God is only a cultural reference point, how can the significance of sacred music be as great as if He does exist? If God is a reality, then the devotion, worship, meditation, contemplation, and all the other attributes of sacred music are surely much more powerful and meaningful? Moreover, if 'sacred' is to be defined as a set of historical and cultural presuppositions that we have inherited from the past, what does that mean for a wide range of music that touches us deeply and yet has no connection with these premises? If we are to identify 'sacred' as something special, then surely it must perform a role that takes us into a deeper understanding of ourselves and of others in relation to

---

[11]   Cianni Vattimo, *Belief*, trans. Luca D'Isanto and David Webb (Stanford CA: Stanford University Press, 1999; Italian edition, 1996), p. 43.

[12]   Scruton, *Aesthetics of Music*, p. 506.

[13]   Ibid., p. 4.

[14]   Ibid.

our existence and death; one that approaches the inexpressible and ineffable in the world, and that enlightens us regarding the deepest theological mysteries of creation, incarnation and redemption? In short, in a real sense, 'sacred' music is that which touches that completely indefinable part of us: the soul.

Sacred Music: A Counter-cultural Phenomenon?

In October 2008, James MacMillan gave the Sandford Lecture at the Royal Institute of British Architects, in which he laid some heavy metaphorical punches against the rise of militant secularism and atheism in society and emphasized the counter-cultural nature of being a Christian musician in Western Europe today.[15] James argued that explicit allegiance to the beliefs expressed in sacred Christian texts and practices, as set to music by composers, is becoming an alien concept to many. He also noted, however, that Christian composers were more productive and inventive than ever. 'Embracing spirituality', he said, 'is now one of the most radical and counter-cultural moves a musician can make'. Indeed, as early as 1997, James MacMillan mused that:

> Religion … is often discussed as an extra-musical starting point for my work. Religion causes one to take positions and can be a confrontational issue at the best of times, even within the supposedly theologically neutral space of the concert hall. So for those people who initially do not want to engage with theology, they should not need to. But to ignore where it's come from is to ignore something of the substance and essence of the music.[16]

Again, in his Sandford lecture, James eschewed the 'Puritanism' of the modernist rejection of the Christian origins of Western music. His music embraces 'the technical gains of the post-war modernists while relinquishing that set's purist avoidance of Western music's tradition.'[17] This too is linked with the notion of faith:

> MacMillan readily accepts that his love of that tradition reflects his own world-view as a Roman Catholic: 'There wouldn't even be Catholicism if there had been an attempt to try and dam up the past in the same, puritanical way.

---

[15]   The lecture was delivered at the Royal Institute of British Architects to mark the thirtieth anniversary of the Sandford St Martins Trust. See http://www.telegraph.co.uk/news/religion/3116598/Composer-James-MacMillan-warns-of-liberal-elites-ignorance-fuelled-hostility-to-religion.html.

[16]   James MacMillan, Interview with Daniel Jaffé, 'Raising Sparks: On the Music of James MacMillan', *Tempo*, no.202 (1997), pp. 1–35, here at p. 12.

[17]   Ibid.

Catholicism needs to have its past as well as its potential future; and therefore I
suppose that conditions the way I look at the past.[18]

James MacMillan is very much a part of that potential future, warning that a liberal
elite with an 'ignorance-fuelled hostility to religion' are trying to drive out faith
from public life and culture. For James, a bridge needs to be built between the
worldview of the Christian, and the secular European culture in which they live.
This is to be done by 'speaking truth to power' and 'expressing their insights in
creativity according to their beliefs'. James' idea finds its inspiration in the words
of Pope John Paul II in his Letter to Artists: 'Even beyond its typically religious
expressions true art has a close affinity with the world of faith so that, even in
situations where the culture and the Church are far apart, art remains a kind of
bridge to religious experience'.[19]

This is particularly true with music of all ages: it is the 'umbilical link with
the sacred', and musicians are the 'midwives of faith'. But, James argued, there
exists a polarized opposition between religion and aggressive atheism: 'A smug
ignorance, a gross oversimplification and caricature that serves as an analytical
understanding of religion, is the common intellectual currency. The bridge has to
be built by Christians and others being firm in resisting increasingly aggressive
attempts to still their voices'.[20]

The language of the battlefield is James MacMillan's own. If this is a fight for
religion's place within society then, he suggests, the common 'assumption that a
war has been won by the forces of the grand secular project' conceals the truth:
'The campaigning atheists, as opposed to the live-and-let-live variety, are raising
their voices because they recognize that they are losing; the project to establish
a narrow secular orthodoxy is failing'.[21] In 2008, therefore, James MacMillan
was convinced that, in what he called a de-humanized world, music brought back
a sense of our humanity: 'I believe it is God's divine spark which kindles the
musical imagination now, as it has always done, and reminds us, in an increasingly
dehumanized world, of what it means to be human'.[22]

When I interviewed James, I wondered if anything had changed in society or in
his opinions about the place of the sacred within it. He mentioned that the hostility
was confined to print rather than expressed in person:

> JA: You mentioned that you were public enemy number one for a while. Do you
> find that you get much antagonism in those conversations – rampant secularism?
> JM: Not in the current situation. Not in the conversations. New Atheism is
> there raging in the press (I write for the *Daily Telegraph*). It's there that you find

---

18   Ibid.
19   http://www.adoremus.org/7-899ArtistLetter.html.
20   MacMillan, Sandford Lecture.
21   Ibid.
22   Ibid.

hostility. People write on my blog. There is a fierceness in the debate that I don't think was there earlier and certainly in critical responses you get some reticence sometimes. But just last week, my *St John Passion* was reviewed in the *Observer* and the reviewer acknowledged in her review that the critical ingredient in my music was my religion and I felt kind of vindicated, because I've always felt that, but there is a mindset about me (from others) that is very, very suspicious.

JA: Is there a sense in which the New Atheists have made you and your colleagues more mainstream because Christianity is galvanizing itself?

JM: It's forced us to think what we're doing and to try to enunciate our position. So in that sense Dawkins has been very good for Christianity. It forces you to gather your thoughts and ideas and arguments – that can't be anything but good. Going back to the Dominicans in Edinburgh, my chaplain there was a young man, 28 years old, Aidan Nicholls. As Catholic chaplain at Edinburgh he laid on these talks [entitled] 'Objections to Catholicism', and it was just one speaker after another coming in and laying into our faith. It was a dialogue. They presented their objections to faith. Some of them were Marxist, some of them were atheists of a pre-Dawkins type and some of them were of an extreme Protestant type – Ian Paisley type figures. One guy came in and scattered unconsecrated hosts to make a point. I'm used to that, because we got a lot of that going on up in the West of Scotland. I think a lot of English Catholics, growing up in the leafy suburbs of the South were absolutely shocked. Not just shocked by that aggression but shocked by hearing strident opposition to the faith for the first time, and saw their faith was not just challenged but undermined by it. But that's the risk you've got to take. Some of us took a different line – let's deal with the objections head on and try to enunciate our response. I think that's what happens in these days of increased aggression against Christianity. The Church will get better for it and purify itself. I think it already has become less slovenly in its actions as well as in its thoughts. I'm quite excited about it. It may be unpleasant at times but I feel it's doing us good.[23]

Religion thrives under opposition and pressure. But, more than this, there is, on the one hand, a process of purification taking place where the Church is being held to account for its wrongs and, on the other, those opposed to religion are also being questioned about the strength of their alternatives to religion in society. Sacred music is playing a strong role in providing a non-verbal, non-confrontational, and non-rational alternative to the public debate in universities, the media and in our homes. Music is indeed a bridge between those who believe and those who do not believe. As a medium of communication that connects people in a common purpose and spirit, music is a superior method by far with which to tackle intolerance, injustice and prejudice in our society. The media's suspicions about James' religious motivations in his writing are being transformed into a respectful

---

[23]   Interview with James MacMillan, 2011.

understanding. He does not see himself as a lone defender of Christianity in the world of music, but as part of a strong tradition of twentieth-century and living composers who very publicly declare a Christian faith as the inspiration for their work. In this context, James believes, criticism of that faith is healthy and good in that it forces the believer to rethink their creed, articulate it with clarity, and demonstrate its continued relevance to the world. One of the most powerful ways in which the complexity, paradox and subtlety of faith is displayed today is in music.

Sacred Music and Cultural Relevance

In today's society, music plays the same role as it did in the pre-Christian world in which Plato wrote: 'Music gives soul to the universe, wings to the mind, flight to the imagination, a charm to sadness and life to everything. Fine music is the essence of order and leads to all that is just and good, of which it is [an?] invisible, but nevertheless dazzling, passionate and eternal form'.[24]

As we have seen in the preceding chapters, there are three possibilities regarding how sacred music is received in today's society. First, as worship or devotion, in which is it used as part of private or organized religion, with prescribed beliefs and practices and in which music may also be used as a means of education and indoctrination as well as devotion. Second, as concert performance, in which organized religion is removed, but a personal, 'live' encounter with the music and its performers creates a relationship of giving, receiving and responding, which can be extremely powerful and life-changing. Reception of the music in this context may vary from a shared experience of sound with few emotional and mental responses, to an extreme sense of mystical transcendence. The third way in which sacred music is received today is in the many forms of media through which the sound can be transmitted, whether it be a live radio broadcast or a recording made thirty years ago and digitally re-mastered. CD recordings, radio stations devoted to promoting classical music, television, DVDs, MP3s and the Internet have opened up more ways to consume the music than ever before. Whilst the presence of these phenomena provides conclusive proof of sacred music's enduring appeal outside the ecclesiastical environment, it is difficult to discern how people choose to listen to this music.[25] The listener may set aside some dedicated time to listen to a recording or may simply play it as background sound. I shall consider each relationship between music and society in turn.

---

[24]   Cited in S. Leventhal (ed.), *Notations: Quotations in Music* (New York: Barnes and Noble, 2003), p. 57. See Michael Mayne, Learning to Dance (London: Darton, Longman and Todd, 2002).

[25]   As I write (on 13 July 2012), a recording of Thomas Tallis's forty-part choral motet, *Spem in Alium*, sung by *The Tallis Scholars*, is top of the classical music chart.

Music and the Church

As Paul Honigsheim has asserted, the idea that music is of value purely in itself without relation to society is relatively new.[26] Indeed, Blanning rightly suggests at the outset of *The Triumph of Music*, music has traditionally been connected with a collective purpose, which is religion.[27] Since music was liberated from its sole function of aiding religion, it was used to invoke negative indoctrination against the Church: 'When a society turns against a traditional religion, music has sometimes been used to place the exponents of that religion, such as priests or ministers, in a comic situation'.[28] For instance, in the Enlightenment and French Revolution comic operas satirized corrupt monks and priests. But what does organized religion use music for today?

Organized religion continues to offer opportunities for musical performances during regular worship services or on special occasions. Today, although church attendance in general has been slowly falling for the last few decades, those attending services in cathedrals have been growing in number, by a massive 30 per cent over the last decade, a growth of approximately 3 per cent on average each year. Cathedrals have seen a rise in visitors, volunteers and midweek attendance as well.[29]

These are heartening figures for the Church, especially when considering that the number of visitors is down, but the number of those attending religious services, those being baptized and those volunteering have all increased. One can conjecture various reasons for these increases, but the quality of the liturgical music may well be a significant factor for many, for it is not just Sunday attendance that has risen but weekday attendance (at Choral Evensong for instance) as well. With the resources at their disposal cathedral chapters are able to offer a high standard of spiritual worship, within the context of beautiful architecture and with sublime music. If one wishes, one can attend a service at any cathedral in Britain with relative anonymity without fear of being coerced into joining a church group or rota. But for those who wish to engage with the community there are many opportunities.

The increase in cathedral attendance indicates that the thirst for the sacred, within the context of our Western Christian and cultural heritage, remains a keen one. The sacred may be represented by the beauty of music and architecture but, as Paul Westermeyer has argued, we do not attend Church worship in order to enjoy a warm glow of self-satisfaction having heard a beautiful sound or seen a grand building. We are there to offer worship, and do not desire to achieve anything beyond that:

---

[26] P. Honigsheim, *Music and Society: The Later Writings of Paul Honigsheim*, ed. K. Peter Etzkorn (New York and London: Wiley, 1973), p. 43.

[27] Blanning, *Triumph of Music*, pp. 7–16.

[28] Honigsheim, *Music and Society*, p. 45.

[29] http://www.churchofengland.org/media-centre/news/2012/03/cathedral-attendance-statistics-enjoy-over-a-decade-of-growth.aspx.

> In the startling economy of the Church, music gathers around the Cross of Christ
> with the rest of creation and gives glory *Deo*, 'to God'. It, like all the rest, is
> simply offered to God and accomplishes nothing. And, lo and behold, God turns
> out to be not only the preacher and the host but the initiator of the dialogue and
> chief singer.[30]

Nevertheless, artistic worth is important 'for it is only by its beauty that music can
signify the sacred'[31] and beautiful music can, and is, warmly received by millions
outside of the Church, so it is to this topic that I now turn.

Sacred Music Outside of the Church

James Herbert has recognized that religion is part of our culture, whether we
consider ourselves to be religious or not:

> Religious issues arise even in seemingly secular works [of art and music]
> where we might not expect them, because Christian mysticism and metaphysics
> thoroughly permeate the rhetoric and sensibility of Western cultural production ...
> While our civilization no longer explicitly professes itself Christian but rather
> considers itself by and large a de-Christianized, post-Christian, lay civilization,
> it is nevertheless profoundly shaped by that heritage at its source.[32]

When a Western audience goes to listen to a concert of music they do so,
consciously or otherwise, with a set of presuppositions that are inextricably linked
to Western Christianity.[33] Thus, to appreciate a concert of sacred music, one does
not necessarily require a belief, merely an acknowledgement that such a belief
was sincerely felt by the composer or the author of the text: 'We need not contend
that God actually descends to analyze how his presence might be felt in art and
music; neither need we assert that such feeling must be nothing more than human
sentiment.'[34] Indeed, it is this crucial issue of the divine in music that is at the heart
of my investigation. I now turn to an interview that sheds some light.

In July of 2012 I was asked by the philosopher, Roger Scruton, to perform
some vocal music as part of a lecture he was giving on 'Music and the Brain'
at a conference in Oxford. I took the opportunity to interview Roger regarding
the place of sacred music in today's society, exploring the question of whether
sacred music was a counter-cultural exercise in a secular society. He has written

---

[30]　P. Westermeyer, 'Liturgical Music: *Soli Dei Gloria*' in E.B. Anderson and B.T.
Morill (eds.), *Liturgy and the Moral Self: Humanity at Full Stretch before God* (Collegeville,
MN: Liturgical Press, 1998), pp. 193–208, at p. 199.

[31]　Ibid., p. 202.

[32]　Herbert, *Our Distance from God*, p. 3.

[33]　Ibid.

[34]　Ibid., p. 4.

extensively on music in his philosophy, especially of the aesthetics of music, beauty and religion. Much of the remainder of this chapter is devoted to that interview, which expresses so much about the relationship between sacred music and secular society. I began by asking him how sacred music and its reception have changed since the Renaissance:

[What] I would like to say is that, first, music has an importance in our civilization which it doesn't have, and hasn't had, anywhere else, I think we have to recognize that. It's not just the Renaissance that exemplifies this – it goes back essentially to Gregorian chant and beyond, it was just assumed that that is how you related to God, through singing, and that music has a divine origin and that a person is automatically in communication with the divinity if they are singing with full heart in communion with others. That was a very important fact in the [early] liturgies: they are forms of communion as well as forms of relation to God, and by singing together people move together and become one. That is a fundamental thought in the Christian religion, and it is also something that has been inherited largely from Judaism. This meant that music was not just planted into the hearts of our civilization in the dark ages, and we emerged with that gift; it also meant that music developed with the understanding of the relation between man and God so that, as we came to understand community in a different way, not as a monastic withdrawal from the world but as part of the world, then the voices began to multiply. Thus, polyphony emerged ... and there was an interchange always between that and the secular dances and songs around it.

JA: So how did music break away from the Church?

RS: Music began to have a life of its own partly because of the profound conception of the integrity of music with the social organ as a whole, which was a religious idea. Then, out of that grew sacred music, the music of the many-voiced choir, which wasn't just something that developed from of a sense of a need to worship God with the best available tools. With the growth of the social importance of the Church, all different kinds of people were united there and the different voices were given a role to play. The choir school emerged from this process too, with the idea that this would be a form of education to the young, for the boys in particular. Of course, the place of women in all this was unclear until very recently, but by Bach's time that was more settled: women were singing in the choir and taking the solos in the cantatas. This development of music into the polyphonic forms that we know was something that reflected the development in our conception of not only human community but a collective way of relating to God. People feel and understand that now. Sacred music has a very important role in people's consciousness today because it is a return always to the concept of pure polyphony.

JA: With the move of sacred music performance, such as oratorios, out of the churches and into purpose-built concert halls, is the music still sacred in any sense, or has it now changed to something else? Has it now been somehow made secular?

RS: That's such a complex question. We shouldn't think that our instrumental music is something completely different to sacred music. They developed in tandem and they grew out of and into each other, the very obvious incidence being the oratorio, which is versatile: it can be sacred or secular; it could be performed in the concert hall or the church. A piece such as [Handel's] *Messiah* had, for English people of my generation and previous generations, the status of a work that united the secular and the sacred so that they were indistinguishable. The melodies resound in the secular world, and the *Hallelujah Chorus* has a ceremonial, nationalistic role to play as well. During the course of the eighteenth century, when the concert hall was coming into existence, it was ancillary to the Church anyway. Moreover, chamber music, which is obviously secular, was composed to be performed in the drawing room, but from the very beginning it began to take on a sacred role. Not just the Romantic music of Beethoven, but the Classical music of Haydn and Mozart; you have works that are clearly designed to put people in their homes into a state of meditation which has a religious object ... So our music, in the Western tradition, takes with it that sacred aura into every space that it invades and converts it from a secular to a sacred space.[35]

For Roger, there may have been a cultural shift away from the Church as the physical space for sacred things, but music has been a constant feature of the sacred, even if that is now encountered more in the home than it has done in previous generations:

One shouldn't think of the secular and the sacred as two contrasting spheres is really what I would want to say. They grew apart because there was the secularization of society, which meant that people were losing their faith and losing the sense that everything depended upon those moments of devotion to God; but music remained as the thread that, nevertheless, attached them to that.

JA: You paint that in quite a positive way: we shouldn't distinguish too harshly between sacred and secular?

RS: Yes, I think that many people come to music by way of rediscovering their connection with the sacred and this can come through the concert hall. Real composers have never thought of the concert hall as totally detached from the acts of worship. There are, of course, atheist composers who will want to believe that; but most atheist composers that I know see their music as something that reconnects at least with what religion meant, even if it doesn't connect with what religion is.

JA: If we consider Wagner's opera *Parsifal*, is that a work of art where Wagner has replaced the old notion of the sacred? Some people would say that *Parsifal* is a more religious music than a Palestrina Mass.

---

[35]   Interview with Roger Scruton, St Anne's College, Oxford, July 2012.

RS: We're talking there about a very special case. [Wagner was] an artist who recognized that art and religion are in the same space and he was somebody who lost what little faith he had but nevertheless profoundly believed that religion was fundamental to the human condition and that art has the task, as he saw it in his time, of recapturing what had been lost, with the loss or religion, and re-presenting it in a symbolic form so that he described *Parsifal* as a sacred work. He had a very intellectual approach to religion but all his works are about religion, [albeit] religion without God and rediscovered in the human condition. That which had been interpreted by previous generations in a religious way, or rather as a relation to God, must be re-interpreted as a relation between people. It's very unclear with *Parsifal* whether he hasn't gone completely through all of that back to the religious experience. Because it retains this very profound meditation on the Eucharist and what it means: this has fascinated anthropologists ever since.

JA: Is there a way, therefore, in today's Western society, that people are choosing to explore ideas of religion, faith and the divine in a non-creedal, non-organized religion way and the concert hall is one of these ways?

RS: I think that could be said. Of course the decline in the attendance at church has also accompanied a decline in the attendance at the concert hall. You have to recognize this, that there is a deeper problem here that modern society substitutes short-spanned addictive forms of entertainment for every kind of large-scale meditative practice. You have to live in an alternative way to this, in order to sit through a church service or a symphony, and not feel you're wasting your time. These are forms of address between human beings and the world which are being eroded by television and pop music. But the optimistic response to that is to say that it can't last, that there is, in human nature, that hunger for the humble recognition of one's created state and the desire to reflect upon this and absorb an understanding of what it is to be and what being is and that comes through long moments of quietness, and music is a form of quietness, as is religion.

So has popular culture reduced our attention spans to such a degree that we are no longer able to engage with long moments of quietness?

People don't have the same conception of how to use leisure time that they had, say, in the seventeenth-century court. People could sit through, in the early days of opera, an opera that lasted five hours and there would be comings and goings and coffee in the course of it and that is how an opera has to be packaged: in two sections with drinks in between. Wagner is a strain for that reason and concerts likewise; the time when they occur has shifted, it gets later or earlier depending on whether people want to eat before or afterwards. That is inevitable I suppose. There probably has not been enough study in the world of scholarship on the difference made to art forms by the structure of the working day and the changes in that have changed the five-act play to the two-act play.

As for the fact that people don't enjoy church services, they were never intended to enjoy them; they were supposed to recognize an obligation to attend them and to feel purified by this. That requires a religious context which has gone: older people have it, and some youth believers can still feel that physical refreshment that people come to church to gain, but the mass of mankind does not. Again, through the music, they understand it.

I wondered whether the breakdown of a distinction between sacred and secular that Roger mentioned is indicative of Eastern Christianity?

The Orthodox Church has integrated music completely into its being. They still have services which go on all day, and people wander in and out and the choir goes on singing, for five hours, things like the Rachmaninov vespers ... In the case of the Russian Orthodox Church there's a use of the human voice which is entirely peculiar to it (and in Bulgaria it's similar): the use of the human voice to create huge imagined spaces in musical terms as though God were being invited to inhabit the music. It's a very wonderful thing and it's a different religious experience from Palestrina or Victoria.

JA: That makes me think about how God perhaps inhabits music that is non-vocal, without a text, say a piece of Bach instrumental music. Is that sacred?

RS: Of course! What's very important here are the words of Schubert's *An die Musik*. It's a prayer of gratitude, but what he's attributing to music is that it transports him to a better world which is the fundamental religious experience and it's indicative of how that experience has found another outlet so to speak.[36]

JA: With the rise of the Internet the way we access music has changed enormously. Has that changed our attitude to music?

RS: That is a change, like the change from the five-act to the two-act play brought about new rhythms of living. It's not internal to any changes in the religious experience; it's that people are used now to consuming music in the home and often in short spells because they've got to get on with work, but it is significant that so much of it is religious. If you talk to someone like James MacMillan he will say that all of his music is religious and people understand it as such, and I suspect that that's true. It would be interesting to look at the charts and see which classical pieces really strike home, and I suspect a lot of them do so because of the religious connotation, and music like the Bach Cello Suites, as you say, can't be understood except as little cathedrals. The same is true of much of the chamber music that we most love, and also of Schubert's Lieder: they have a profoundly religious connotation for most people today because they are talking about a world in which there really was loneliness, there really was romantic love, there really was distance between people – all the things that made the world full of wonder.

JA: ... and that's something we've lost?

---

[36]   The text is found at the beginning of the introduction to this book.

RS: Well, it's something we have to recreate in imagination because we're surrounded by comforts and we don't have to suffer from loneliness, we just have to turn the telly on. Of course there is a deeper sort of loneliness that is involved in that.

Having talked about religious music, I ask Roger what *is* the relationship between music and theology? Is music a metaphor for God, or is music in itself a theological language that enables us to understand God where words fail?

There is a profound question here about the difference made by music to our understanding of God. The growth of the Christian liturgy went hand in hand with the great musical discoveries that Western civilization has made. That has meant that we understand God as a real presence among us, who comes among us as we unite our voices in song; and that's our most profound experience of the real presence of the Eucharist and so on. All beautifully captured by Mozart in the *Ave Verum* of course. It's not that music as metaphor is a bridge to God, it's rather that our understanding of God and His relation to us has been shaped from the beginning by music and has developed with the development of music. At a certain stage music developed at such a point that it took off on its own, like a child at last leaving home, and took that message into the world … Western tonality is not just a style among others, it involved huge discoveries. The equivalent in the world of sound of the discoveries of Newton and Einstein in physics.

JA: Does that start with Pythagoras?

RS: It starts there, yes, with the discovery of the pure, geometric harmonies, but it took off with polyphony. Something like *Summer is a cumin in*: if you look at that with the eye of scholarship you'll see a tremendous amount of knowledge contained within what looks like a single line of melody. It's knowledge of all the relations those notes can have to each other in the space of tonal music. And that, when it took off, there was no stopping it. So you get the whole common practice tradition beginning, which is essentially in place with fifteenth-century polyphony, and it's certainly there by the time of Palestrina. The music of Wagner and the developments right through to jazz are genuine discoveries which made it possible for people to make music in ways that they couldn't have done in the ancient world and produce a different kind of pleasure. I think the most important thing, with polyphonic music, is the sense of so many different things coming together in a unity: unity in variety. The traditional symphony is an amalgamation of people playing completely different instruments, colours, techniques, pitches and so on, and yet somehow the whole thing doesn't just harmonize vertically but it moves logically and horizontally into a complete whole. That sense of the whole, of a community of completely distinct individuals all united in a common meaningful totality, is a symbol of the social order: of the reconciliation of individuality and freedom within the social order which is maybe what Western civilization is all about.

Thus, the symphony orchestra is an embodiment of our community in music, and that community includes the listeners, players, conductor and composer. But, I wonder, how much of our understanding of music, in that role, goes back to the pre-Christian times of Plato and Aristotle, the importance of aesthetics of music, song and dance as a civilizing influence?

> The Greeks recognized the importance of music and Plato, in particular, recognized the dangers of the wrong sort of music. He began a tradition of criticism of pop music that is still relevant today. That is, people dance to the wrong thing, with the wrong movements and by imitating them, develop in themselves the wrong character.
>
> JA: Which brings me on to this idea about what is good music and what is bad music. Not all music is the same and not all music is sacred.
>
> RS: All I will say is that there are experiences that we cherish, that we obtain in and through music; experiences of being transported out of ordinary anxieties and given the vision of the completeness of things which comes to us only because we are attending to this complex argument of tones which is taking us through a space of its own. We are relying upon instincts like desire to move in harmony with each other, desire to be taken, as it were, to drift forwards in the clouds of sounds, but engaging the most contemplative and concentrated part of ourselves.
>
> Those same instincts, the instinct to move in time to rhythm, the instinct to follow a line of music to its closure and so on, these can be used in another way to provide short-term gratification, to get people into a state of surrender to their surroundings and close their mind to the meaning of it. Obviously much pop music is of that latter kind. It's a way of closing the mind rather than opening it … There is a way in which our musical instincts can be used to produce a form of addiction which closes the mind to any higher social experience; or they can be, on the contrary, disciplined and used to create a door into another world, which is the act of the Schubert song.
>
> JA: Can I ask you then, in today's society, what is the purpose in music? Is it anything more that purely pleasure?
>
> RS: Many people don't find any other purpose in life [than pleasure] anyway! It's the same with everything else … But I think really musical people would say that music is a source of understanding rather than pleasure. It's a way in which we understand the world of human relations and also the wider way in which we relate to reality as a whole.
>
> JA: Which we cannot do with words?
>
> RS: Yes, that's true. Obviously there's a mystery here. Why is it that people stand still when a beautiful piece of instrumental music sounds? They might stand and just listen; it's the nearest we have to the experience of wonder.
>
> JA: Is that something that has to be experienced communally and at first hand? Does it have to be in a live performance?
>
> RS: For very few people now it's live. How many people have heard a string quartet live? Very few compared to the number of people who have heard string

quartets [on recordings]. For many people the great moments of their musical experience have been on their own, but that doesn't alter the fact that the experience is an intimation of community. You are at one with others who are sharing it, even if you don't know who they are. You are certainly locked on to a wavelength which unites us around a sense of what we really are. I think that's what happens when people have those encounters with music.

JA: And would you say that God is in there somewhere?

RS: Well yes. That's what the 'real presence' is. That goes back to the Old Testament concept of God being among us, which is there from the beginning of Genesis: the peace of God which is suddenly made available without any explanation.

Today, then, where sacred music, in its broadest sense, is being consumed on such a massive level through concerts, recordings, Internet and radio, I ask Roger how music justifies itself in a world of scientific explanation? Are materialists missing the point that there should be some mystery and power in things that cannot be explained?

I think that many atheists would say that there's something in us that hungers for something beyond ordinary sensory experience, and some people look for that in religion but some also find it in music too. I think that they would say that that's a more rational approach because it doesn't come with a whole collection of false beliefs ... Although the majority of people are not officially religious anymore I suspect very few of them are atheist. All of them have a space in their heart for the religious idea, and there's no barrier between them and the appreciation of sacred music.

JA: Are you concerned at all in the decline in church attendance and popularity of organized religion?

RS: I am of course. I would be much happier if we still lived in a Christian country where people regularly renewed their religious commitment and regularly rehearsed their own sinfulness. I think it's a very important part of living properly. [Decline] has been going on for all my lifetime. It's not as though much has changed really. It also presents one with an interesting challenge, to live in another way if you can, in the middle of all of this.

JA: Does that make music that is overtly Christian, like that of James MacMillan, a counter-cultural exercise?

RS: Well it is. All culture, all *real* culture now, is counter culture because we're surrounded by totally ephemeralized pseudo-culture which is the official culture. The culture of grinning politicians, the cultures that are taught through the media ... We live in a cultural catacomb. Nevertheless, we keep the memory of *real* things alive. It has ever been so probably, in one way or another.[37]

---

[37] Ibid.

Thus we end where we began this chapter, with a sense that great music, deeply rooted as it is in the development of Christianity in Western civilization, will always be counter-cultural to some extent as it seeks to embody a 'real presence' that cannot be found in a materialist and consumerist secular pseudo-culture.

Conclusion

This chapter began with a reflection upon James MacMillan's discussion of his adoption of a counter-cultural stance simply by being a Christian believer in Western society today. This notion of counter-culturalism has pervaded his music and his approach to his work. *Real* culture, as Roger Scruton put it, always has to fight for its place in communities where individuals are drawn to more easily consumed and more swiftly gratifying pleasures. Plato was writing about such 'real culture' in relation to the quality of music long before the development of Christianity and the great musical discoveries of Western civilization. Nevertheless, both MacMillan and Scruton emphasize the positive elements of this struggle today. MacMillan does not see himself as isolated in his task, but part of a tradition of great Christian composers of the twentieth century. Likewise, Scruton sees the twentieth century as one of the greatest centuries for music, and especially religious music.

We have seen in this chapter that music within the religious context continues to be an attractive option for those seeking a spiritual 'real' alternative to popular culture. Cathedral attendance in Britain has grown remarkably in the last decade, indicating the desire to keep the bond between Christian worship and its music. Yet even outside of the Church, as James Herbert has observed, the Western cultural heritage of Christianity cannot be ignored in the arts, for music and art are saturated with the language and context of our Christian past. It is simply part of the vocabulary, without which much of our culture makes no sense. Roger Scruton elaborated upon this idea, arguing that music is peculiarly important to Western society, which is not the case throughout the world, and that the development of Western musical tonality has an importance for Western civilization that is not the case anywhere else.

In the West, music developed through the centuries alongside humanity's growing understanding of God. Our understanding of how we relate to God as a 'real presence' among us has been shaped by musical development itself. As music gained a life of its own outside the church walls, like a child growing up and leaving home, it retained its sacred use. Even in the privacy of the drawing room, chamber music became sacred. Thus Roger Scruton urges us not to distinguish too harshly between sacred and secular, for they do not signify contrasting spheres. Even after the secularization of society and the loss of the idea that we are dependent on devotion to God for our happiness, music still threads the sacred and the secular together, for instance in Schubert's lieder which, like Bach's instrumental music, have 'profoundly religious connotations'. Wagner recognized the loss of religion and sought to re-present it, albeit non-theistically. But today, individuals struggle to find time and space to allow music to transport them to another 'world' or 'reality'.

Nevertheless the development of Western music alongside and in tandem with Western Christianity, Roger argues, means that we relate music, even subconsciously, to 'real presence'. That 'real presence' may be epitomized in the idea of the musical symphony, where unity is formed from variety of people, instruments, tones and sounds; a community given meaning through polyphonic sound that draws listener, performer, conductor and composer together. It symbolizes a social order that is at the heart of our ideals for Western civilization and if there is grounds for more optimism regarding sacred music it is that humans have an innate hunger for 'the humble recognition of one's created state' and 'the desire to reflect upon this and absorb and understanding of what it is to be … which comes through long moments of quietness, and music is a form of quietness as is religion'.[38]

Sacred music, whether vocal or instrumental, may be competing with less demanding forms of culture today, and with more immediate sources of pleasure; but there is much evidence that, now as ever before, there is a genuine hunger to encounter music that requires quietness and stillness, concentration of mind and body, and takes one to a place that is beyond the merely material to a 'real' place of understanding, which cannot be accessed by speech or word. Music at its most profound is not just pleasure, but a means of understanding reality, and even if you are listening alone, you join with a community of those who also seek, through music, 'a sense of who we really are'.

---

[38] Interview with Roger Scruton.

Chapter 6
What is the Future of Sacred Music?

The world is charged with the grandeur of God.

Gerard Manley Hopkins[1]

So far there has been a great deal of discussion in this book about how sacred music is performed, practised and received, and about its status in society today. But what about its future? How will music contribute to society and what predictions are there in terms of how it may change?

In this final chapter I will be using interview material and analysis to examine how musicians, theologians and philosophers perceive the future of sacred music in Western culture, both from within the Church and without. I begin with the latter.

Sacred Music Without the Church

In a recent interview, the conductor Sir John Eliot Gardiner bemoaned the general state of musical culture in Britain:

> Things are getting worse. But I've been used to a back-to-the-wall entrenched position really since the word go. I was very lucky, I suppose, in the 1980s with the arrival of CDs and the interest in early music, that suddenly there was a fashion which seems to have tailed off. Or have the record companies become fat cats and made the wrong decisions? I don't know the answers to that … There is this perceived crisis of classical music. How much that is to do with successive governments – and particularly the Blair government – for not keeping music in schools as a vibrant and essential part of the curriculum, it's difficult to say. I feel that Blair has got just as much to answer for as Margaret Thatcher had in different ways – certainly in the dumbing-down of culture.[2]

Sir John Eliot's concerns about the dumbing-down of culture are shared by others, such as Roger Scruton, as we have seen. But another conductor has concerns regarding musical education even at the highest level. Harry Christophers has seen no improvement in musical conservatoires being willing to prepare singers for professional choral work:

---

[1]   G.M. Hopkins, 'God's Grandeur' in R. Bridges (ed.), *The Poems of Gerard Manley Hopkins* (London: Humphrey Milford, 1918).

[2]   John Eliot Gardiner, interview with Rusbridger.

There is still that brick wall you face with any conservatoire in this country: if you're going to be a singer, you're expected to go on the opera stage. It's a real battle. You've got to give up singing in choirs, which makes absolutely no sense at all. If you're an orchestral player at an academy or college, you have your private lessons, just the same as a singer would, but you also play in the orchestra. It's a discipline. You do exactly the same as a singer. This completely nonsensical attitude by singing teachers is part and parcel of the fact that when they were growing up in the business, choirs were viewed as choruses, which has an 'amateur' tag to it. But from the 1970s there have been more and more [professional] choirs. Today there are many choirs with really excellent singers. People who've come through the *The Sixteen*, like Mark Padmore, Christopher Purves and Sarah Connolly [all international soloists and opera stars] recognize their grassroots and realize that [singing in a] choir was a great discipline. It's a complete nonsense to me that music colleges don't accept that fact, which is something we're trying to change. In terms of nurturing new singers, we're at a dangerous time because ... there are fewer and fewer people coming through [Oxford and Cambridge] into the world of choral concert music and we're not necessarily getting the natural singers wanting to enter the profession.

That's why we started our *Genesis Sixteen* for 18–23 year olds ... Thank God that there are now so many groups about that people do feel they can make a living by going into this type of music. That's great. But also, when you consider those who are present-day choral scholars at Oxbridge, many of them will not wish to go into the music profession. They may have a wonderful voice but they're high flown academics or medics or bankers or whatever.

So what about the future of sacred choral music?

The choral tradition is alive and healthy and going from strength to strength because new groups are emerging. The profile of groups like *The Sixteen* and *The Monteverdi Choir* is ever increasing, so therefore younger groups and younger singers are looking up to that. I think it's great that more girl choristers are singing [in cathedrals] because there will be fewer parents who want to send their children away as borders. That culture has changed a lot; people don't want to be separated from their children. So that's going to have an impact on a lot of these places, in particular London, where you have to be boarders, and other cathedrals, such as Canterbury. Again there's the financial implication of maintaining these choirs ... The more people that can encourage girl and boy choristers the better. They've got to make singing in a cathedral choir trendy and as good as playing football. People often talk about how music and sport tend to go together. Talk to most people when they're sixteen and they love sport! I was an absolute maniac for sport. The two have to go hand in hand. It's up to schools to work out this problem and not get in the way. It does worry me; there are more music departments going under, particularly in the state system, so that's therefore up to people to get Saturday and Sunday music going. Some areas it's brilliant, but in others, it's absolutely terrible.

We have great organizations such as the National Youth Choir. These institutions are expensive for students and, sadly, it all boils down to finances and government policy and tinkering with education. The awful mistake would be to allow this rise in the appeal for choral music not to be maintained at the lower levels. People like Gareth Malone, who has really brought singing to the nation is a good example. Also Eric Whitacre possesses a talent for inspiring the younger generation, with his emphasis upon multimedia. That's all great.[3]

From a performer's point of view, therefore, there are areas of optimism for the future of professional music, but also areas of concern, particularly in the sphere of education. Harry has started an educational project that will help to train young singers for a future professional career:

The *Genesis* project is free, which is a big bonus for students. This was the first year that we had over 400 applicants to whittle down to 22. The standard of all those 400 was very high. That also goes to show that, through the radio, television and the Internet, youngsters are listening to this music; people from all walks of life and different schools. We've made it our aim, through our advertisers, to travel to as many state schools as possible. We're not focused on those public schools where music is already flourishing at a high level. Our project is centred on less privileged schools and it's fascinating to see what results are possible, and that's wonderful to see.[4]

Harry, like other conductors and performers, is taking responsibility for nurturing the future of sacred music and passing on the tradition to future generations. Francis Steele has chosen another way of fostering musical growth, after many years as a professional performer, in his courses for singers in Roujan, France. I asked him how he saw the future of sacred choral music in our culture:

Music which descends directly from the Lutheran chorale – choral in the broadest sense – gospel music, for example, will I imagine continue to burgeon. I don't mean to suggest that J.S. Bach was the musical *papa* of gospel; gospel is fed by tributary streams of music of popular origin, jazz, folk, spiritual, rock. Rather, that what *Jesu meine Freude* and *Deep River* have in common is an attitude to this mortal life which renders the loss of it desirable. Hope for another, better, life, beyond the grave, is common to the oppressed and deprived, to slaves, be they on a sugar plantation or in early Christian Rome. Suffering begets music, and since the human condition is unlikely to improve, the source is unlikely to run dry. Exploring the depths of human misery in his cantata *A Child of our*

---

[3]   Interview with Harry Christophers, 2011.
[4]   Ibid.

Time, Sir Michael Tippett replaced Bach's chorales with spirituals which ache for 'that land where all is peace'. This music will flourish as long as suffering itself, because it expresses something deep within the human psyche, and it will remain in the hands and mouths of the chorus – the congregation, unmediated by any authority other than popular belief.[5]

Suffering and music have often been related in history and, no doubt, will continue to be, for music relates to our basic humanity. Roger Scruton reminds us that our society is linked with music in a way that no other civilization has ever been. However, there is still a problem with postmodernism for Scruton, which is blocking many from experiencing music properly.[6] Perhaps, therefore, the return to the beautiful harmonies of Renaissance and later choral music is a restoration of something essential to our society, whilst leaving the formal and creedal aspects of the religion it represents in the churches. One thing that might have directed interest back to the harmonic world of the sacred is the rise of great performers and performances around the globe. But it may also be partly due to a reaction against the failed atonal experiments of the twentieth century:

> The avant-garde persists only as a state-funded priesthood, ministering to a dying congregation. We have seen the demotion of serialism from the obligatory language of modern music to a stylistic eccentricity in free competition with the tonal styles; we have witnessed too the renunciation of experiment for experiment's sake and the attempt to integrate the modernist discoveries into a lingua franca that will be not so much post-tonal as pantonal. Atonal music proved unable either to find an audience or to create one. Its harsh interdictions and censorious theories threatened the musical culture, by disparaging the natural bourgeois life on which it depends.[7]

This harsh criticism, or perhaps accurate assessment, of the avant-garde portrays the modern, twentieth-century, concert hall as a bleak landscape in which atonal sounds failed to provide a genuinely transcendent or profound experience for either performer or listener. Roger Scruton, however, does see a glimmer of hope for the future, albeit a delicate one, in which the sacred is, once again, emerging as meaningful and necessary. This involves a return to two things, the 'old' and the 'religious':

> At the same time, a new bourgeois audience is emerging – one which does not feel the force of modernism's bleak imperatives. It is as yet a fragile audience: its ears muddied by pop music, its body starved of rhythm, and its soul untutored in religious hope. Yet it has encountered the old musical culture, and been inspired by it.[8]

---

5   Interview with Francis Steele, 2013.

6   Scruton, *The Aesthetics of Music*, pp. 500 and 506.

7   Ibid., pp. 506–7.

8   Ibid., p. 507.

This hope for the future of sacred music and a 'sacral community' is, therefore, built upon the notion that a new generation has been *inspired* by the sounds of the 'old' and the 'sacred'. However, the sacral, to use a term favoured by both Scruton and Saliers, is a community which is, as yet, not fully formed. This is because too much damage has been inflicted by popular culture, Scruton argues, and due to a lack of understanding about where this music comes from and what it means:

> Nor should we be surprised if the new audience is animated by a religious longing, while being unable to distinguish the religious from the religiose, content with a sentimental image of faith that, in its real vision, stands too severely in judgement over the post-modern world-view.[9]

Is sacred music, however brilliantly performed in the concert setting, merely evoking a 'sentimental' response from the listeners? Concert-goers no longer wish to engage with religion in its entirety and are positively averse to any idea of judgement, but wish to extract a sense of the sacred that fulfils a religious need, a longing: the sacred, without the religion; liturgical music, without the liturgy; pathos without confession. Scruton is faintly condemning of the modern religious music to which this type of bourgeois audience subscribes:

> Such an audience finds in the morose spirituality of Górecki the perfect correlative of its musical taste. For his is serious music, with a promise of release from the alienated world of popular culture, yet composed as pop is composed, with monadic chanting over unvoiced chords. It is as though serious music must begin again, from the first hesitant steps of tonality, in order to capture the postmodern ear. There is no doubt that, thanks to composers like Górecki and Tavener, the bourgeois ear is again being opened to music. Nevertheless, the thinness of this new music reminds us of the great task which lies before the art of sound: the task of recovering tonality, as the imagined space of music, and of restoring the spiritual community with which that space was filled. I doubt that this act of restoration can be accomplished in Tavener's or Górecki's way: a musical equivalent of [T.S. Eliot's] *Four Quartets* is needed – a rediscovery of tonal language, which will also redeem the time. Many of our contemporaries have aimed at this ... But none, I think has yet succeeded.[10]

Whilst considering how this rediscovery might be found, it is perhaps worth remembering that all great religious composers of the past, such as Victoria, Tallis, Byrd and Bach, have demonstrated a serious wrestling with belief; and their music is rooted in the theological, political and cultural heritage of their time. The danger we have today is, as Ivan Hewitt has recently reminded us, that religious music becomes feel-good music for the 'commitment-phobe' who wishes neither to

---

[9] Ibid.

[10] Ibid, pp. 507–8.

engage with faith *or* doubt.[11] Perhaps Hewitt is right. Maybe there are too many commitment-phobes. But is there also a more aggressive antagonism towards the sacred from secular society today? In relation to this question, I asked James MacMillan, first, whether sacred music was seeing a revival; and, second, how secularism was impacting upon the world of sacred music-making:

> JA: How do you see the future of sacred music? A revival?
>
> JM: I do. One of the things that Pope Benedict has done is to refocus the Church on its liturgical heritage and richness and that every time he talks about liturgy he's taking about music, and that can't help but have an effect. It is having an effect. It's a top-down approach at the moment, and one wonders just how grass roots it will be but, I think we've been through the sixties and that something else is beginning to emerge. But I do lots of different things and I like that varied life. I like my association with confessional religion and using music as best I can, and that is plugged in to a sense of authenticity; but I'm also aware that I'm involved in the secular world as well. There are grey areas overlapping all the time.[12]

There may be antagonism for what James MacMillan and other Christian composers are doing, but in personal conversations and in the concert hall itself, when the encounter is first hand, the conversations tend to be more constructive than destructive:

> I love going to concerts where people appreciate and are given the opportunity to applaud the music, but I'll enjoy the conversations about it afterwards with people who don't share my faith at all. I think my *St John Passion* confronts a lot of people (the quality of the music apart) with the vernacular text in a way that they've never encountered, even if they're devotees of the Bach Passions. They don't hear them in the modern language; they hear them in German and are just one step removed all the time. But with any modern vernacular setting of the passion, they're hearing a retelling of the passion story that, perhaps, they've never heard, especially younger people or, with older people, haven't heard properly enunciated for maybe decades. And that leads to very interesting conversations with the agnostic music lovers.[13]

Not all confrontation is bad, therefore, if it leads to a refining and purifying of what really matters and shows how to achieve it. Is there, then, a possibility of the creation of a 'spiritual community' in our society?

---

[11]   http://www.telegraph.co.uk/culture/music/proms/9528897/Religious-music-for-the-commitment-phobe.html. See above, pp. 26–8.

[12]   Interview with James MacMillan, 2011.

[13]   Ibid.

The Restoration of the 'Spiritual Community'

We have discussed the notion of the 'sacral' or 'spiritual' community in this book, by which is meant the breaking down of the barriers between sacred and secular in music. This would mean joining together as a community, whether in a church or a concert hall, in order to be moved out of our ordinary existence and our superficial engagement with popular culture, (television, radio, and so on) when we give our wholehearted attention to music that speaks of the 'deep elemental facts of our existence'.[14] That is, music that points to our mortality, our ability to love, our suffering.

The evidence suggests that there are composers of sacred music today who are achieving a rediscovery of a musical language that deeply expresses the human longing for seriousness and for God. The music of James MacMillan, Arvo Pärt, Jonathan Harvey, Morten Lauridson, Gabriel Jackson, Judith Weir and Jonathan Dove (amongst many others) has achieved a level of expression that has spoken profoundly of, and to, our human desire for the divine. Moreover, with the rise of the professional sacred music concert and the plethora of world-class choral and orchestral groups able to provide first-class performances through the world, there has never been greater access to the world of the 'spiritual community' of the arts.

But beyond this world of striving for a twenty-first century sacred music is the return, rediscovery and sometimes discovery of the music and religion of the past. The music of the Renaissance and the 'golden age' of polyphony, and the tradition of chant from which it grew, is an endless draw for audiences worldwide. I believe this is true for three reasons: the publication of new editions and works previously undiscovered; the rise of performance practice and great professional choirs; and the quality of the music itself and what it represents. Let's look at this last point first.

The Unsurpassed Greatness of Renaissance Polyphony: Complexity and the Mind of God

In my discussion with James MacMillan he acknowledged his debt to the Renaissance composers of polyphony, what he called the 'great contrapuntalists': I am fascinated by this notion of a connection between complex polyphony and the mind of God – that through music we have a window onto the divine. One of the ways this is enacted in ourselves is by use of our voice, which '*enacts* the praise, thanksgiving, and blessing. Singing also *enacts* sorrow, anger, lament, and the questioning of God'.[15]

So singing in itself is a theological act. Moreover, this is not related to the fact that the polyphony is a setting of sacred words. The music is sufficient to express the divine:

---

[14]   Saliers, *Music and Theology*, p. 60.
[15]   Ibid., p. 61.

A certain use of the voice – as in the polyphony of Palestrina or Victoria – automatically transports us into the religious context. We hear the God-wards intentionality in religious music, just as we see it in the upturned face of the sculpted saint. And the example is all the more telling in that God cannot be represented, except in forms that misrepresent him. He is always, from the point of view of representation, 'off-stage'.[16]

For some Renaissance composers, it is the passion of their faith that we encounter and with which we engage, and that is capable of transporting us away from the concerns of our individual lives:

> The unbroken tradition of polyphonic writing enables us to hear, in Victoria's great *Responsories for Tenebrae*, exactly *what it was like* to believe as Victoria believed, seeing the world in terms of the Christian drama. This experience is overwhelming: it redeems for us a moment of past time, which could never be redeemed by factual knowledge. It makes a vanished experience present in our own emotions, and instructs us, through the imagination, in spiritual possibilities that our lives deny. Such experiences could not be obtained, if musical performance were merely a kind of scholarly reconstruction. Every performance would then be an affirmation of the distance between the audience and the music. Performance should be part of a tradition: a practice which is constantly amended in the light of new examples, which in turn owe their life to what has gone before.[17]

A New Age of Technology and Fast Living

In the new *Cambridge History of Musical Performance*, Sir Nicholas Kenyon, one-time controller of Radio 3, Director of the Proms and now Managing Director of the Barbican Centre in London, begins his article on 'Performance Today' with this quotation from Gleick:

> Once upon a time, before music television, before remote controls, before books on tape and internet streaming media, a possible method of enjoying a basic art form was this: a person would sit down and listen to an entire symphony, for however long that took. It is not so easy anymore … Halfway through the adagio they feel a tickle somewhere between the temporal and occipital lobes and realise they are fighting an impulse to reach for a magazine … With all the arts making their small sacrifices to hurriedness, music lovers can hardly expect

---

[16]   Scruton, *The Aesthetics of Music*, p. 167.

[17]   Ibid., p. 449; see also T.S. Eliot, 'Tradition and the Individual Talent' in *The Sacred Wood* (London: Methuen, 1920; reprinted in *Perspecta*, 19 (1982), pp. 36–42), which, Scruton asserts, is the 'classic account of tradition in artistic matters'.

to be immune. There is a special kind of pain, though. Music is the art form most clearly about time.[18]

The way we consume sacred music is vastly different from fifty years ago, through a vast variety digital recordings, Internet downloads, radio and television as well as live performance. Thus, the media through which sacred music, along with all other music, can be delivered has altered the way it is performed and packaged. The chapel choir in my Oxford College (Worcester) made a recording in 2012 that was distributed throughout the world without any physical copies being sold. Everything is available to buy online and to be downloaded, from the whole recording (for a few pounds) to single track (for a few pence). The marketing of the recording and the raising of the profile of the choir was achieved by means of the Internet and social networking sites.[19]

The ability to buy single tracks of sacred music was a distinct advantage to me when preparing a lecture on 'Music in the age of Renaissance and Reformation'. In compiling a PowerPoint presentation I was able to purchase single tracks of sacred choral music from plainchant to Perotin and Palestrina to Praetorius, and load them into the presentation to use as musical illustrations.

This is music written for the Church but now being heard in a context, and in a manner that would have been unimaginable to those who composed it. Even those church, chapel and cathedral choirs where sacred choral music is provided for services throughout the year, broadcast their performances and liturgy in podcasts, live streaming on the Internet, through their own websites or through the BBC on Radio 3, as well as by means of regular recordings and television. But Kenyon argues that the age of new media has also provided the opportunity to promote and commission the work of contemporary composers as well as singing traditional repertoire:

> The annual service of Nine Lessons and Carols from King's College Cambridge, in many respects a perfect example of an invented tradition, has admirably commissioned a new carol each year from composers including Arvo Pärt, Judith Weir, James MacMillan and Gabriel Jackson. In April 2011, millions watched a royal wedding in Westminster Abbey, whose traditional musical values were articulated through the dominance of the music of Hubert Parry, a commission from John Rutter and a work by Welsh composer Paul Mealor.[20]

So, how has all this affected performance practice?

---

[18]   J. Gleick, *Faster* (New York: Random House, 1999), pp. 191–3, quoted in N. Kenyon, 'Performance Today' in C. Lawson and R. Stowell (eds.), *The Cambridge History of Musical Performance* (Cambridge: CUP, 2012), pp. 3–34, at p. 3).

[19]   Worcester College Choir, *This Christmas Night*, conducted by Stephen Farr, was *BBC Music Magazine* Christmas disc of the month, December 2012.

[20]   Kenyon, 'Performance Today', p. 5.

For a long time tradition developed directly. The only places where a corpus of the music of the distant past existed were in the cathedral tradition (where old music was always sung) … Until the revival of 'ancient music' began in concerts in the eighteenth century, most people listened essentially to contemporary music.[21]

However, a key change in society has been not just the lack of religious and historical education (as Roger Scruton observes) but a lack of musical knowledge, as Kenyon asserts:

Now the audience is changing and changing fast. Thanks to crises in our education system, the assumptions about how new generations enter the world of classical music have been repeatedly challenged in recent years. (The arguments about applause at concerts between movements in symphonies and song cycles surely relate to varying levels of knowledge among the audience, and uncertainty about concert behaviour).[22]

Why has this regression in musical literacy occurred? The music philosopher Adorno blamed popular culture:

Adorno attacked something that he called the 'regression of listening,' which he believed had infected the entire culture of modern America. He saw the culture of listening as a deep spiritual resource of Western civilization. For Adorno the habit of listening to long-range musical thought, in which themes are subjected to extended melodic, harmonic, and rhythmic development, is connected to the ability to live beyond the moment, to transcend the search for instant gratification, to set aside the routines of the consumer society, with its constant pursuit of the 'fetish,' and to put real values in the place of fleeting desires. And there is something persuasive here that needs to be rescued from Adorno's intemperate and over-politicized critique of just about everything he found in America. But Adorno reminds us that it is very hard to criticize a musical idiom without standing in judgment on the culture to which it belongs. Musical idioms don't come in sealed packets, with no relation to the rest of human life. And when a particular kind of music surrounds us in public spaces, when it invades every café, bar, and restaurant, when it blares at us from passing motor cars and dribbles from the open taps of radios and iPods all over the planet, the critic may seem to stand like the apocryphal King Canute before an irresistible tide, uttering useless cries of indignation.[23]

---

[21]   Ibid., pp. 17–18.

[22]   Ibid., p. 30.

[23]   R. Scruton, 'Music and Morality', *The American Spectator*, February, 2010: http://spectator.org/archives/2010/02/11/music-and-morality (accessed 19 September 2013).

The fact that musical arts organizations (such as choirs, orchestras and opera companies) are increasingly being awarded funding for educational ventures as well as their artistic projects points towards an increasing need in society for education in the world of classical music. This decline in musical literacy combined with a decline in church attendance and religious belief more generally may lead one to expect a corresponding decline in interest in sacred music – an art form that combines both classical music and religion.

However, this is not the case. As has already been discussed, the number of people worldwide who have access to sacred choral music and listen to it through recordings, radio, television or the Internet has never been higher in history. Having considered sacred music's future in wider society, I now turn to ask how it will fare within the liturgy of the Church.

Music Within the Liturgy: The State of Sacred Music Today and in the Future

In order to assess the state of sacred music in our cathedrals and churches, and how it will develop in the future, I asked Francis Steele, as a singer and choral coach who has thought for many years about this subject, what his opinion was about music within the liturgy. He began by considering the roles of the Church and the composer:

> Both have roles which entail responsibilities. For the Church, the privilege of patronage entails commitment to sacred choral music and, by extension, support for the means and places of its dissemination – choirs and buildings. It is responsible too for consensus in doctrinal terms, generally reflected by a constant and stable liturgy: that the Latin Mass was once the common focus of composers' attention derives from the relative stability of liturgical use over a long period of time, stability which offered the composer future as well as present renown. Liturgy with built in obsolescence is unlikely to engender or nurture great music. In the Roman Catholic Church it is still too soon (only fifty years!) to assess the effects of Vatican II's preference for the vernacular over the Latin Mass on the production of music. The Anglican liturgy is more fluid in terms of the music it can accommodate, though it is perhaps worth observing that its vast repertoire of service settings in the vernacular remains virtually unknown outside the anglophone world, or even the United Kingdom. The responsibility of the composer is to respect the liturgy and to conform to its legitimate demands, to the doctrinal consensus it elaborates.

But do we live in a different world now, where the dual responsibilities of patron and composer have broken down, or is the Church no longer dictating the relationship? Is the public now the real patron of music, freeing composers to choose whatever text they wish? Francis continues:

In surveying the vast expanses of sacred choral music, it's difficult to make out clear trends. But if Bach wrote primarily liturgical works for his patron, the Lutheran Church, Handel, in his oratorios, wrote sacred music for a new patron – the public – thereby gaining the choice of subject and text. When we come to Brahms, despite the liturgical resonance of its title, *Ein Deutches Requiem* is a far cry from the Latin *Requiem*: by choosing the texts himself, Brahms avoided reference to the terror of the last judgment, selecting instead words that express to the living the peace and consolation to be found in death. Just as in *Deep River*. By omitting any mention of Jesus, the work becomes non-denominational, and Brahms the man looms large, not only as composer but as compiler of the text. Delius's *Requiem* is more radical still, in that it sets atheistic texts. Stravinsky wrote for two rites, the Roman Catholic in his *Mass*, and the pagan in *Le Sacre du Printemps*, dual service which would not have been tolerated in the sixteenth century. Britten's *War Requiem* incorporates the poetry of Wilfrid Owen, whilst Tippett wrote his own text for *A Child of our Time*.

So has the role of composers changed over time, granting them greater personal status and attendant freedom to remove compositions from liturgical restrictions?

That the composer seems to loom ever larger – even to the extent of disqualifying his work from liturgical performance – will not surprise us when we consider the history of European thought and art from the late eighteenth century onwards, nor would I expect this trend to alter, but it does beg the question of the relationship between an authoritative, dictatorial Church – one which, in the twentieth century, still referred to its laity as 'subjects' – and the artist as demigod. Vatican II acknowledged for the first time, in 1962, the fundamental right to freedom of conscience for all; it also advocated the value of 'noble simplicity' and 'active participation' in the liturgy. Whilst there are at present, and will always be, a few composers offering fealty to these values, in general, if sacred choral music is not finally to be divorced from the liturgy, the composer's task in realizing the latter 'ideal' will be just as herculean as will be the assimilation of the former ideal by the Church. As I don't think that either ideal is currently endemic among or natural to either party, I think that sacred choral music is likely to slip its moorings to the liturgy and drift offshore for a while.[24]

Whilst it certainly seems true that there have been trends that have freed composers of sacred choral music from liturgical straightjackets, James O'Donnell, Organist and Master of the Choristers at Westminster Abbey, is nevertheless optimistic and takes a positive approach concerning the major developments in cathedral music, linking it firmly with education. The introduction of girl choristers in cathedrals is welcomed, as is the influence of professional choral groups who sing

---

[24]   Interview with Francis Steele.

cathedral repertoire in concert settings, but whose performances are also available throughout the world by various recorded media:

> My impression is that things are extremely healthy, and when you're talking about the English choral tradition, you're talking about lots of other things as well, in particular education. One of the most rewarding aspects of being involved in a place with a choir school is that you're absolutely immersed in an enterprise that is educational, in the largest sense of that word. I don't just mean the classroom, but formational education. I think that choristers learning to sing well and to become musicians is only the tip of the iceberg; in many ways it's the lead activity but there are many others as well and who knows what they can then contribute? It's great to see, for instance, over the years, so many choristers going on to university, studying music and becoming professional musicians or, alternatively, becoming investment bankers! They bring their education, sense of organization and their self-possession and all of their skills and apply them in their chosen careers. The cathedrals are very healthy … The introduction of girls into cathedral choirs has been an extremely valuable development and a positive thing.

How is the practice of sacred music faring outside of the liturgical context?

> What has really benefited the Church music scene, and the cathedral music scene particularly, has been the development of groups such as *The Tallis Scholars*, *The Sixteen*, *The Monteverdi Choir* and others that are singing this repertoire and, of course, the explosion of available music on CD and the Internet – the fact that you can now hear almost anything, no matter how recondite, at the flick of the switch, the click of the mouse, has totally changed things for the better. It's broadened everybody's minds.

James O'Donnell works for the Anglican Church, although he is himself a practising Roman Catholic. So what is the picture like for the future in the Roman Catholic Church? James MacMillan has given a very definite point of view in his article: 'Throw out the guitars and bring back sacred silence – a liturgical wish-list from a young Catholic':[25]

> I received this eight-point wish-list from a young Catholic student which seems as clear-headed, moderate and sensible as anything else I've seen recently. What is it about the young that they 'get' Benedict, when all we see with some of their elders is truculent annoyance?

---

[25]   James MacMillan, *Daily Telegraph*, 3 November 2010: http://blogs.telegraph.co.uk/culture/jmacmillan/100048506/throw-out-the-guitars-and-bring-back-sacred-silence-%E2%80%93-a-liturgical-wish-list-from-a-young-catholic/ (accessed 19 September 2013).

1. Instrumentation. Explicit rules about exactly what is and is not appropriate for liturgical use, with a particular promotion of a) the organ; b) the choir; and c) congregational singing ...

2. Rhythms. Excessive use of syncopated rhythms produces a very secularized effect since it draws attention to itself and is therefore incongruent with its purpose as an aid to prayer.

3. Plainchant. A much greater promotion of and respect for plainchant – the original musical language 'of the people' in church ...

4. Investment. The main reason the Anglican Church excels musically in many of its churches (and certainly its cathedrals) is simply because it invests in musicians ...

5. Text. Care should be taken to avoid some of the over-saccharine poems that have replaced either good-quality poetry or sacred texts. Poetry does not need to be sentimental to be accessible to a wide audience.

6. Silence. This is perhaps the greatest loss of all. The whole nature of the user-friendly, post-Vatican II liturgy seems to have become synonymous with the tax collectors in the temple ...

7. Notices. These always seem excessively long, especially given that all the information is printed on newsletters ...

8. Refusing to sing? There should be much, much more publicity of St Augustine's famous 'Quis cantat, bis orat' – 'he/she who sings prays twice' ... People don't obstinately stand with their mouths closed during the spoken recitation of the Creed, so why do they feel so comfortable to do so during a hymn – or even a sung part of the Ordinary? This schism between those who sing and those who refuse is deeply problematic, as it weakens the whole point of Sunday worship: to do so as one body – as the Church.

The themes of centuries of tradition in sacred music within the liturgy are rehearsed in this wish list: the fluent and competent use of voices and chant, setting of beautiful poetry that feeds the souls, and time and space for silent meditation, reflection and prayer. But the young Catholic also makes the practical point that financial investment in the future is as important as changing the instruments. Somehow the Anglican Church held on to its choral tradition after the Reformation and, although many cathedral choirs are very expensive to run (St Paul's Cathedral Choir costs over £1 million a year) they are valued and funded by whatever means are available, because they are not just an extra part of the liturgy, nor even a quaint custom to be kept alive for the sake of nostalgia. They are a living and creative part of our national culture that is part of our musical and religious heritage and its influence is felt far beyond the cathedral walls.

Conclusion

In this chapter we have been considering the future of sacred music in Western culture. We have found that, for some performers, such as Sir John Eliot Gardiner and Harry Christophers, there are some grounds for concern in the areas of classical music education in schools and the place of choral training in music conservatoires. These concerns may lead to questions about where future generations of composers and performers may come from and what the implications of Internet technology and social media might have upon society's desire for live performance of sacred music. Moreover, Roger Scruton believes that, as a society, we still need to recover the art of listening, and rediscover tonality as the imagined space of music and restore the spiritual community with which that space was filled.

However, we have also found much to be optimistic about the future of sacred music, from the emergence of new recording labels such as *The Monteverdi Choir and Orchestra*'s *SDG* label, to *The Sixteen*'s Genesis education project for young singers, and every professional exponent of sacred music benefits from the advances in technology, which has helped more people to have access to excellent performances of sacred music than ever before. As to the appetite for listening to sacred music in a 'live' setting, the evidence suggests that there is far from being a decline in this area. Added to this is that fact that the act of singing remains fundamental to our self-expression as human beings and much of the greatest vocal music is sacred repertoire. Indeed, composers of sacred music today stand at the end of an unbroken tradition through the centuries that leads back to the great contrapuntalists of the Renaissance. Francis Steele finds optimism in the fact that human suffering has often been the inspiration for music, from Luther to the Spirituals of the American Deep South. Roger Scruton finds that the minimalist style of composition has been a reaction to the failure of the postmodern avant-garde, as a means of recovering tonality.

Not only has sacred music maintained and increased in popularity in the secular setting of the concert hall, but professionalized music making within the Church at cathedral level has also seen a rise in those turning up to listen and participate in the liturgy over recent years. Why? I wish to suggest that there are several reasons for this.

As Roger Scruton has identified, there has been a failure in postmodernism and the avant-garde in music, especially reflected in the areas of atonality and irreligious attitudes. There is now a reaction against this, and sacred music provides a sound world and seriousness that is warmly welcomed by many who are seeking an alternative aesthetic to consumerism and popular culture.

There has also been a rise in the number and quality of professional ensembles offering world-class performances of great sacred works, whilst many previously undiscovered works have been brought to light. With the advent of multimedia access to this music there has been an inevitable rise in demand. The *Classic FM-*style promotion of classical and choral music as 'relaxing' has given rise to a sense that this type of music, regardless of its religious origins, provides a relaxing antidote to the busy modern world. However, as Nicholas Kenyon has observed, music is about time, and people's ability to sit and listen to a piece of music, such as a whole symphony, has now been compromised by competing forms of instant gratification.

Thus, I suggest that there is a deeper need that is being satisfied when people attend concerts in order to set aside time for listening. This is the most difficult aspect to identify and define, as it must be individual to each participant in the performing/listening relationship. For some it is a specifically religious experience of hearing a cathedral choir as part of a service of prayer and praise. For others it may be the sentimentality of a half-forgotten religion of their childhood, and memories of a world where life was perhaps slower and simpler, rather like those who are fond of the Book of Common Prayer for the sound of the language but not the creedal content. Francis Steele pointed out that sacred music may drift away from the Church if the 'noble simplicity' within the liturgy, advocated by the Second Vatican Council in the Catholic Church, cannot be combined with a desire for 'active participation' from composers.

However we approach this music, it is *great* music by any standards and, as such, will inevitably create a profound effect wherever it is well performed. The 'profound' impact may take many forms: a sense of other-worldliness, transcendence, spirituality; or perhaps an experience that touches the emotions and the mind, stirring new thoughts and feelings that encourage, inspire or distress even. It may stir religious affection or devotion, whether this be overt or unarticulated. Whatever happens, perhaps we can be optimistic that wherever great sacred music is performed, there is created a 'sacral community' that, rather like the Church itself, contains a variety of starting points and destinations but that is able to cultivate emotions, beliefs, doubts and ideas of time, space and transcendence that collectively break down the barriers between the sacred and the secular. When we encounter the beauty of art, music and word in the singing of voices, whether in concert or in the liturgy, we each begin a journey, whether as composer, performer or listener, and we do not know where it will take us. At the end, we have been transported; but we may not be able to define the place where we have arrived. Indeed, we cannot and do not wish to define the journey, for the music and the expression of the minds and bodies that produced it cannot be analysed and put into words. The inexpressible beauty of music is enough. All we can say is that the journey was worth it and was unique. There will never be another one like it. Each performance will be different and evoke a different result. Music enables us to be human: to encounter a spiritual community through music is to glimpse something of the divine spark and reminds us 'in an increasingly de-humanized world, of what it means to be human'.[26]

---

[26]   James MacMillan, Sandford Lecture.

Conclusion

Music expresses that which cannot be said and on which it is impossible to be silent.

Victor Hugo [1]

After silence, that which comes nearest to expressing the inexpressible is music.

Aldous Huxley [2]

In the Introduction to this book I examined the nature of sacred music and began by asking what is sacred music, exploring how music is fundamental to our civilization and language, as well as its development in the West and its liberation from its function in organized religion. I considered how sacred music might be defined by its relation to the intentions of the composer and the explicit purpose of inspiring devotion to a God, or perhaps by the context in which the music is performed, that is, a sacramental role within a religious church service. However, the evidence of the interviews undertaken for this book suggests that when the art of music is perfected by a great composer and performed by accomplished musicians, then sacred music could be defined better as that which appeals to those needs, desires and doubts that are experienced by all thinking and truly human individuals. Thus, there can be no divide between the church and the concert hall, or between religious and secular society, for the art of music is received by everyone alike. Each may receive as they are able or willing and they may benefit in many and various ways. The music may lead them to God, to contemplate, for instance, suffering, loneliness, joy, peace or anger. Music provides for us the means to explore the indefinable, the inexpressible, that unknown to us and yet that for which we search and long. Those desires, articulated by Augustine as a thirst for God, still exist whether we call our age 'secular', 'Christian' or any other name.

In Part I, I explored the ideas of those who practise sacred music, both composers and performers within and outside of the Church. An examination of the role of composers considered the role of text and subtext in composition, the necessity or otherwise of sincerity of faith on behalf of the composer, music as a possible witness to truth and the traditions of composition that today's composers inherit, from plainchant to contrapuntal technique. I concluded that the quality of compositions of sacred music in the West are as strong as they have ever been,

---

[1] V. Hugo, *William Shakespeare* (Paris: Librairie internationale, 1864), Part 1, Book 2, Chapter 4, p. 58.

[2] A. Huxley, *Music at Night and Other Essays* (London: Chatto and Windus, 1931), p. 19.

and remain part of a tradition stretching back over a thousand years and more of musical and religious development. Good or great sacred music requires not merely sincerity on the part of the composer, but also conviction, rigour and engagement with the difficulties and ambiguities of faith and with the influence of past composers. Sacred music, both in its ideology and compositional form, is part of a long tradition of believing, but also one of doubt, and that the context in which the music is performed is neither a defining factor, nor a constraint.

For those who perform sacred music within the religious settings of church, cathedral or chapel services, the notion of performance is embraced, emphasizing the duty and service offered by professionals to an overall excellence of liturgy, in which music plays its role amongst the words, preaching and sacraments. There remains a thirst for this kind of religious offering and, from the musical point of view, the human voice continues to play a significant role in how such music is communicated. We discovered, with James O'Donnell, that any performer cannot legislate for the listener's experiences, one simply offers the music and, within a liturgy that is greater than the sum of its parts, there is no single recipient in mind, even God, but the music plays its part and, at its best, avoids any attempt at emotional manipulation. The role of chant is at the heart of the tradition of Church music, reflecting a rhythm of life.

The evidence of those who perform sacred music within a concert setting, such as Peter Phillips, Harry Christophers and Francis Steele, suggested that music is potentially theologically stronger when it is performed well, leading to a possibility that God might be more truly venerated through music in a concert setting than in a religious service. Theologically, the idea that we are bidden to praise God with our music and voices is most powerfully performed when it is done well. In offering the very best of art, we too, as human beings, receive the most from creation. Moreover, in the concert hall, music in itself is unfettered by denominational boundaries, whether the composer is Catholic of otherwise. Thus, the divisions of belief are harmonized by engagement with the sacred sound. A concert is uncompromised by religion and uninterrupted by speaking, leaving the audience free to receive as they wish. Nevertheless, it is crucial that really good sacred music is not seen as simply a 'wallpaper' background sound. The use of religious terminology in concert programmes, such as Choral Pilgrimage and Bach Pilgrimage emphasizes the religious historical heritage from which the music descends, whatever the current cultural *zeitgeist*. The purpose of the performer is, therefore, is to be faithful to the music, to deepen the drama and elucidate what is in the score, so that the music that is within time also transcends time and thus the individual experience of that music embraces both past and future.

In Part II, I explored the reception of sacred music: what it means to listen, the relationship between music and culture and the future of sacred music. I began by considering music's power to express notions of redemption and death and to effect the emotions. However, if one uses music as a spiritual wash to bring about calm and stasis, without engaging with the true essence of the music, whether its text, context or subtext, then one will not reach a maturity of listening or experience the spiritual depths of music, which can teach us to live with and before God. In the interview with Rowan Williams the role of plainchant was once again emphasized as a thread through the history of sacred music embodying something about good listening practice that takes time, attention; a physical settling and a patience that goes beyond mere emotional manipulation. Likewise the role of great instrumental music was that which demands the listener to be quiet, to be still, and allow the music to create a space into which a deeper reality can enter. Thus instrumental music cannot be separated from the sacred, just as the sacred cannot be separated from the secular or the concert hall from places of worship. Even after secularization and, for many, the loss of dependence on a devotion to God, music remains a thread that attaches us to that devotion.

Through the ideas of Christian apophatic theology and of William James, I conjectured some ways in which music touches the soul, even to those who have no faith. God is unknowable, inexpressible, invisible, uncertain, only known by faith and by experience that leads every believer, inevitably and ultimately, to silence before the divine. However, sacred music can offer a perspective on faith and an experience, personal and communal, that can take us beyond the realm of words. No other art form comes close to opening up the pathways to experiencing the inexpressible divine. That is why words like soul and spirit, transcendent, divine, heavenly, paradise and transfiguration are legitimate because, whether a believer or not, they are the only vocabulary we have that approximates to the reality that the music conveys. Good sacred music, therefore, is not merely manipulative of our emotions, but insists that we stop and engage with something greater than the sound itself.

In examining the relationship between music and culture, I explored James MacMillan's notion of Christian counter-culturalism that has pervaded his music and his approach to his work, as well as Roger Scruton's (Platonic) idea that *real* culture has always had to fight for its place in communities where individuals are drawn to more easily consumed and more swiftly gratifying pleasures. Both interviewees, however, emphasized that the twentieth century had been one of the greatest for sacred music in history. Music within the ecclesiastical context continues to attract those seeking a spiritual, 'real' alternative to popular culture, with a dramatic rise in cathedral attendance in the first decade of the twenty-first century. Outside the Church the music and the arts are saturated with the language and context of our Christian past: music is peculiarly important to Western society. Music has developed through the centuries alongside humanity's growing understanding of God. Initially this was in the Church, but as music gained a life of its own outside the Church walls it retained its sacredness. Even in our homes chamber music became sacred in that it requires time and attention, which is easily distracted by popular culture, and which is indicative of a hunger for the humble recognition of one's created state. Thus, for Scruton, the instrumental music of Bach and Schubert, for instance, have 'profoundly religious connotations'. Thus, 'sacred' and 'secular' do not signify contrasting spheres. Rather, music threads the sacred and the secular, harmonizing society, and becomes a means of understanding reality. Our understanding of God has been shaped by music. Polyphonic music is resonant of unity within variety, forming a community from distinct individuals in a common meaningful tonality, which is a symbol of social order. For Scruton, therefore, the counter-cultural battle is between religion and good music, or 'real' culture, and ephemeralized pseudo-culture. Good music is that which transports us out of ordinary anxieties, using instincts like desire to move in harmony with each other, engaging contemplation. Therefore the non-believer will still have a space in their heart for the religious idea, for there is no barrier between them and the appreciation of sacred music.

In the final chapter I considered the future of sacred music in Western culture and discovered that there are some justified concerns for the health of classical music in school education and of choral training in music conservatoires as well as a wider anxiety for our culture and the place we give to listening. However, the emergence of new ensembles, recording labels, educational projects and developments in cathedral choirs, technology and the abundance of excellent composers of sacred music give grounds for much optimism. For Francis Steele, the source of optimism for the future is a paradoxical one: suffering. Suffering begets music and as long as suffering continues music will be created. For Roger Scruton the advent of minimalism is a reaction to the failure of the postmodern avant-garde. It is as if music needs to begin again with composition from first principles. In terms of future of ancient music, to listen to piece by Tomas Luis da Victoria, Scruton suggests, is to be shown what is was like to believe what he believed. Thus an academic and scholarly reconstruction of the music in performance will only put distance between the audience and the music. Performance must be 'real' if it is to be meaningful.

Findings

I conclude that not only does sacred music have a significant contribution to make to our society, but also that it meets a deep and intrinsic human need for the spiritual, mystical, transcendent, or unearthly. These terms are increasingly used without reference to God, but in fact find their most pertinent and meaningful significance within a theistic setting. People will continue to flock to hear professional musicians perform on concert platforms and in cathedral concerts because of the aesthetic value of the music, as long as the high standards of the performance continue. Our appreciation of the great works will inevitably vary according to the quality of the performance and the atmosphere of the venue, but however it is conveyed, the sacred will always be a part (and the most valuable) of music that was specifically intended as a response and a prayer to God.

Music has always been at the heart of our civilization, the basis of our language and, in Western society, has always been associated with the sacred.[3] What makes a work of music sacred is not simply the intentions of the composer, or a religious or liturgical context, but rather the very nature of that music itself, providing a

---

[3] McGilchirst, *The Master and his Emissary*, pp. 1–14, 94–132, 298–329.

'real presence' of spirituality in our lives by virtue of its temporal, incarnate form of sound.[4]

Music has always been an essential expression, not only of what it is to be a religious believer, but what it is to be human. To engage with both religious texts and music is to touch the numinous, and to indulge the need for the spiritual in all of us. As MacMillan so eloquently puts it: 'I believe it is God's divine spark which kindles the musical imagination now, as it has always done, and reminds us, in an increasingly de-humanized world, of what it means to be human'.[5]

Sacred music is not defined by context, text, or creed, but is that beautiful art that illuminates us to attributes of the divine, such as sacrifice and love. The greatest music will always lead the composer, performer and listener towards these subjects. In contemplation of these two attributes, through musical beauty, the sacred is encountered.

Sacred music demands time and space in order to listen, engage and be transformed by it. It offers society an art form that comprises a presence of spirituality that draws the individual away from self and back into a relationship with community, and away from selfish desire towards a sacrificial relationship with others that leads to love; great sacred music stands in contrast to individualism and consumerism and leads towards greater cohesion, harmony and community. This leads towards the chief subject of all artistic and natural beauty, which is love and, ultimately, God.[6]

But this argument leads me on to a second and, perhaps, paradoxical point, that in sacred music, in whatever context, God appears to be venerated as effectively in the secular concert performance, and in many cases a great deal more so, than in sacred liturgical worship.

The prevalence of sacred music, being regularly commissioned, composed and performed by the best musicians of our age, is a challenge to those who are members of believing communities, that is, the Churches, who need to recognize that sacred music and those who practise it bear witness to a profound desire for an alternative to a desecrated and dehumanized world. The popularity of sacred music, which can lead the listener, composer and performer from one reality to another, provides an indication of the spiritual health of our society as a whole. This is, surely, something to be celebrated and embraced by Christians and those of other faiths. Thus, we need to accept a new sense of the sacred.

A New Sense of the Sacred

Music can retain its integrity as an instrument of connection between the human and the divine, regardless of context or purpose. Karl Barth went so far as to connect apparently secular music with the divine, if it is great music: 'Why

---

[4]   R. Scruton, *Beauty*, pp. 43–5, 99–101, 104–5, 108–11, 147–8, 156–64.

[5]   MacMillan, Sandford Lecture.

[6]   Scruton, *Beauty*, pp. 160–61.

shouldn't we see a divine spark in the genius of a Mozart or a Wagner?', hailing *Tannhaüser* as a piece of 'powerful preaching'.[7] Bach's *Passions* are heard more now than in their own day, of course, but that need not suggest that a secular society finds something completely different in the music than Christians did in Bach's day. The intention of the composer, the context for which it was written, the Biblical text it sets, and the glorious beauty of the music are still intact and speak directly to the same human needs that it did nearly 300 years ago.

Although society may change and social emphases may be reconfigured, human nature and its need for the transcendent remains a constant presence. The sacred music of the past, as well as that being composed today, is equally as relevant and rich irrespective of the context in which it is performed. For, in fact, 'every religious tradition and indeed every human culture, inherits a set of acoustic images and convictions that define what makes music "sacred". ... the very notion of "sacred sound" is thus demythologized into another genre of "social construction".'[8] So perhaps in our own age, we need to explore again what 'sacred' means and whether that is to be confined to the religious context or does it have a place in the wider world, where the spheres of sacred and secular cannot be separated.

Even in a noisy and busy world we remain, as individuals and as a society, drawn to the sounds of sacred music. As a society that has had music at its heart since before the historical records begin, we are attracted most fundamentally to the music of the voice.[9] If we turn from our busy lives and sit for a while within the sounds of beauty, dedicated to expressing the mysteries of the divine or that which is inexpressible in words, we re-connect with something deep within ourselves that is fundamental to our humanity. We are re-humanized by the experience in whatever context it is presented. For those who see sacred music as a means of facilitating prayer in the context of worship, then, they may find a religious building the most conducive place to engage with it. For others, who are more ambivalent about faith, the concert hall may be the setting of choice, where the specific function of the music is not so strongly emphasized. In either case, the important performative duty of the musicians, and indeed a theological point in terms of how the art achieves its aim of communicating something genuine to the listener, is the standard of the performance.

It is for this reason that I conclude that there is no grand divide between the church and the concert hall, between religious and secular society, for the art of music is received by everyone alike. Each may receive as they are able or willing and they may benefit in many and various ways. The music may transport us, transcend language and definition, so that we cannot express where we have

---

[7]   D.J.R.S. Moseley, '"*Parables*" and "*Polyphony*" in *Resonant Witness*, pp. 240–70, at p. 245, quoting K. Barth in E Busch, *Karl Barth: His Life from Letters and Autobiographical Texts*, trans. John Bowden (Philadelphia: Fortress Press, 1976), pp. 29–30.

[8]   Saliers, *Theology and Music*, pp. 56–7.

[9]   McGilchrist, *The Master and his Emissary*, pp. 102–32.

travelled from or to; but we know we have experienced something profound and meaningful that could only come through music and not through the word. For Peter Phillips a concert should take the listener away from the ordinary business of life for a space of time; focus them on something other than daily chores and allow another, perhaps deeper experience, to take place. They are transported: the listener, engaging with the performer, is somehow taken from one place to another, be that spiritually or emotionally to an inexpressible experience that, for some people can only be completely explained in religious terms, as approaching the divine or glimpsing God.[10]

Sacred music should not be confused with, or confined to, organized religion, for, encountered in a wider context, it can lead people to consider the most profound aspects of human life and lead them to the threshold of faith. Music is a bridge that can connect the religious congregation or listener to their secular counterparts. There is so much in our experience that we cannot express or hope to define, and we cannot hope to pin definite attributes upon the ultimate truth. But music does not demand a process of initiation or catechesis; it does not judge or require confession and absolution; it has no argument except in its own beauty and no authority except in its irresistible power to transcend worldly values that are constantly bargained over in words. Music does no more than to *exist* in sounds created by composer and performer. The listener can choose to be prepared, to focus the attention, to open up to possibilities that it can bring in the transience of time. Alternatively, the listener can choose to ignore these potentialities. There is no compulsion, confinement or coercion, except in the sound itself. It is a conduit, through brief moments of time and experience, of something we cannot articulate. In music there is no pursuit of filling in the missing gaps of comprehension, merely the pure existence of sound with which we can choose to engage or ignore. The experience will not give us scientific truths that we can take away as rational argument for, or against, the existence of the divine, but if we take the music seriously, we will be changed by what we have heard in a way that ultimately leads to the deepest truths of our reality: of joy, suffering, pain, loss, forgiveness, sacrifice, mortality and, ultimately, of love, which is God.

No one can ever experience a concert by reading the newspaper review. No one can ever say they know a painting by a description only. No words of description will adequately capture the true nature of a performance. Therefore, we must continue to strive for the highest standards of musical performance, to break down the barriers that divide the sacred and the secular in society, to acknowledge that, in music, we have not just a metaphor for the divine, but a totally different, non-verbal way of experiencing reality that is of great significance in our society, for those who are seeking to know more of the world than can be put into words.

Sacred music is for all. It can be heard in more ways than ever before by a greater number and breadth of population than ever, and is more popular than ever. Is it, then, the means by which many people in society are tapping into a spiritual

---

[10]   Interview with Peter Phillips, 2012.

side to their lives without the need for confessional religion? Is sacred music now the language of the divine more than ever?

Music is the bridge between two places: sacred and secular. Whether we are Christian, of another faith, or of none, there is no absolute knowledge of truth, reality or the divine in this lifetime. But in music, sometimes, we come close.

Select Bibliography

Printed Primary Sources

Acts of John, 94–97, translated in J. McKinnon (ed.), *Music in Early Christian Literature* (Cambridge: CUP, 1987), p. 25.

Ambrose of Milan, *Expositio Euangelii Secundum Lucam*, in Patrologia Cursus Completus Series Latina, ed. J.P. Migne, 221 volumes (Paris, 1857–64), Vol. 15, cols. 1762–63: commentary on Luke 15: 25.

Arnobius, *Adversus Nationes* 2: 42, quoted in J. McKinnon (ed.), *Music is Early Christian Literature* (Cambridge: CUP, 1987), p. 49.

Aristotle, *Politics*, VIII, Chapter 5.

Augustine, St, *Confessions of S. Augustine* XXXIII, 49, trans. E.B. Pusey (J.M. Dent & Sons Ltd., 1907 (first published 1838)).

——, *Sermons*, The Works of St Augustine: A Translation for the 21st Century, Part III, Vol. 2, trans. Edmund Hill (New York: New City Press, 1990), Sermon 34.

Babylonian Talmud (Megillah 32a), cited in 'Jewish Music, §III, 2(ii)(a): Synagogue Music and its Development: Biblical Cantillation' in *The New Grove Dictionary of Music and Musicians*, Vol. 13, ed. S. Sadie and J. Tyrrell (London: Macmillan, 2001), p. 41.

Council of Trent, 22nd session, canon 8. For a full text of the Council see http.history.hanover.edu/texts/trent.html.

Dionysius the Areopagite (known now as Pseudo-Dionysius), *Mystical Theology*, trans. T. Davidson, *Journal of Speculative Philosophy*, 22 (1893).

Ficino, M., *De Vita Coelitus Comparanda: Three Books on Life*, A Critical Edition and Translation with Introduction and Notes, by Carol V. Kaske and John R. Clark (Binghamton, NY: Medieval and Renaissance Texts and Studies, 1989), Book 3, Chapter XXI.

Hildegard of Bingen, *Hildegardis Bingensis Epistolarium, Pars Prima I–XC*, ed. L. Van Acker, Corpus Christianorum Continuatio Mediaeualis, 91 (Turnhout: Brepols, 1991), pp. 61–6: Epistle 23, translated in P. Dronke, *Women Writers of the Middle Ages* (Cambridge: CUP, 1984), pp. 196–8.

——, *The Letters of Hildegard of Bingen*, ed. J.L. Baird and R.K. Ehrman, 3 volumes, Vol. I (New York: OUP, 1994) , pp. 76–80, Epistle 23.

Ignatius, St, *Epistle to the Ephesians*, in *The Ante-Nicene Library*, Vol. 1: *The Apostolic Fathers*, ed. Alexander Roberts and James Donaldson (Edinburgh: T&T Clark, 1870), pp. 149–50.

Isidor of Seville (d. 636), *Etymologiarum sive Originum Libri XX*, Book III.

James, W., *The Varieties of Religious Experience: A Study in Human Nature*, ed. M.E. Marty (New York: Longmans, Green and Co., 1902; New York: New American Library, 1958; Harmondsworth: Penguin, 1982).

Kepler, J., *Harmonices Mundi* (1619).

Luther, M., 'Letter to Ludwig Senfl, 1530' in *The Letters of Martin Luther*, ed. M.A. Currie (London: Macmillan, 1908).

——, 'Preface to Georg Rhau's *Symphoniae Iucundae*', 1538, in *Luther's Works*, Vol. 53, *Liturgy and Hymns*, ed. U.S. Leopold (Philadelphia: Fortress Press, 1965), pp. 321–4.

——, Commentary on Psalm 4 (*Luther's Works*, 10: 42) and Letter to Ludwig Senfl: *Luther's Works*, Vol. 49 (Philadelphia: Fortress Press, 1972), p. 426.

Messiaen, O., 'Réponses à une enquête', *Contrepoints* 1, no. 3 (March–April, 1946), pp. 73–5.

——, Interview with Patrick Szersnovicz, 29 May 1987, *La Monde de la Musique* (July–August, 1987), pp. 29–35.

Second Vatican Council, *Constitution on the Sacred Liturgy (Sacrosanctum conilium)*, §83.

Stravinsky, I., *Poetics of Music in the Form of Six Lesson*, trans. Arthur Knodel and Ingolf Dahl (Cambridge MA: Harvard University Press, 1947).

The Constitution of the Sacred Liturgy (The Second Vatican Council of the Roman Catholic Church; Rome, 1963).

Weiss, P. and Taruskin, R., *Music in the Western World: A History in Documents* (London: Macmillan, 1984).

Secondary Sources

Aldridge, D., *Music and Altered States: Consciousness, Transcendence, Therapy and Addictions* (London: Jessica Kingsley, 2006).

Allen Seel, T., *A Theology of Music for Worship Derived from the Book of Revelation* (Metuchen, NJ, and London: Scarecrow Press, 1995).

Anderson, E. and Morill, B.T., *Liturgy and the Moral Self: Humanity at Full Stretch before God: Essays in Honour of Don E. Saliers* (Collegeville, MN: Liturgical Press, 1998).

Bachelder, L., *The Gift of Music* (Mt Vernon, NY, the Peter Pauper Press, 1975).

Banks, J., 'Performance in the Renaissance: An Overview' in C. Lawson and R. Stowell (eds), *The Cambridge History of Musical Performance* (Cambridge: CUP, 2012), pp. 297–317.

Barenboim, D., *Parallels and Paradoxes* (London: Vintage, 2004).

Barth, K., *Church Dogmatics*, 31 vols. (Edinburgh: T&T Clark, 1961).

——, *How I Changed My Mind*, ed. and trans. John Godsey (Edinburgh: The Saint Andrew Press, 1969).

——, 'Music for a Guest – a Radio Broadcast' in E. Busch (ed.), *Final Testimonies*, trans. G.W. Bromiley (Grand Rapids, MI: Eerdmans, 1977), pp. 23–4.

——, *Wolfgang Amadeus Mozart 1756/1956* (Zurich, 1956), trans. C.K. Pott (Grand Rapids, MI: Eerdmans, 1986).

Begbie, J., *Music in God's Purposes* (Edinburgh: The Handsell Press, 1989).

——, *Voicing Creation's Praise: Towards a Theology of the Arts* (Edinburgh: T&T Clark, 1991).

——, *Beholding the Glory: Incarnation through the Arts* (London: Darton, Longman and Todd, 2000).

——, *Theology, Music and Time* (Cambridge: CUP, 2000).

——, *Sounding the Depths: Theology through the Arts* (Canterbury: SCM, 2002).

——, *Resounding Truth: Christian Wisdom in the World of Music* (London: SPCK, 2008).

——, 'Created Beauty: The Witness of J.S. Bach' in J.S. Begbie and S.R. Guthrie (eds), *Resonant Witness: Conversations between Music and Theology* (Grand Rapids, MI: Eerdmans, 2011), pp. 83–108.

——, 'Faithful Feelings: Music and Emotion in Worship' in J.S. Begbie and S.R. Guthrie (eds), *Resonant Witness: Conversations between Music and Theology* (Grand Rapids, MI: Eerdmans, 2011), pp. 323–54.

Benitez, V.P., 'Messiaen and Aquinas' in A. Shenton (ed.), *Messiaen the Theologian* (Farnham: Ashgate, 2010), pp. 101–25.

Benson, E.B., 'Improvising Texts, Improvising Communities: Jazz, Interpretation, Heterophony, and the *Ekklēsia*' in J.S. Begbie and S.R. Guthrie (eds), *Resonant Witness: Conversations between Music and Theology* (Grand Rapids, MI: Eerdmans, 2011), pp. 295–319.

Black, L., *Franz Schubert: Music and Belief* (Woodbridge: Boydell, 2003).

Blackwell, A., 'The Role of Music in Scleiermacher's Writings' in *Internationaler Schleiermach-Kongress, Berlin* (Berlin: de Gruyter, 1984), pp. 439–48.

——, *The Sacred in Music* (Cambridge: Lutterworth Press, 1999).

Blanning, T., *The Triumph of Music: Composers, Musicians and their Audiences, 1700 to the Present* (London, Allen Lane, 2008; Harmondsworth: Penguin, 2009).

Bohlman, P.V., Blumhofer, E.W. and Chow, M.M., *Music in American Religious Experience* (Oxford: OUP, 2006).

Bonds, M.E., *Music as Thought: Listening to the Symphony in the Age of Beethoven* (Princeton: Princeton University Press, 2006).

Bonhoeffer, D., *Works*, Vol. 5 (Minneapolis: Fortress Press, 1996).

Borthwick, A., Hart, T. and Monti, A., 'Musical Time and Eschatology' in J.S. Begbie and S.R. Guthrie (eds), *Resonant Witness: Conversations between Music and Theology* (Grand Rapids, MI: Eerdmans, 2011), pp. 271–94.

Bowman, W.D., *Philosophical Perspectives on Music* (New York: OUP, 1998).

Breuggemann, W., *Israel's Praise: Doxology Against Idolatry and Ideology* (Philadelphia: Fortress Press, 1988).

Brown, F.B., *Religious Aesthetics: A Theological Study of Making and Meaning* (Princeton NJ: Princeton University Press, 1989).

Busch, E., *Karl Barth: His Life from Letters and Autobiographical Texts*, trans. John Bowden (Philadelphia: Fortress Press, 1976).

Butt, J., *The Cambridge Companion to Bach* (Cambridge: CUP, 1997).

Byron Anderson, E. and Morill, B.T. (eds), *Liturgy and the Moral Self: Humanity at Full Stretch before God* (Collegeville, MN: Liturgical Press, 1998).

Campling, C.R., *The Food of Love: Reflections in Music and Faith* (London: SCM, 1997).

Chadwick, H., *Boethius: The Consolations of Music, Logic, Theology and Philosophy* (Oxford: OUP, 1981).

Chua, D.K.L., *Absolute Music and the Construction of Meaning* (Cambridge: CUP, 1999).

——, 'Music as the Mouthpiece of Theology' in J.S. Begbie and S.R. Guthrie (eds), *Resonant Witness: Conversations between Music and Theology* (Grand Rapids, MI: Eerdmans, 2011), pp. 137–61.

Clapper, G.S. and Saliers, D.E., *John Wesley on Religious Affections: His Views of Experience and Emotion and their Role in the Christian Life and Theology* (Metuchen, NJ: Scarecrow Press, 1989).

Clarke, E.F., *Ways of Listening: An Ecological Approach to the Perception of Musical Meaning* (Oxford: OUP, 2005).

Clarke, M.V., *Music and Theology in Nineteenth-Century Britain* (Farnham: Ashgate, 2012).

Clement, Theophilis, *Oratorios Displayed in a Letter to a Friend: Shewing the Evil Tendency of Performing Sacred Music, in the Manner in which it is now Frequently Exhibited* (London, Printed by Augustus Applegath and Edward Cowper, [Between *c.* 1820 and 1822?]).

Clines, D., *The Theme of the Pentateuch* (Sheffield: Sheffield Academic Press, 1994).

Cobussen, M., *Thresholds: Rethinking Spirituality Through Music* (Aldershot: Ashgate, 2008).

Cone, J., *The Spirituals and the Blues* (Maryknoll: Orbis Books, 1972, 1991).

Cook, N., *A Guide to Musical Analysis* (London: OUP, 1987).

——, *Music: A Very Short Introduction* (Oxford: OUP, 1998).

Costen, M., *African American Christian Worship* (Nashville: Abingdon Press, 1993).

Croucher, T., *Early Music Discography: From Plainsong to the Sons of Bach*, 2 vols (London: The Library Association, 1981).

Dahlhuas, C., *The Idea of Absolute Music*, trans. R. Lustig (Chicago: University of Chicago Press, 1990).

Deacy, C. and Arweck, E., *Exploring Religion and the Sacred in a Media Age* (Farnham: Ashgate, 2009).

Dingle, C.P. and Simone, N., *Olivier Messiaen: Music, Art and Literature* (Aldershot: Ashgate, 2007).

Dow, J., *Engaging Emotions: The Need for Emotions in Church* (Cambridge: Grove Books, 2005).

Drake, S., 'Renaissance Music and Experimental Science', *The Journey of the History of Ideas*, 31 (1970), pp. 497–8.

Dyson, G., 'False Relation' in L. Macy (ed.), *Grove Music Online*, http://www.oxfordmusiconline.com/public/book/omo_gmo (accessed 16 February 2007).

Eisenstein, J.K., 'The Mystical Strain in Jewish Liturgical Music' in J. Irwin (ed.), *Sacred Sound: Music in Religious Thought and Practice*, Journal of the American Academy of Religion Studies, Vol. 50, no. 1 (Chico, CA: Scholars Press, 1983), pp. 35–53.

Ekman, P., and Davidson, R.J., *The Nature of Emotion: Fundamental Questions* (New York: OUP, 1994).

Eliot, T.S., 'Tradition and the Individual Talent' in *The Sacred Wood* (London: Methuen, 1920; reprinted in *Perspecta*, 19 (1982), pp. 36–42).

Farndale, N., Interview with Sir John Tavener, *Daily Telegraph*, 29 July 2004.

Faruqi, Ibsen al, 'What Makes "Religious Music" Religious?' in J. Irwin (ed.), *Sacred Sound: Music in Religious Thought and Practice*, Journal of the American Academy of Religion Studies, Vol. 50, no. 1 (Chico, CA: Scholars Press, 1983), pp. 21–34.

Fassler, M., 'Music for the Love Feast: Hildegard of Bingen and the Song of Songs' in J.S. Begbie and S.R. Guthrie (eds), *Resonant Witness: Conversations between Music and Theology* (Grand Rapids, MI: Eerdmans, 2011), pp. 355–81.

Flynn, W.T., '"The Soul is Symphonic": Meditation on Luke 15:25 and Hildegard of Bingen's Letter 23' in D. Zager (ed.), *Music and Theology: Essays in Honor of Robin A. Leaver* (Lanham, MD, Toronto, Plymouth, UK: Scarecrow Press, 2007), pp. 1–8.

Foley, E., *Foundations of Christian Music: The Music of Pre-Constantinian Christianity* (Collegeville, MN: Liturgical Press, 1996).

Ford, D., *Self and Salvation, Being Transformed* (Cambridge: CUP, 1999).

Garside, C., 'Calvin's *Preface to the Psalter*: a Reappraisal', *The Musical Quarterly*, 37 (October, 1951), pp. 570–91.

Gleick, J., *Faster* (New York: Random House, 1999).

Godwin, J., *Harmonies of Heaven and Earth: The Spiritual Dimension of Music from Antiquity to the Avant-Garde* (London: Thames and Hudson, 1987).

Gundry, I., *Composers by the Grace of God: A study of Religion and Music* (Thames Publishing, London, 1998).

Gunton, C., *The One, the Three and the Many* (Cambridge: CUP, 1993).

Gurlitt, W., *Johann Sebastian Bach: The Master and his Work*, trans. O.C. Rupprecht (St. Louis: Concordia, 1957).

Guthrie, S.R., 'The Wisdom of Song' in J.S. Begbie and S.R. Guthrie (eds), *Resonant Witness: Conversations between Music and Theology* (Grand Rapids, MI: Eerdmans, 2011), pp. 382–407.

Gyulai, G., *The Theology of Pope Benedict XVI: The Christocentric Shift* (New York, 2010).

Hanslick, E., *Geschichte des Concertwesens in Wien*, 2 vols (Vienna, 1869), Vol. I.

Hargreaves, D. and North, A.C., *The Social Psychology of Music* (Oxford: OUP, 1997).

Harrison, C., 'Augustine and the Art of Music' in J.S. Begbie and S.R. Guthrie (eds), *Resonant Witness: Conversations between Music and Theology* (Grand Rapids, MI: Eerdmans, 2011), pp. 27–45.

Hart, D.B., 'Beauty of the Infinite: The Aesthetics of Christian Truth', *Pro Ecclesia*, 4 (2005), p. 283.

Hawn, C.M., 'The Truth Shall Set You Free: Song, Struggle, and Solidarity in South Africa' in J.S. Begbie and S.R. Guthrie (eds), *Resonant Witness: Conversations between Music and Theology* (Grand Rapids, MI: Eerdmans, 2011), pp. 408–33.

Hendrickson, M.L., *Musica Christi: A Lutheran Aesthetic* (New York: Peter Lang, 2005).

Herbert, J.D., *Our Distance from God: Studies of the Divine and the Mundane in Western Art and Music* (Berkeley, CA: UCLA, 2008).

Higgins, K.M., *The Music of Our Lives* (Philadelphia: Temple University Press, 1991).

Holloway, R., *On Music: Essays and Diversions, 1963–2003* (Brinkworth: Claridge Press, 2003).

Honningsheim, P., *Music and Society: The Later Writings of Paul Honigsheim*, ed. K.P. Etzkorn (New York and London: Wiley, 1973).

Hooker, M.D., *The Gospel According to Mark*, Black's New Testament Commentary (London: A&C Black, 1991).

Hopkins, G.M., 'God's Grandeur' in R. Bridges (ed.), *The Poems of Gerard Manley Hopkins* (London: Humphrey Milford, 1918).

Hughes, G., *Hebrews and Hermeneutics* (Cambridge: CUP, 1979).

Huxley, A., 'Seven Meditations' in C. Isherwood (ed.), *Vedanta for the Western World* (Hollywood, CA: The Vedanta Society of Southern California, 1945), pp. 163–70.

Irwin, J., *Neither Voice nor Heart Alone: German Lutheran Theology of Music in the Age of the Baroque* (New York: Peter Land, 1993).

——, '"So Faith Comes from What is Heard": The Relationship between Music and God's Word in the First Two Centuries of German Lutheranism' in J.S. Begbie and S.R. Guthrie (eds), *Resonant Witness: Conversations between Music and Theology* (Grand Rapids, MI: Eerdmans, 2011), pp. 65–82.

Ito, J.P., 'On Music, Mathematics, and Theology: Pythagoras, the Mind, and Human Agency' in J.S. Begbie and S.R. Guthrie (eds), *Resonant Witness: Conversations between Music and Theology* (Grand Rapids, MI: Eerdmans, 2011), pp. 109–34.

Jaffé, D. 'Raising Sparks: On the Music of James MacMillan', *Tempo*, no.202 (1997), pp. 1–35.

——, Interview with Jonathan Harvey, *Classic CD*, July 2009.

James, J., *The Music of the Spheres: Music, Science, and the Natural Order of the Universe* (London: Abacus, 1993).

Juslin, P.N., and Sloboda, J.A., 'Music and Emotion: Introduction' in *Music and Emotion: Theory and Research*, ed. P.N. Juslin and J.A. Sloboda (Oxford: OUP, 2001), p. 3.

Kenyon, N., 'Performance Today' in C. Lawson and R. Stowell (eds), *The Cambridge History of Musical Performance* (Cambridge: CUP, 2012), pp. 3–34.

Kilfoyle, M., Programme note for *The Sixteen*'s Choral Pilgrimage Concert Series, 2008.

Kivy, P., *Music Alone: Philosophical Reflections on the Purely Musical Experience* (Ithaca: Cornell University Press, 1990).

Kretzmann, O.P., 'Bach in the Twentieth Century' in *The Little Bach Book*, ed. T. Hoelty-Nickel (Valparaiso, IN: Valparaiso University Press, 1950), pp. 3–4.

Kung, H., *Mozart: Traces of Transcendence* (Grand Rapids, MI: Eerdmans, 1992).

Larkin, P., *Philip Larkin: Collected Poems*, ed. Anthony Thwaite (London: Faber & Faber, 1988).

Lavezzoli, P., *The Dawn of Indian Music in the West: Bhairavi* (New York: Continuum, 2006).

Lawson, C. and Stowell, R., 'The Future?' in C. Lawson and R. Stowell (eds), *The Cambridge History of Musical Performance* (Cambridge: CUP, 2012), pp. 817–33.

Leaver, R.A., *Music as Preaching: Bach, Passions and Music in Worship* (Oxford: OUP, 1982).

——, *J.S. Bach and Scripture: Glosses from the Calov Bible Commentary* (St. Louis: Concordia, 1985).

——, *Luther's Liturgical Music: Principles and Implications* (Grand Rapids, MI: Eerdmans, 2007).

Leaver, R.A. and Trautman, C., *Bachs Theologische Bibliothek: Eine Kritische Bibliographie* (Neuhausen-Stuttgart: Hänssler, 1983).

Leppert, R.D. and McClary, S., *Music and Society: the Politics of Composition, Performance and Reception* (Cambridge: CUP, 1987).

Leventhal, S., (ed.), *Notations: Quotations in Music* (New York: Barnes and Noble, 2003).

Löwith, K., *Meaning in History* (Chicago: Chicago University Press, 1949).

Lungu, N., Costea, G. and Croitoru, I., *A Guide to the Music of the Eastern Orthodox Church* (Brookline, MA: Holy Cross Orthodox Press, 1984).

McCleery, D., Interview with Sir John Tavener, transcribed from 'John Tavener Reflects … A Recorded Interview' on the CD recording *John Tavener: A Portrait* (Naxos, 2004).

McGann, M.E., *Exploring Music and Worship and Theology: Research in Liturgical Practice* (Collegeville, MN: Liturgical Press, 2002).

McGilchrist, I., *The Master and His Emissary* (New Haven and London: Yale University Press, 2012).

McGrath, A., *Scientific Theology*, Vol. 1 (Grand Rapids, MI: Eerdmans, 2001).

McKinnon, J., *Music is Early Christian Literature* (Cambridge: CUP, 1987).

McLary, S., 'The Blasphemy of Talking Politics during Bach Year' in R. Leppert and S. McLary (eds), *Music and Society: The Politics of Composition, Performance and Reception* (Cambridge: CUP, 1987), pp. 13–62.

MacMillan, J., Blog, *Daily Telegraph*, 3 November 2010: http://blogs.telegraph.co.uk/culture/jmacmillan/100048506/throw-out-the-guitars-and-bring-back-sacred-silence-%E2%80%93-a-liturgical-wish-list-from-a-young-catholic/ (accessed 19 September 2013).

——, 'Why I Wrote a Piano Concerto Based Upon the Rosary', Blog, *Daily Telegraph,* 18 April, 2011.

Macmurray, J., *Reason and Emotion* (London: Faber and Faber, 1935).

Mahrènholz, C., *Musicologica et Liturgica: Gesammelte Aufsätze,* ed. K.F. Müller (Kassel: Bärenreiter, 1960).

Manning, J. and Payne, A., 'Vocal Performance in the Twentieth Century and Beyond: an Overview' in C. Lawson and R. Stowell (eds), *The Cambridge History of Musical Performance* (Cambridge: CUP, 2012), pp. 752–77.

Marini, S., 'Rehearsal for Revival: Sacred Singing and the Great Awakening in America' in J. Irwin (ed.), *Sacred Sound: Music in Religious Thought and Practice,* Journal of the American Academy of Religion Studies, Vol. 50, no.1 (Chico, CA: Scholars Press, 1983), pp. 71–91.

Maritian, J., *Art and Scholasticism* (New York: Sheed and Ward, 1933).

Massin, B., *Olivier Messiaen: une poétique du merveilleux* (Aix-en-Provence: Éditions Alinéa, 1989).

Mayne, M., *Learning to Dance* (London: Darton, Longman and Todd, 2002).

Mellers, W., *Music and Society: England and the European Tradition* (London: Faber, 1946), second edition, ed. K.P. Etzkorn (1950) (New York: Wiley, 1973).

——, *Bach and the Dance of God* (London: Faber, 1980).

——, *Music and the Dance of God* (London: Faber, 1980).

——, *Beethoven and the Voice of God* (London: Faber, 1981).

Milbank, J., '"Postmodern Critical Augustinianism": A Short *Summa* in Forty Two Responses to Unasked Questions', *Modern Theology,* 7 (1991).

Milsom, J., 'Soundclips and *Early Music*', *Early Music,* 31 (2003), p. 3.

Mitler, P.D., 'The Psalms as Praise and Poetry', *The Hymn,* 40 (October, 1989), p. 15.

Moseley, D., '"*Parables*" and "*Polyphony*": The Resonance of Music as Witness in the Theology of Karl Barth and Dietrich Bonhoeffer' in J.S. Begbie and S.R. Guthrie (eds), *Resonant Witness: Conversations between Music and Theology* (Grand Rapids, MI: Eerdmans, 2011), pp. 240–70.

Myers, D.G., *Psychology* (New York: Worth Publishers, 2004).

Nauman, M.J., 'Bach the Preacher' in *The Little Bach Book,* ed. T. Hoelty-Nickel (Valparaiso, IN, 1950).

Niebuhr, R.H., *Christ and Culture* (New York: Harper and Row, 1951).

Norris, C., *Music and the Politics of Culture* (London: Lawrence and Wishart, 1989).

——, Interview with Sir John Eliot Gardener, *Daily Telegraph,* 20 January 2005.

Nussbaum, M., *Love's Knowledge: Essays on Philosophy and Literature* (New York: OUP, 1990).

O'Connor, M., 'The Singing of Jesus' in J.S. Begbie and S.R. Guthrie (eds), *Resonant Witness: Conversations between Music and Theology* (Grand Rapids, MI: Eerdmans, 2011), pp. 434–53.

Pelikan, J., *Bach Among the Theologians* (Philadelphia: Fortress Press, 1986).

Phillips, P., *What We Really Do* (London: Musical Times, 2003; second edition, 2013).

Pickstock, C., 'Music: Soul, City and Cosmos after Augustine' in *Radical Orthodoxy: A New Theology*, ed. J. Millbank, C. Pickstock and G. Ward (London, Routledge, 1999), pp. 243–77.

——, *'Quasi Una Sonata*: Modernism, Postmodernism, Religion, and Music' in J.S. Begbie and S.R. Guthrie (eds), *Resonant Witness: Conversations between Music and Theology* (Grand Rapids, MI: Eerdmans, 2011), pp. 190–214.

Pike, A.J., *A Theology of Music* (Toledo: Gregorian Institute, 1953).

Plantinga, R.J., 'The Integration of Music and Theology in the Vocal Compositions of J.S. Bach' in J.S. Begbie and S.R. Guthrie (eds), *Resonant Witness: Conversations between Music and Theology* (Grand Rapids, MI: Eerdmans, 2011), pp. 215–39.

Polkinghorne, J., *Science and Christian Belief* (London: SPCK, 1994).

——, *The God of Hope and the End of the World* (New Haven, CT: Yale University Press, 2002).

——, *Belief in God in an Age of Science* (New Haven CT: Yale, 2003).

Potter, J. And Sorrell, N., *A History of Singing* (Cambridge: CUP, 2012).

Routley, E., *Church Music and Theology* (London: SCM Press, 1959).

Rusbridger, A., Interview with John Eliot Gardener, *The Guardian*, 12 December 2005.

Saliers, D., 'Beauty and Terror: What Have We to Sing: What Has Worship to Pray?' in D. Zager (ed.), *Music and Theology: Essays in Honor of Robin A. Leaver* (Lanham, MD, Toronto, Plymouth, UK: Scarecrow Press, 2007), pp. 213–27.

——, *Music and Theology* (Nashville: Abingdon Press, 2007).

Saliers, D and Saliers, E., *A Song to Sing, A Life to Live: Reflections on Music as Spiritual Practice* (San Francisco: Jossey-Bass, 2005).

Saxton, R., *The Wandering Jew* (CD), with Roderick Williams in the title role, BBC Singers and Symphony Orchestra, cond. André de Ridder (London: NMC, 2011).

Schiller, F., *On the Naïve and Sentimental in Literature* (Manchester: Carcanet New Press, 1981).

Scholl, R., 'The Shock of the Positive: Olivier Messiaen, St Francis, and Redemption through Modernity' in J.S. Begbie and S.R. Guthrie (eds), *Resonant Witness: Conversations between Music and Theology* (Grand Rapids, MI: Eerdmans, 2011), pp. 162–89.

Scruton, R., *The Aesthetics of Music* (Oxford: Clarendon Press, 1997).

——, *Death-Devoted Heart: Sex and the Sacred in Wagner's Tristan and Isolde* (Oxford: OUP, 2004).

——, 'Music and Morality', *The American Spectator*, February, 2010: http://spectator.org/archives/2010/02/11/music-and-morality (accessed 19 September 2013).

——, *The Face of God: The Gifford Lectures 2010* (London: Continuum, 2012).

Service, T. 'On the Trail of the Sacred', *Guardian* blog, 11 March 2010.

Shenton, A. (ed.), *Messiaen the Theologian* (Farnham: Ashgate, 2010).

Sholl, R., 'The Shock of the Positive: Olivier Messiaen, St Francis, and Redemption through Modernity' in J.S. Begbie and S.R. Guthrie (eds), *Resonant Witness:*

Conversations between Music and Theology (Grand Rapids, MI: Eerdmans, 2011), pp. 162–89.

Smith, H.L., *Where Two or Three are Gathered: Liturgy and the Moral Self* (Cleveland: Pilgrim Press, 1995).

Smith, R., *Handel's Oratorio and Eighteenth Century Thought* (Cambridge: CUP, 1995).

Söhngen, O., *Theologie der Musik* (Kassel: Johannes Standa Verlag, 1967), pp. 262–340.

——, 'Music and Theology: A Systematic Approach' in J. Irwin (ed.), *Sacred Sound: Music in Religious Thought and Practice*, Journal of the American Academy of Religion Studies, Vol. 50, no. 1 (Chico, CA: Scholars Press, 1983), pp. 1–19.

Spencer, J.M., *Protest and Praise: Sacred Music of Black Religion* (Minneapolis: Fortress Press, 1990).

——, *Theological Music: Introduction to Theomusicology* (London: Greenwood Press, 1991).

Steiner, G., *Real Presences* (Chicago: Chicago University Press, 1989).

Stiller, G., Leaver, R.A., Herbert, J. and Bouman, A., *Johann Sebastian Bach and Liturgical Life in Leipzig*, (trans. from the 1970 German edition (Kassel: Bärenreiter, 1970), St. Louis: Concordia, 1984).

Stoltzfus, P.E., *Theology as Performance: Music, Aesthetics and God in Western Thought* (New York: T&T Clark, 2006).

Thielemann, S., *The Spirituality of Music* (New Delhi: A.P.H. Publishing Corporation, 2001).

Thomas, D.A., *Music and the Origins of Language: Theories from the French Enlightenment* (Cambridge: CUP, 1995).

Thomas, J.L.H., 'The Idea of Absolute Music by Carl Dahlhaus: Roger Lustig. Review by J.L.H. Thomas', *Music and Letters*, 72 (1991), pp. 89–92.

Tillich, P., *Systematic Theology*, 3 vols. (Chicago: Chicago University Press, 1951–73).

——, *Dynamics of Faith* (New York: Harper Collins, 1958).

Van Deusen, N., 'Material: Philip the Chancellor and the Reception of Aristotle's *Physics*' in J.S. Begbie and S.R. Guthrie (eds), *Resonant Witness: Conversations between Music and Theology* (Grand Rapids, MI: Eerdmans, 2011), pp. 46–64.

van Maas, S., 'Messiaen's Saintly Naïveté' in A. Shenton (ed.), *Messiaen the Theologian* (Farnham: Ashgate, 2010), pp. 41–59.

Vattimo, G., *Belief* trans. Luca D'Isanto and David Webb (Stanford, CA; Stanford University Press, 1999; Italian edition, 1996).

Vendrix, P., *Music and the Renaissance: Renaissance, Reformation and Counter-Reformation* (Farnham: Ashgate, 2011).

Watson, P.S., *Let God be God: An Interpretation of the Theology of Martin Luther* (Philadelphia: Fortress Press, 1947).

Weber, W., 'Political Process, Social Structure and Musical Performance in Europe since 1450' in C. Lawson and R. Stowell (eds), *The Cambridge History of Musical Performance* (Cambridge: CUP, 2012), pp. 35–62.

Weil, S., *Waiting for God*, trans. E. Cranford (New York: Putnam, 1951).

——, *Notebooks of Simone Weil*, ed. A. Wills, 2 vols (London: Routledge, 1956), Vol. I.

——, *Gravity and Grace*, trans. E. Cranford (London: ARK, 1987).

Weiss, P., and Taruskin, R., *Music in the Western World: A History in Documents* (London: Macmillan, 1984).

Westermeyer, P., *Let Justice Sing: Hymnody and Justice* (Collegeville, MN: Liturgical Press, 1998).

——, 'Liturgical Music: *Soli Dei Gloria*' in E.B. Anderson and B.T. Morill (eds), *Liturgy and the Moral Self: Humanity at Full Stretch before God* (Collegeville, MN: Liturgical Press, 1998), pp. 193–208.

——, *Liturgical Music: Soli Deo Gloria*. (Westminster: Knox, 2000).

Williams, R., 'Keeping Time' in *Open to Judgement: Sermons and Addresses* (London: Darton, Longman and Todd, 1994), pp. 247–50.

Wittgenstein, L., *Culture and Value* (Chicago: University of Chicago Press, 1980).

Witvliet, J.D., 'Afterword: Mr. Holland's Advice: A Call to Immersive, Cross-Disciplinary Learning' in J.S. Begbie and S.R. Guthrie (eds), *Resonant Witness: Conversations between Music and Theology* (Grand Rapids, MI: Eerdmans, 2011), pp. 453–63.

Wolterstorff, N., *Art in Action: Toward a Christian Aesthetic* (Grand Rapids, MI: Eerdmans, 1980).

Wren, B., *Praying Twice: The Words and Music of Congregational Song* (Louisville, KY: John Knox Press, 2000).

Wright, D., 'Music and Musical Performance: Histories in Disjunction?' in C. Lawson and R. Stowell (eds), *The Cambridge History of Musical Performance* (Cambridge: CUP, 2012), pp. 169–206.

Young, F., *The Art of Performance: Towards a Theology of Holy Scripture* (London: Darton, Longman and Todd, 1990). Republished as *Virtuoso Theology: The Bible and Interpretation* (Cleveland: Pilgrim, 1993).

Zager, D. (ed.), *Music and Theology: Essays in Honor of Robin A. Leaver* (Lanham, MD, Toronto, Plymouth, UK: Scarecrow Press, 2007).

Websites

http://www.adoremus.org/7-899ArtistLetter.html

http://www.churchofengland.org/media-centre/news/2012/03/cathedral-attendance-statistics-enjoy-over-a-decade-of-growth.aspx

http://www.classical-music.com/feature/meet-artists/sir-john-eliot-gardiner.

http://www.guardian.co.uk/music/2010/mar/11/sacred-music-simon-russell-beale

http://www.telegraph.co.uk/culture/music/proms/9528897/Religious-music-for-the-commitment-phobe.html

http://www.telegraph.co.uk/news/religion/3116598/Composer-James-MacMillan-warns-of-liberal-elites-ignorance-fuelled-hostility-to-religion.html

Index

CPSIA information can be obtained
at www.ICGtesting.com
Printed in the USA
LVHW080813041022
729859LV00010B/355